A Monster for Many

THE
ROBERT H. WAUGH
LIBRARY OF
LOVECRAFTIAN
CRITICISM

A Monster for Many

Talking with H. P. Lovecraft

Robert H. Waugh

Hippocampus Press
New York

Early versions of "'Cool Air,' the Apartment Above, and Other Stories," "Lovecraft's Rats and Doyle's Hound: A Study in Reason and Madness," and "Where Lovecraft Lost His Telescope: His Kingston and the Towns around It" appeared in *Lovecraft Annual* Nos. 5 (2011), 7 (2013), and 12 (2018). "Lovecraft's Influence in Science Fiction" appeared in *Lovecraft and Influence: His Predecessors and Successors* (2013).

Copyright © 2021 by Hippocampus Press
Works by Robert H. Waugh copyright © 2021 by Robert H. Waugh

Published by Hippocampus Press
P.O. Box 641, New York, NY 10156.
www.hippocampuspress.com

All rights reserved.
No part of this work may be reproduced in any form or by any means without the written permission of the publisher.

Cover art and frontispiece by Josh Yelle, pencilmancer.com.
Cover design and series logo by Daniel V. Sauer, dansauerdesign.com.
Hippocampus Press logo designed by Anastasia Damianakos.

First Edition
1 3 5 7 9 8 6 4 2

ISBN 978-1-61498-340-8 paperback
ISBN 978-1-61498-356-9 e-book

Contents

Introduction 7
Part One: Histories and Stories 13
   Of the Midnight Ride 15
   Lovecraft Dallies with Historiography 23
   Where Lovecraft Lost His Telescope: His Kingston and the Towns around It 41

Part Two: Wells, Mirages, Madness, and Academe 51
   The Brimming Wells 53
   Looming at the Mountains of Madness 61
   At Home in Miskatonic U. 75
   Lovecraft's Rats and Doyle's Hound: A Study in Reason and Madness 95

Part Three: Apartments and Books 111
   "Cool Air," the Apartment Above, and Other Stories 113
   Lovecraft's Influence in Science Fiction 140
   Lovecraft Dallies with the Nobel Prize 155

Part Four: Apologies and Defenses 181
   An Apology in Kadath 183
   An Apology for John Keats et Alii 211

Works Cited 221
Index 233

Introduction

Once more I am happy to say that my work across the wide range of Lovecraft's creative life allows me to state what is now obvious; he has been accepted from practically every side of the American canon. He may be slightly embarrassed, given his love for the English Crown; but he knows perfectly well that the presence of America in his creative world is deeply accepted. He can't escape it; he is an American. As Jason C. Eckhardt has said, Lovecraft has been teaching us all how to be a "cosmic Yankee." But of course it is fairer to say that he was a New Englander, and that he could accept. I say this with full diffidence since I was born and raised in Indiana, far from New England. What do I know?

One of the peculiarities of these essays is that a number of them were conceived in my three-hour drive home from the 2017 NecronomiCon, where I had completed my stay in Providence by sitting on a panel that dealt on the subject of Lovecraft, the New England author; one of these essays that clearly began in that way was that devoted to Kingston and Lovecraft, as I inform the reader in that first paragraph, which began with a meditation on the gaps and losses within what we know of history. I had already been concerned with the stories about the worlds carven on the sides of ancient, silent temples; Virgil was on my mind, and so was Kleist, and very swiftly I was thinking about Henry Wadsworth Longfellow and Paul Revere, two artists resolutely in the violent pressure of our contemporary America. Yet I should also keep in mind that Longfellow was an early example of comparative literature, my own academic study.

Next I am dealing with some words, *wells* and *looming* and *litten* and *strange,* words important to the texture of Lovecraft's stories. Not one of these words, however, or others live by themselves. Though these words belong to their own stories, there is a good deal of spillage; also I should point out that these particular stories, "The Rats in the Walls," *At the Mountains of Madness,* and "The Colour out of Space" are works that I have already spent some time on. Next to these essays I spend some space on Brown University, which represented to Lovecraft the values of the academic life that he found impossible to join; only Miskatonic University could heal that loss.

Finally I spend a good deal of space devoted to that quiet story "Cool Air," which is surrounded by a rich culture that I could not cease from reading, both in itself and for the echoes it excites. My last essay in this part of the collection opens the speculative question what Lovecraft might have reacted to in the yearly presence of the Nobel Prize. Here are such old names as Carducci, France, and Undset.

I conclude here with a close reading of *The Dream-Quest of the Unknown Kadath.* No doubt Lovecraft was right in deciding to put that fantasy aside; yet the more often we read that dream away, the better sense it makes and the more dreamlike it seems. So I am reading it once more in the expectation that it shall carry me away, listening to the words I am chanting as I pull in the car that has brought me here: O Boston! O Nyarlathotep! In a short piece I look once more at Lovecraft and Keats, as well as Baudelaire and Leopardi.

Many people supported me in these endeavors. First I want to thank the people of the Sojourner Truth Library who helped me through many problems, despite my private status as a professor emeritus. John Langan and Laird Barron provided me excellent examples of where the genre of horror fiction should be moving. Fiona Paton introduced me to the wonders of Hugh MacDiarmid's *A Drunk Man Looks at the Thistle,* which has brought me home so often. Jan Schmidt, Andrew Higgins, Thomas Olsen, and Cyrus Mulready gave me good ideas and creative support, often in the nick of time; for years I have been very lucky in my debt to the English Department of SUNY New Paltz. My wife Kappa, as so often, did not allow me any escape from the virtues of her critical eye.

Thank you, S. T. Joshi, David E. Schultz, and Derrick Hussey, for seeing me through the difficulties of editing; and thank you for your encouragement from the beginning.

Abbreviations

CE	*Collected Essays* (2004–06; 5 vols.)
CF	*Collected Fiction: A Variorum Edition* (2015–17; 4 vols.)
ET	*Letters to Elizabeth Toldridge and Anne Tillery Renshaw* (2014)
FLB	*Letters to F. Lee Baldwin, Duane W. Rimel, and Nils Frome* (2016)
JVS	*Letters to J. Vernon Shea, Carl F. Strauch, and Lee McBride White* (2016)
MWM	*Letters to Maurice W. Moe and Others* (2018)
RB	*Letters to Robert Bloch and Others* (2015)
RK	*Letters to Rheinhart Kleiner and Others* (2020)
SL	*Selected Letters* (1965–76; 5 vols.)
SR	*The Spirit of Revision*

Behold, there is a woman that hath a familiar spirit at Endor.—I Sam. 28:7

Doubts, may be, it might suggest, but not knowledge; for how, by examining the book. should I think I knew any more than I now think I do; since, if I think it is the true book, I think it so already; and since if it be otherwise, then I have never seen the true one, and don't know what that ought to look like.—Melville, *The Confidence Man,* ch. 10

Der *Satz* soll ausdrucken, *was* das Wahre ist, aber wesentlich ist es Subjekt; als dieses ist es nur die dialektieshe Bewegung, dieser sich selbst erzeugende, fortleitende und in sich zurückgehende Gang. (The sentence should express what the truth is, but essentially it is the subject; as the subject it is giving birth, showing you the pathway, and showing you the true way in return.)—Hegel lxxxiii

> Ma seule *étoile* morte,—et mon luth constellé
> Porte le *soleil* noir de la *Mélancolie.*
> [My lone star dead, my starry lute
> Bears the black sun of Melancoly.]
> —Gérard de Nerval, *Les Chiméres*

> This living hand, now warm and capable
> Of earnest grasping, would, if it were cold
> And in the icy silence of the tomb,
> So haunt they days and chill thy dreaming nights
> [. . .] See, here it is—
> I hold it towards you.
> —Keats, *Poems* 503

Part One:
Histories and Stories

Of the Midnight Ride

> It was then young flood, the Ship was winding, and the moon was rising.—Paul Revere, cited in Triber 103.

One of the charming aspects of "Pickman's Model," if there is anything charming about this story of a New England ghoul, is its description of the map of Boston, whether the time is circa 1863, when in the middle of the Civil War Longfellow wrote "Paul Revere's Ride"; or 1926, when Lovecraft wrote "Pickman's Model"; or 1775, when Revere's Ride in fact did occur, a prologue to the American rebellion that Lovecraft in retrospect loathed. It is very striking how these different ways of telling this story circle one another; and I mean in this essay to trace how these very different stories occur within their different histories.

The center of "Pickman's Model" takes place on some such civilized place as Beacon Hill in the 1920s, during the afternoon tea of two gentlemen, the subject of their conversation the painter Pickman, who preferred the North End. True, the tea yields its place to a decanter of strong coffee, black (*CF* 2.71). Despite the details of the story, Pickman's scorn for Newbury Street and Back Bay is evident; the reader has the impression that Lovecraft has walked up and down those streets; it was easy for him to visit Boston throughout his life, though in a letter in 1934 he admitted that the ancient charm of Boston had vanished, "swept away by civic change" (*FLB* 140). He seldom mentions Cambridge, though that important suburb may be present in the mind of the reader; Lovecraft did make potent use of it in his later story *At the Mountains of Madness*. There is much about the North End that Pickman does not mention. In a letter from 1936 Lovecraft still remembers with great fondness the maze of those alleys. More important, many might think, is Paul Revere, the silversmith and patriot who did live in the North End, the protagonist of the famous poem by Longfellow. Longfellow, of course, is mentioned in Lovecraft's story, but only as the striking and perhaps stinking dish of a ghoul (*CF* 2.67).

It may seem odd to turn our attention to Lovecraft and Longfellow, but it is difficult for any American of the first half of the twentieth century to escape Longfellow and his poem "Paul Revere's Ride." We have good evidence that Lovecraft had carefully read "Lady Wentworth," a charming poem that occurs later in Longfellow's sequence *Tales of a Wayside Inn* than does "Paul Revere's Ride," which introduces the sequence. Lovecraft intimates his pleasure in the surprising conclusion of "Lady Wentworth," perhaps because it has the same kind of conclusion, the terminal climax (Leiber 56–57), as so many of his own stories do, though we must confess that Longfellow does not achieve that conclusion as beautifully as Lovecraft might have. For our purposes, however, we see that Lovecraft was familiar with Longfellow and with the Boston of yesteryear.

In the spring of 1930 Lovecraft wrote to Elizabeth Toldridge that "most of the northern cities have ten times as much structural ugliness cluttering up their streets—downtown Boston being an especially depressing example" (*ET* 145). At the end of the summer, however, he found the sea-approach to Boston "highly impressive" (*ET* 158), an impression he repeated a month later (*DS* 231). A survey of his letters indicates that Lovecraft's attitudes toward Boston change according to his place and time. He abhors the changes in the modern city; but just like Pickman he is fascinated by the antique city, both its architecture and its history. He loves it all the more because it is falling apart.

We should keep in mind that Lovecraft's childhood was passed in the suburbs of Boston; something of that childhood is expressed by his alter ego Randolph Carter, especially in the conclusion of *The Dream-Quest of Unknown Kadath:* "he was come again to the fair New England world that had wrought him. [¶] So to the organ chords of morning's myriad whistles, and dawn's blaze thrown dazzling through purple panes by the great gold dome of the State House on the hill, Randolph Carter leapt shoutingly awake within his Boston room" (*CF* 2.213), catching himself out of the dream in which Pickman played a cataclysmic part. This is the light side of Pickman's dark alley-ways that Lovecraft bestowed upon him. Longfellow the poet, however, might have found the language a bit too rich and fanciful; and we might have been embarrassed on Lovecraft's side.

Given Lovecraft's familiarity, then, with Boston, this omission of Revere should strike us as rather odd. Cotton Mather was worth two paragraphs of Lovecraft's vituperation (*CF* 2.60, 62). Now Pickman is deep in his rant. "There's hardly a month," he asserts, "that you don't read of workmen finding bricked-up arches and wells leading nowhere" (*CF* 2.61). On the other hand, pirates lived there and "what they brought in from the sea" (*CF* 2.61); smugglers and privateers, familiar with the North End, lived there, people who knew "how to enlarge the bounds of life" (*CF* 2.61). These are arches, wells, and a criminal life, symbols of a renewal of life, that Revere may have known little of, although as a child he probably took note of the head of a pirate, well-pickled, publically displayed (Triber 11); and though Revere may not have understood these symbols, he certainly led a life that was to change the world profoundly and, as he was to say, "enlarge the bounds of life."

We should keep in mind the several events that took place leading up to the Lexington and Concord Battles, which Revere and others rode apace for, but which Longfellow ignores; the past is not as important in the poem as the present danger and the ride. The Stamp Act in 1765 was important for many people; and they would not forget. Even more unforgettable and violent was the Boston Massacre, for which Revere cut a famous engraving in 1770. More baroque doubtless was the Tea Act in 1774, which led to the Boston Tea Party and which Revere probably took part in (Fischer 25-26). The Powder Alarm in 1774 and the Salem Alarm in 1775 called forth many people, afraid that the English were marching against the colonial supplies of gunpowder, just as the events in the spring of 1775 did, for which Revere and Dawes and others rode out. By that time, riding to and fro most of the Whigs of Boston and the East Coast were intimately connected against the English colonial power; Revere took an important part in those connections, but he was not the only person who took part in the weight of history; this is the great difference between the history and the poem.

Let us read Longfellow's poem as though we were reading it next to Pickman and Lovecraft, not in the light of what we know now of Revere and his great ride, as though we were the children that the poet summons in the first stanza of the poem. The Landlord of the Inn who is about to tell the tale of Revere's ride is probably right to say that "Hardly a man is now alive / Who remembers that famous day and year" (ll. 4-5). This comment on the Landlord's tale is probably all the stronger now in the twenty-first century. Which of us now knows a child who can quote Longfellow's poem? Which of us has read the poem recently, or which of us has read a history of that time with all its pretensions? It is frightful to lose that past.

Given this commentary in the first stanza, the second stanza introduces the two main characters, Revere who shall ride from the Charlestown shore if his nameless friend should hang two lanterns from the tower of the old North Church when he sees the English on the march, especially if the soldiers leave the *Somerset*, "A phantom ship, with each mast and spar / Across the moon like a prison bar" (ll. 20-21). There is a touch here that resembles a passage in *The Rime of the Ancient Mariner* when the Mariner sees the hot sun barred as though it was in a prison:

> And straight the Sun was flecked with bars
> (Heaven's Mother send us grace!)
> As if through a dungeon-grate he peered
> With broad and burning face. (ll. 177–80)

Of course, this is the sun not the moon, but the grate of this hell denies any grace in a horrible fashion; in the frequent language of the Romantic period, the moon is a symbol of the imagination. So here the imprisoned moon acts out the imprisoned imagination and the world such as the colonized world might know it. But it is not simply our imaginations that are imprisoned; this is a hulk, and it may be a hulk that is literally a prison that is more than "like a prison bar," No, this is a dungeon that bars men in. This is an actual prison that may be worse than a warship; and no doubt the prisoners' taste improves with time.

The problem with this understanding of the *Somerset* is that we have the material that outlines the size of the ship and the number of people, soldiers and sailors, aboard it (Fischer 308-10). We cannot be led astray by the metaphoric language of the poet's account of the scene, powerful as that is. Pickman is at least at third or fourth remove from the reality that Revere and other men suffered.

Here we should pause to confess that if we know little about the ship that threatened the North End, we also know little about this church from which the two lanterns will swing; and the fact that Revere and Lovecraft do know this old church indicates an erasure here in the story. In fact this is an Anglican church, devoted to the service and liturgy of an English congregation (Fischer 99); and at the end of the war it becomes Episcopalian. Also this "phantom ship" that we shall encounter in the following stanzas prepares the reader for the frequent characterization of the ghosts surrounding the Old North Church, or this is what the friend seems to see:

> Beneath, in the churchyard lay the dead,
> In their night-encampment on the hill,

> Wrapped in silence so deep and still
> That he could hear, like a sentinel's tread,
> The watchful night-wind, as it went
> Creeping along from tent to tent,
> And seeming to whisper, "All is well!" (ll. 42-48)

The effect of these passages, however, is not to increase the several Gothic passages, but to hint that the English rulers of the colonies are already dead; they certainly do not understand that all is not so well, though they believe that it is. "Yum yum," however, says the apparently apolitical Pickman, who eats a dish that has a tang to it.

Revere decided not to carry a gun, probably saving his life thereby. When an English Regular stopped his ride and threatened to blow his brains out, it was the fact that Revere carried no arms that calmed the man (Fischer 103, 133). The tradition in Longfellow's aesthetic does not allow a man to leave a weapon behind; it is not heroic, so the poem has nothing to say in the matter. In Pickman's tradition, if we may speak of such a thing, a man who leaves a weapon behind is akin to a chef who uses no hot sauce.

This is a poem in which much is surprisingly steep. The nameless friend climbing the ladder inside the steeple climbs something "steep" indeed. When Revere leaves Charlestown on the other side of the river from Boston, he "mounted the steep, / And beneath him, tranquil and broad and deep, / Is the Mystic, meeting the ocean tides" (ll. 81-83). And we should notice also how often the sound of the syllable "ee" occurs; something difficult is that the two characters meet. And Revere encounters this moment also: "The meeting-house windows blank and bare, / Gaze at him with a spectral glare, / As if they already stood aghast / At the bloody work they would look upon" (ll. 96-100). This is pure Lovecraft, emphasizing "blank and bare" windows that look out "with a spectral glare." They recall the "the silent, sleepy, staring houses" in "The Picture in the House" which "blinked with bleared windows" (*CF* 1.208). He may have aesthetic problems with Longfellow's career, but I don't believe he can have problems with this complex Witch's Dance.

Looking back at the structure of the poem, it begins very simply, in stanzas that are six or seven lines long, mostly in couplets. In the center of the poem the stanzas are often eight or nine lines long, and rather discursive in nature, with rhymes that have become more complex. The last three stanzas are longer than all, and the complexity even more increased, of the sort we are liable to find in in the sestets of the Petrarchan sonnets. Thus civic orders discover and create themselves; in our case, America still begins to come into being; we still hear about the Midnight Ride in political discussions late at night on television. This Midnight Ride, however, calls forth every journey in the darkness from which we are liable to die, a horror of life that we are all to experience, one after another. For Revere it happens one dark hour after another as he knocks upon a door.

Longfellow asserts in the next to the last stanza, "You know the rest" (l. 111), taking up the theme of what we know and do not know with which the poem began. Yes, in this stanza we know how the battle ended at "at the turn of the road" (l. 117), but this is not a useful knowledge. That is what the last stanza offers:

> A cry of defiance and not of fear,
> A voice in the darkness, a knock at the door,
> And a word that shall echo forevermore! (ll. 122-24)

A cry, a voice, a knock, a word! That is all very well, but we sense once more that something has been left out, perhaps the "blank and bare / Windows" that watch Revere as he thunders past on his steed, perhaps the taste for that which has been left in death.

Enough of historiographies, symbols, themes, enough of the political temperatures of Longfellow's poem. Let us turn to Robert Browning's poem, "How They Brought the Good News from Ghent to Aix," also about a long horseback ride that life depends on. I am not saying that Longfellow's poem has been influenced by Browning's, but it does have features that are suggestive. First of all are the similar meters of the two poems, four anapests in a line with often a caesura in the middle of the line. The great difference in metrics is that Browning's poem is solid in inexorable couplets; Longfellow's poem with couplets on occasion is rather nervous in its effect. Both poems in their handling of the two metrics possess a great sense of urgency, conveyed through the power of the two horses. In Browning's poem two horses die of exhaustion, but not the narrator's horse, Roland, though that horse has almost offered up its life. We should keep in mind, however, that the Palatine Roland does suffer an enormous defeat. In Longfellow's poem readers see very clearly the reality of the battle of Concord:

> And one was safe and asleep in his bed
> Who at the bridge would be first to fall,
> Who that day would be lying dead,
> Pierced by a British musket-ball. (ll. 107-10)

There is a great difference here between the pyrotechnics of Browning and the sobriety of Longfellow, who all things considered is writing to save not the battles of the past but the battles of the Union now engulfed in the Civil War, very much "In the hour of darkness and peril and need" (l. 127).

Though the two poems move from darkness to light, the Longfellow poem remains lost in the darkness, since Lincoln's armies have some way to go before they reach Appomattox. "Pickman's Model" remains also drenched in such darkness; it does not matter that teatime has passed and the two men have moved to the North End to confront that darkness. Lovecraft does not seem to be writing for the darkness that is eternally in the cellar, and neither the tea nor the spirits will alleviate what stirs beneath it.

Lovecraft Dallies with Historiography

> Den Zahn schlägt sie in seine weisse Brust,
> Sie und die Hunde, die wetteiferden,
> Oxus und Sphinx den Zahn in seine rechte,
> In seine linke sie.

[She stabbed her tooth into his white breast, / She and the hounds, the contending ones,/ Oxus and Sphinx their teeth in his right breast,/ She in his left breast.] (Kleist 219)

In a small but significant number of stories Lovecraft attempted to construct a history of the prehistoric, prehuman world. "The Mound," *At the Mountains of Madness*, and "The Shadow out of Time" are all concerned with this apparently extra-literary project in great detail; and he made an early outline of this interest in "The Nameless City." Not that Lovecraft was alone in this tendency. Robert E. Howard provided him something of a model as the Texan constructed an exotic background for his Conan cycle. But in the 1920s and 1930s we meet several authors whose attention was turned to the project of history, as though the tendency that began in Vico and Herder had now reached complex flower in the volumes of Spengler and Toynbee, challenging counter-histories, myths dressed in the garb of the *Geisteswißenschaften*. Tolkien had been constructing his history of Middle-Earth since the first decade of the century. And others such as Yeats and Joyce, in their different ways, had pursued their own histories, Yeats with some light self-irony in *A Vision* and Joyce with great humor and intelligence in *Finnegans Wake*.

I am not concerned in this essay to establish the degree to which Lovecraft was consistent in his details as others have done; instead, I wish to compare his histories in order to meditate on their fictional significance. In addition, I think it is important to pay some attention to the media of his histories, so often carved as hieroglyphic murals on the ceilings and walls of his lost civilizations.

We examine Lovecraft's histories with a full awareness of the engagement of the West's meditation on histories. In the Enlightenment the concern for history was rooted in the possibility that history, once comprehended, could be laid in human hands; we could create our own history, our own future, with no possibility of return. In the modern age, in part because of Nietzsche's emphasis upon the *Ewige Wiederkunft,* considering the possibility that history was cyclic or in whatever its shape inexorable, we surrendered the possibility of creating it. We were its predications, not its subjects. Soviet Russia, like Augustinian Christianity, saw the matter rather differently of course; each in a different way believed in the City of God, even if it was Hegel or Marx who sat on the throne. Lovecraft is rather different in that his histories are not cyclic and possess no inexorable shape; yet they impend upon his alien races and upon humanity in a way that leaves no escape from destruction. Time is not for us forever.

I

Vidi Cammilla e la Pantesilea (Dante, *Commedia* 1.4.124)

Before addressing Lovecraft's works directly it will be useful to examine his model for such a procedure in Virgil's *Aeneid.* I have already examined this passage as an act of fantasy (Waugh, *Voices* 278-82), so my examination here will be rather different. After his far wandering Aeneas meets his Trojan history carved in the walls of a temple dedicated to Juno which Dido has constructed in a grove "laetissimus umbrae" (1.441), not only happy in having this temple built but happy in the shadows. In this wall he is first struck by Achilles, who is fighting both Agamemnon and his brother; then he gestures to the artist's rendering of Priam and sums up his feelings in the famous line, "sunt lacrymae rerum et mentem mortalia tangent" (1.462). Our sense of history never escapes the personal engagement, for Aeneas is indeed "multa gemens" (1.465) as he points out the salient work. He concludes by returning to the striking figure of Achilles and wrestling with the figures of Memnon, the black warrior who is the son of the Dawn, and Penthesilea, the queen of the Amazons and the bellatrix who dares fight men. These contrasts that have come down from the past world are not to be ignored, and shortly we will say more about them.

For very good reasons S. T. Joshi has little regard for Lovecraft's story "The Nameless City" (*I Am Providence* 380–82), since it is his first attempt at outlining the history of an alien race, which is the very reason why we wish to address it. Before we speak of that history, however, we need to pay some attention to the framework of the story. Two elements from the opening of the story play the part of a refrain at the conclusion. First, we have the couplet from the *Necronomicon:* "That is not dead which does eternal lie, / And with strange aeons even death may die" (*CF* 1.232), a strong expression of the race's attempt to achieve an earthly immortality and thus to escape the earthly change, especially geological change. Lovecraft was himself sufficiently taken by the couplet to recall it in a number of later stories, so we cannot overlook it, though it expresses the desire that history should come to an end, leaving behind a time and place of "strange aeons," the time and place that is extraordinary, outside the world that we know (*Webster's,* "strange" and "extra"). The word "strange" is slightly more formal than the world of the Outsider that we readers of Lovecraft are familiar with; but both strange and outside point to a world that is more than we know.

The second detail that brackets the story is the allusion to Memnon. This is the potent myth to which Virgil had referred, the handsome black hero of the Trojan War who is the son of Eos, the goddess of the dawn; every morning she weeps for his death, and every morning at sunrise his elegant statue in Thebes emits a single, pure note. This myth concerns reconciled contraries, though it is difficult to see any reconciliation at Troy. Memnon slays many warriors before he meets his death; it is as though he died through meeting his own double, that being the warrior Penthesilea; Memnon dies, but he achieves a new life in the art of the statue and in its pure musical salute to the sun. Still, there is something ironic in this moment as this narrator alludes to this Trojan moment; stone and air work together for the sake of art. He traditionally dies at the hands of Achilles, as does Penthesilea, but we need to deal with them further.

Our difficulty is that we have two accounts of the deaths of these heroes. Homer gives a very short account of their matter, and Quintus Smyrnaeus too extended an account, twelve thousand years after Homer; in the two books in which they die they deliver only the most accustomed orations, at which Achilles slays Memnon in the first book and then Penthesilea in the second.

We are liable, however, in the noise to miss the explanation that Smyrnaeus offers for the horror of Penthesilea, who has killed her sister in the hunt. She has come now to Troy:

> Of murder's dread pollution thus to cleanse
> Her soul, and with such sacrifice to appease
> The Awful Ones, the Erinnyes, who in wrath
> For her slain sister straightway haunted her
> Unseen. (1.27–30)

We find here once more the theme of the double and the attempt to erase the double; and once more this scene is truly erased, for Smyrnaeus, after this introduction of the sister, will seldom mention her again.

There is nothing for us then to do but to turn to Kleist's difficult, blood-soaked tragedy in which Penthesilea, violently in love with Achilles, turns her dogs on him and joins them at the glut. It was a play that Goethe found impossible and which we find impossible also and fearful, wondering whether Achilles has unconsciously taken the part of Memnon and the sister. Writing the life of Kleist, Joachim Maass discovered there no more than suicide on the side of Achilles and on the side of Penthesilea; or he finds here an internal portrait that Kleist has drawn of himself before his suicide in 1812. This is a violence that refuses to be understood. So Virgil devotes three lines to Penthesilea and a mere two to Memnon, breaking the expected symmetry. History is too stylized in these works to make sense.

II

> Nubes—incertum procul intuentibus ex quo monte (Vesuvium fuisse postea cognitum est)—oriebatur [. . .] [A cloud arose—that observers found uncertain, though afterwards we knew it was Vesuvius [. . .] (Pliny, *Natural History* 2.61.5)

With some relief we turn to Zamacona, the Spanish adventurer who twice fails to find his way into the ruins of K'n-yan, but after many similar attempts he discovers a steep staircase into the abyss. There he finds the frescoes that he was certain existed and that he was searching for, "the nameless city," not so difficult we should think, for the phrase "the nameless city" occurs twenty times in the story, as though it did in effect harbor a tongueless race; though it achieves an alphabet, nevertheless the race communicates its world through a pictorial art and pageantry.

We need to pause here for a moment to consider the language that Lovecraft is using here, a language that depends upon the context of the King James Bible. Lovecraft made a very conscious decision that he would use a language that depended upon the Elizabethan and Jacobean tongue. For instance, he would render Psalm 106:2 as "Who can utter the mighty acts of the Lord? who can shew forth all his praise?" In the same fashion he would render Luke 20:47 as "Beware of the scribes [. . .], which devour widows' houses, and for a shew make long prayers." In Colossians 2:23 we read "Which things have indeed a shew of wisdom and humility," understanding the word "shew" immediately, but within the context of twentieth-century fiction it will always seem strange, bearing with it the suggestiveness of King James religiosity, especially if the word is used more often than we expect, just as it is in "The Nameless City" where the word "shew" occurs seven times. We have already learned in various stories that Lovecraft knows how to paint with words; and he paints with this word often.

The history that this narrator reads from these frescoes begins with a seacoast glory; there is no indication of a past before this golden age. This glory, however, cannot hold out against the steady pressure of geological change as the sea sinks away and the desert rises. The narrator says that he reads in the frescoes "its wars and triumphs, its troubles and defeats" (*CF* 1.240), but recounts no individuals and no nations involved in these convulsions. As for the narrator, he is only interested in the geological disaster; he does not say whether this narrative that bypasses particularities is his responsibility to the nameless people in the nameless city. Let us add that Lovecraft in his several histories is not interested in individual responsibility. The aliens are simply too monstrous for any one human to deal with them, submerged in the action.

At this point a further complexity enters the story that this narrator offers, for he has admitted that the people who inhabit the city in the frescoes are reptile-like, but of a kind like the crocodile, the seal, the cat, the bulldog, the satyr or the human being, which is to say that they were "outside all established categories" (*CF* 1.240). He cannot, however, accept them in any of these guises, so he argues that they were a mere allegory (*CF* 1.240); he never, however, offers a reading of this allegory.

Dubious as the allegory may be, it proceeds to its utopian conclusion; the race, whatever that race might be, burrows into the earth hoping to find there "an ideal of earthly immortality" that the skeptical narrator regards as "a cheering illusion" (*CF* 1.241). According to the frescoes as he reads them, the race discovers for itself a place in the abyss of the earth where it shall live in its own flesh eternally. Unfortunately, as the narrator recounts this allegorical history, he is taking note of other evidence alternating in the frescoes that might suggest another, rather different history. The tunnel is ringed with coffins in which reptile-like creatures lie mummified, but the narrator refuses to understand these bodies.

These details lead us to emphasize a number of them in a picture of Lovecraft's history, one which the history of the nameless city often confronts. The language of the symbolic carvings is often described as a cartouche, a gun cartridge that contains gunpowder, quite deadly, or an oval figure that might enclose a sovereign's name. The tunnel is leading to an underworld, one that seems closely associated with the intricate afterworld of the Egyptian. Insofar as the cartouche is connected with language, we may think of it as a letter, a single letter that does not manifest a meaning. I daresay, however, that the cartouche is most often associated with the Egyptian *Book of the Dead*.

III

But march away.
Hector is dead; there is no more to say.
(Shakespeare, *Troilus and Cressida* 5.10.21–22)

After writing "The Nameless City" in 1921, from 1921 to 1935 Lovecraft wrote three works that extrapolated a history and society other than the Western model of the last two-thousand years, and therewith began writing something that strongly resembles science fiction, at least in its old-fashioned sense that he began to write utopian fiction, though he might not have minded to grant that this is a speculative fiction. These are "The Mound," *At the Mountains of Madness*, and "The Shadow out of Time." Other works such as "The Shadow over Innsmouth," "The Shadow out of Time," and "The Whisperer in Darkness" make utopian gestures, which is to say that they meditate upon a society outside of time, but their histories hardly have the sense of a time that is always in change, subject to the sweep of all other fictions. I understand *utopian* in this essay in a critical fashion. The commentary that a utopia offers upon the present time is often ironic, running the gamut from Plato to Orwell. And so we must not read the stories as though they were wish-fulfillments or as though they were satiric; he has learned the lesson of H. G. Wells that no human construction, not even the utopian plans we construct, can be static. But neither is Wells teaching in these stories; that is to say he is not using normal discourse to model what he knows and what the reader ought to know. He is historically speculating, mirroring this world in a broken manner and restructuring the contemporary pressures and political thought of the twenties and thirties.

"The Mound," the novella that Lovecraft ghostwrote for Zealia Bishop and that was his first work to offer a full-scale other society and culture, has several elements we need to take note of, though this underworld is so spacious that it almost loses the quality of a closed space. Traditionally a mound is "a burial-place or ceremonial dais" (*CF* 4.161). The natives of the region, however, tell stories of an invisible battle in the air, at least that is what the first narrator, a very sober "American Indian ethnologist" (*CF* 4.158) records.

A secondary narrator, the ageless Grey Eagle, chooses not to descend, but he tells stories of several descents and ascents that others have made, the last story being the most circumstantial since it is the oldest, coming from the manuscript of a Spanish conquistador. In his story the descent begins through a doorway giving upon Cyclopean masonry with carvings that concern the figures "Yig and Tulu" (4.190). Only later in the story do we learn that the natives in the underworld are telepathic and do not require speech. "The carvings must have been loathsome and terrible" (4.190). Yes indeed, so terrible as to introduce Yig and Tulu and to introduce the theme of the monstrous cosmic intrusion. Later as Zamacona crawls across "a sinister cartouche or hieroglyphic on the wall," he sees "occasional cartouches with shocking bas-reliefs" (4.190). It is not necessary for Lovecraft to describe in detail these fetishistic objects or to bestow upon them any temporal order.

Once more as at the Nameless City a wind starts up, "some perverse gust of wind" (4.178), but this wind seems "almost as if the air thickened in front of me, or as if formless hands tugged at my wrists" (4.178). Near the conclusion of the novella this wind appears once more, "a sudden wind blowing against me." At the swing of his machete the narrator senses "a cave-in and uprush of curiously chill and alien air" (4.237). Lovecraft is very careful about this wind, which is so important to the shape of the novella, important enough that we may wonder whether it incarnates the persona of Memnon, which is twice figured in the "mem" and "non."

This triad twice over in the name of this character is odd enough that we should pursue it further. "No" is an act of refusal, so powerful that in Middle English it is doubled, producing the "non" we find in "Memnon" and in the "non" of Latin (*American Heritage* 1226). The roots of "mem" are more complicated. As we thought, "memory" (in doubled "m's") comes from (s)smer, as does "remember" and "Mimir, the giant guarding the well of wisdom" (1147). We had not expected the gigantism of Mimir to be confirmed in Memnon. Pokorny suggests that Mimir has other possibilities in "emporragen" or "denken, geistig erregt sein," a spiritual confirmation of the gigantistic theme, nor had we expected that the neck, "Nacken" or "Hals" would appear at the end of the story in the beheadings or, in more of a strain, that a monstrous "Ungeheuer" would appear (1.726-27). But this is that kind of monster.

In his account Zamacona begins to read the various sliding, crawling, clambering and walking that are the ascents and descents of three days, followed by a series of caves until at last he comes out into a space so large he cannot see the height or breadth of it, lit by "a bluish, quasi-electric radiance" (*CF* 4.191), at which the narrator compares him to Balboa discovering the Pacific from "that unforgettable peak in Darien" or to "an intruder on an alien planet," allusions to Keats's sonnet "On First Looking into Chapman's Homer" (*Poems* 64). This is the point at which Lovecraft's historiography begins, though just like Keats this narrator misremembers the detail, as though our history suffered from a touch of *Trägheit,* be it inertia or a tendency to suffer from inadvertent mistakes.[1]

This allusion to Keats's sonnet also subtly introduces the theme of the "dry, temperate climate," its "delightfully spring-like stability" (*CF* 4.193), which ought to surprise us. Usually in Lovecraft's framework of this sort of story the climate is extreme; in "The Nameless City" the desert is often referred to, in *At the Mountains of Madness* the world is bitterly cold. We are liable to forget the lines in the sestet: "Then felt I like some watcher of the skies / When a new planet swims into his ken" (ll. 9–10). Its gigantic intimacy subtly transforms the Mediterranean imagery of the "many western islands" (l. 3) in the octet, just as the imagery of the Pacific had done in the twelfth line of the sestet, which magnified the new ocean at which the men stared in silence.

This description of the novella does not do justice to the complexity of the ways in which the action and the presentation unroll, only because this essay is interested in the full understanding of these four stories within a philosophic understanding of history, not in their four individual details. To put it another way, there is much more presentation than action in this story. Beyond this consideration of

---

1. I have dealt with this matter in *The Monster in the Mirror* 118–19 and 260.

the frame that Lovecraft uses in Keats's use of the oceanic and cosmic imagery in the Chapman sonnet, transforming that imagery to a meditation on the realm of the poet, we should also have in mind the overt use he makes of Keats's two *Hyperion* fragments as a future frame to the theme of the pathos of history. There is no getting past the fall of the Titans, though they have each "sifted well Nature's law" (*Hyperion* 2.181), which moves ahead through the Lucretian "atom-universe" (2.183), with no promise of a swerve. Oceanus claims to be an aesthete, but it is in fact mechanistic. Lovecraft had good reason to brush up his Keats.

But it is not enough to describe the descents and ascents here, for "The Mound" and "The Shadow out of Time," which we will shortly examine, share with *At the Mountains of Madness* a historiography that introduces Lovecraft's prejudices in a new fashion. He did believe that India, Indo-China, and China had a prehistoric influence in Central America (*ET* 113 and *SL* 5.87). In "The Mound," with its millennial history in which the cosmic race, more alien than Zamacona or we readers at first recognize, has slowly grown decadent, we can trace his view of China as ancient and slow, a stereotypical view most famously expressed in the exclamation of Tennyson's speaker in "Locksley Hall," "Better fifty years of Europe than a cycle of Cathay" (l. 184). In that aspect China was so foreign to European expectations of change that a number of times during the 1930s Lovecraft expressed sympathy with the Japanese invasion of China (*JVS* 175-76 and *RB* 201), at the same time it seemed probable that "in spite of all conquerors there will be a virtually unchanged China for generations after the present European world is forgotten" (*ET* 205).

After this long presentation, which is not very detailed, in the fourth chapter, the narrator Zamacona has much more to say in the final seven chapters. Here we learn much more about the three levels of this underworld, heavily colored in blue, red, and black as though this universe were a volume colored by L. Frank Baum. More interesting are the gods Tulu and Yig and the relationship between Yoth and Tsathoggua; the toad figure that is devoted to Tsathoggua no doubt has an arcane relation with the city Tsath that creates a strong feeling of expectancy; I would pronounce it with a short, nasty *â* or *ae*. Gradually, however, the demonic aspect of the dark city becomes more evident. "The dizzy giganticism of its overawing towers" (*CF* 4.220) gradually becomes more suggestive of Lovecraft's experience of New York, with no escape to Rhode Island. "The arenas of Tsath," the witness of Zamacona assures us, "must have been accursed and unthinkable places—Zamacona never went near them" (*CF* 4.226). This indirect discourse refuses to say what the horror might be—often, Edgar Rice Burroughs tells us with some relish (102-9).

IV

"I don't hate it," Quentin said, quickly, at once, immediately; "I don't hate it," he said. (Faulkner 378)

In "The Mound" the introduction to the body of the work is quite long, but that is nothing to the introduction of *At the Mountains of Madness*. The introduction of "The Nameless City" was far shorter, and you may be assured that the introduction to "The Shadow out of Time" is massive, though a bit shorter than *At the Mountains of Madness*. "The Hound" may rhyme with "The Mound," but that is the least of their likenesses.

I would like to suggest that *At the Mountains of Madness*, despite its title, may be one of the most orderly and balanced works that Lovecraft produced. First, we have the steady approach of the expedition across the antarctic plain that in the first four chapters leads to the several messages from Lake's sub-expedition and the loss of Gedney's party. The next four chapters contain the discovery of the great mountains that leads to the destruction of Lake's camp, culminating in the decision of Dyer and Danforth to fly across the mountains and their gasp at the sight of the enormous city beyond them. This is the first half of the novella, moving along slowly. The second half is the more important, careful section of the work, containing within it the history of the city and state of the Old Ones, Gedney's body, and the sudden appearance of the shoggoth. The decrescendo of the last four chapters thereafter is nicely muted, accompanied by the assertion that the Old Ones were "men," human by any standard of rationality, measured by the shoggoth and by Danforth's clever madness. This handling of the several materials, including the drawing of the different human characters, is one reason, I think, for the popularity of the work.

Let us consider this history that Dyer and Danforth slowly piece together, and much of this history is work that they have made more coherent after the fact. But both the Great Old Ones and these two men are together eager to create this history in which they are engaged: "It is this abnormal historic-mindedness of the primal race—a chance circumstance operating, through coincidence, miraculously in our favour—which made the carvings so awesomely informative to us" (*CF* 3.89). It is only this mutual engagement in the meaning of their walls that makes the readers, our readers, and the alien race so obsessive. We should admit, however, that it is only a New Englander—or a Southerner—who can understand this obsession with history, and only they can feel the force of these "terrible mural sculptures" (3.90), these "omnipresent" (3.81) and "oppressive walls" (3.121). But anyone may suffer the sense of being enclosed by our history. More generally, we live within our history. We carve and shape it; we are protected and shaped and destroyed by it. We have no escape from it. We recognize that those alien creatures are us, both in our rationality and in our sensuality that they had "filtered down from the stars when earth was young" (3.92). Dyer and Danforth, however, cannot be certain of the order of things. "Disordered time and alien natural law" (3.94) confuse them greatly. So great is this confusion that we might as well admit that since we are related to the Old Ones we are the makers of the shoggoths. I repeat, it is this moral shock that favors many of us to suffer this fiction.

The next stage in the history of the Old Ones lay in their creation of the shoggoths, which they had already accomplished on other planets "under hypnotic influence and thereby forming ideal slaves" (3.95). Through their strength they build their civilizations as easily under the sea as above in dry land. The history is now more complex, "evidently complex and probably socialistic" (3.99). In the late sculptures there is a "shambling primitive mammal used sometimes for food" that shows distinct signs of simian, human life (3.100). But barely had a civilized world come into being than signs of decadence appeared, at the same time that Dyer and Danforth saw the monstrous albino penguins. Also they realized that the art of the murals was now pastoral, "like, yet disturbingly unlike" (*CF* 3.138) the earlier work of the Old Ones, who had been deeply artistic. For the first time in these ancient histories the aspect of the aesthetic world enters into consideration, at the same time that it begins to fall apart.

The eleventh chapter is the climax of the entire work, as on the one hand Dyer and Danforth discover the body of Gedney and realize that the aliens who treated him as they would have treated any person they had encountered were precisely as much men as the men who had amputated them. This scene is followed quickly by the appearance of the shoggoth uprising through the fog, which leads to the trauma of Danforth. The two men escape, but they cannot escape the psychic traces of the creature, nor can the reader.

V

Habet quidem oratio et historia multa communia, sed plura diuersa in his ipsis, quae communia uidentur. Narrat illa narrat haec, sed aliter [. . .]

[Certainly an oration and a history have much in common, but there is much that is different between them. One narrates and the other narrates, but each with a striking difference] (Pliny 5.8.9)

Each of these works to some extent is composed as an experiment in time. "The Nameless City" has two plots, that of the narrator and that of the ancient history. "The Mound" in speech has a number of different plots, or different times, at work. *At the Mountains of Madness* would seem in its first half to be quite straightforward in its plot, but the second half is much more complicated in the history that is driven by the complex double plot and the complex moral problems. These three works, however, are not at all as complicated as "The Shadow out of Time." There is a problem in the immediacy of that title, but we will leave that problem to the conclusion of our reading.

Let us leave that to our reading of the double plot, that in which Peaslee finds himself engulfed and that in which the Great Race exists. On the one hand we have the difficult psychic problem that Nathaniel Wingate Peaslee faces, a problem that we sense in his reticence of speaking his name; on the other hand is the problem of his other self, but let us put that self aside first. "Nathaniel" means "Gift of God"; "Wingate" is a good old fashioned name, and that good son becomes "a professor of psychology at Miskatonic" (*CF* 3.368); and "Peaslee" is a good old New England name. Perhaps this is a name only too positive to be borne. In any case, he names his son first before he gives his own name, but that first name of his son, Nathaniel, has inexplicably been lost. His wife has found it necessary two years into his experience to divorce him, and his daughter and elder son have copied her.

Obviously these two plots, as two plots are wont to do, flow together often, but Lovecraft is careful, as he did in *At the Mountains of Madness,* to shape the work in its chapters, here in eight chapters that are divided into two sets of four chapters. In the first chapter Peaslee introduces himself and the dates that make his life so difficult, especially 1914, which he hardly regards as so important as any other person would in the Western World; he is as dissociated from that world as he is from himself. In the second chapter he reassures the reader that he is now as sane as he was before, taking up as any professor would his work in the 1914 term. He can no longer teach economy, so he addresses himself to the most outré psychologies, especially those that use mythic materials, as we can see in these simple sentences: "I *shewed* no sign of consciousness," he says of his first collapse (*CF* 3.366; emphasis added). "I haunted the college library at all hours," he admits, his first reaction to his new self (3.367). The third chapter traces how he tries to cope with his fragmentary dreams, and the fourth chapter extends those dreams into visions that are a shade more timely but "shewing no physical variation" (3.395). The fourth chapter concludes with a shewing forth of visions "untroubled by the monstrous entities" (3.408).

The fifth chapter opens with Mackenzie's letter from Western Australia, the other side of the world, as Peaslee prepares his expedition, using the photos that Mackenzie sends him and having secured the backing of Miskatonic University and the aid of William Dyer, the man who led the exhibition into *The Mountains of Madness* (*CF* 3.414). We are about to learn the large extent to which "The Shadow out of Time" summarizes other of Lovecraft's late novellas. Meantime he learns how well-read Mackenzie is. When they arrive in Australia as this fifth chapter concludes they meet "a late wind [that] had wholly altered the hillocks of shifting sand" (3.418), a broken, pneumatic wind that is very like the wind in "The Nameless City." In the sixth and seventh chapters "dreams welled up" (3.422), and elements of them are "well-remembered" (3.430). Toward the close of the seventh chapter he studies a book "with a haunting, half-aroused memory" (3.435).

Now in the eighth and final chapter three shewings occur, though Peaslee is certain he is alone there. But the intensity of his experience increases, leaving him hopeless. Walking forward he passes a "draught-giving abyss" (3.442), "where cold draughts welled up from unguarded depths" (3.443). It is as though in these last two chapters of this narration Lovecraft had wrestled together the words and themes that had been most important to the secret horrors of his career.

Narrations are important in this story. On the one hand, we have Peaslee's narration that he works as meticulously as is possible for him, ransacking the libraries of the world in the faith that day by day his life will make sense. On the other hand, we have the time of the Great Race, whose universe is totally broken up; it does not move according to the chronology shared by all races, the humdrum chronologies of days and years. These chronologies break up the universe, as does every race, and once more the principal time, according to the shoggoth, rules all; but we are all out of the shadow of time, and out of time.

No doubt Penthesilea has much to do with it, devouring her beloved just as a historian would and leaving not a bite behind.

Where Lovecraft Lost His Telescope: His Kingston and the Towns around It

It is time to record the origins of my place in Lovecraft criticism, which was the Lovecraft Forum that I founded thirty years ago through the efforts of a fan who appeared one day in the office of the English Department of SUNY New Paltz, saying to the Chair, "You need to have a Lovecraft Forum." "Why?" she asked mildly, and he answered that we must because Lovecraft had visited New Paltz in 1929. At this the Chair suggested that the fan should see Professor Waugh. I was only casually interested in Lovecraft at the time; but when the fan said he could provide me with his copies of *Lovecraft Studies* and *Crypt of Cthulhu* and bring such scholars as S. T. Joshi and Peter Cannon to the event, I acquiesced and have been running the Forum ever since. The few times I was gone students ran the Forum. The fan, whose name I have forgotten to my shame, has disappeared, on his way to Florida with his mother.

During the many years I lived in New Paltz and environs, I never took to heart the point of doing the Forum in that town. Later, when I moved seventeen miles north, preparing to retire to Port Ewen upon the Esopus Creek, I happened to read in Lovecraft's copious letter to Elizabeth Toldridge that besides the city Kingston he also visited the small towns of Hurley and New Paltz (*ET* 64–72), towns I am very familiar with and which Lovecraft visited at the same time as he visited Kingston. I had moved from one Lovecraft site to another; I could not escape him. So I gave up, and in this short essay I would like to outline what Kingston and those towns were like in the late 1920s when he visited them and to explore how he reacted to those towns.

Chartered in 1661, halfway up the Hudson River between New Amsterdam and Albany, for several years Kingston grew until 1797, when it became the first capital of the new State of New York, its name acknowledging for some years its fealty to King George III. One can still see many of the old government buildings, reared in the solid rock and stone of the eighteenth century and in the ornamental brick that is now the signature of the city. It was his interest in architecture that led Lovecraft to put aside his telescope, searching out the details of the upper friezes; it was here, however, that someone stole his diary and telescope, which is now something of the true cross that we Lovecraftians still have to recover (Joshi, *I Am Providence* 731). In this city the Dutch Reformed Church and the Episcopalian Church vie for interest, but the Victorian style of the Episcopal church would not have excited Lovecraft's interest.

"Kingston itself interested me prodigiously," he wrote in a letter in May 29, 1929, "for it is a highly venerable & historic place full of reliques of the past" (*ET* 64). Let us consider this statement: "reliques of the past." Twice over he emphasizes that it is the past that he has come to admire. Thus it is "venerable," a place to be approached in adoration. Now adoration is difficult, no matter what its object may be, so we shall see that Lovecraft does adore as far as he can.

"Kingston" can then be many things to many people. Lovecraft is meticulous in describing the shape and history of the city, the history of Kingston proper and the history of Rondout and the Strand, which in Lovecraft's time had its own ferry across the Hudson to Rhinebeck. The vibrant scene of the railroad and the commercial trucking had led to the stagnant world of the Strand that Lovecraft knew. He, however, was quite fascinated by the society of the Strand, in his day "a somewhat picturesque slum" (*ET* 64). One may well think of the slums of Eastern Providence that attracted Charles Dexter Ward as a young man or "the queer dark courts on the precipitous hillside" where Professor Angell died upon being jostled by "a nautical-looking negro" (*CF* 2.22). These were slumming places that I believe sang to Lovecraft's secret sensibility.

Now things are very different along a Strand that has been quite renovated, as has the arcade in the center of the city where people slowly built the Stockade District. A great variety of pleasure boats dock at the Strand; the restaurants are excellent, thanks to the Culinary Institute across the Hudson, and the art galleries are interesting. The Strand has become gentrified. At least, that is how it seems at first; but when you walk to the west along the shore of the Esopus, things become a bit more sleazy. Consider, in comparison to this present, what Lovecraft thought of the area some eighty years ago: "Hilly Rondout on the river has become a sort of declassé section largely given over to foreigners, from whom Kingston proper is almost wholly free" (*ET* 66).

What shall we say, then, of the foreigners in the city of Kingston and the towns of Hurley and New Paltz? The building of the Delaware and Hudson Canal in the 1820s brought a great influx of Irish, especially to the work on what became known as Rosendale Cement (Evers 220–21). Rosendale is a town that came into existence between Kingston and New Paltz; but in his description of his trip to New Paltz Lovecraft has no word to spare on Rosendale; this is a shame, since he might have found the caverns of Rosendale of some interest. From 1905 to 1915 Italians arrived to work on the Ashokan Reservoir (Evers 388); later the work in the farms became important for Jamaican labor. Finally we must mention the State Teachers College that became one of the state universities with a strong emphasis in the last twenty years on a diverse student body. Clearly Lovecraft could not see what was in front of his nose when he said that Kingston and New Paltz were free of foreigners.

As I have suggested, Kingston provided Lovecraft with a wealth of architecture. Yes, there were the gambrel roofs in which he reveled.

There were the stone houses of Hurley and New Paltz, and the ancient stone buildings in Kingston that survived the fire of the Revolution. Lovecraft is happy to speak for "a Dutch diplomat, visiting the place not long ago, [who] declared that as a whole [Hurley] is more typically & historically Dutch than anything now left in Holland!" (*ET* 68). He is happy to trip off his tongue "the railway station, P. O., public library, city hall, hospital, & Y M C A" (*ET* 66).

Lovecraft has considerably more interest in the streetcar line, to which he devotes two long, complex sentences, and the motor coach service, to which he devotes two more spacious sentences; these vehicles he believes must have "all the freshness, charm, & simplicity of a small village" (*ET* 66). It is easy to see what sorts of cities and villages Lovecraft preferred. It is possible, of course, that he appreciated the streetcar lines, the motor coach, and the rail line because he traveled by them.

From Kingston Lovecraft visited Hurley for a day, a pleasant backwater of Kingston that had a number of old stone houses. To call Hurley a backwater today, however, is to forget the historical turmoil that the town suffered in its early life, for it and Kingston did become a part of the Indian Wars, which Lovecraft wisely took note of: "Severe Indian warfare harassed the town throughout its early history—incidents not unprovoked by the high-handed seizure of lands & arbitrary and cruel treatment of Indians by the Dutch settlers" (*ET* 65). In 1663 the Natives burned Hurley to the ground and carried off a number of women and children. Lovecraft, we see, pays attention not only to the architecture but to the history. It was the search for those captives that brought some of the French Huguenots to the valley they named New Paltz, which as Lovecraft put it brought him on his next "sub-pilgrimage" after visiting Hurley (*ET* 68).

New Paltz founded in 1687 by French Huguenots who had arrived in the New World via the Netherlands and stayed first in Hurley. They bought the land from the Natives lawfully, "a step which would have delighted Roger Williams," the Rhode-Islander within Lovecraft cannot help himself from remarking (*ET* 70). Once more they built the stone houses that properly fascinated Lovecraft and which lured him to the town, houses built in the seventeenth and eighteenth centuries that were still inhabited by the original families when he arrived. The main church was the Dutch Reformed Church, which had slowly superseded the French Huguenots. By Lovecraft's time there had been a great influx of Italian families, drawn by the cement works in the nearby town of Rosendale, a town with no architectural or historical interest for Lovecraft. Through the first half of the century many more Italians arrived to exploit the earth for the sake of vineyards and apple orchards. A Roman Catholic church had been built in the heart of New Paltz, not far from the State Teachers College, which he did notice. A small Episcopal church existed for the sake of the Anglican managers of the cement works. It was a very quiet town, on the verge of expressing its new tensions and of discovering the treasures it possessed in the old stone houses.

Did any of this material find its place in Lovecraft's fiction? Yes, in 1924 in "The Shunned House," but before he went to Kingston, Jacques Roulet, the horrible creature of that story, comes from a family of Huguenots who have settled in the neighborhood of the French Provence. More striking are Lovecraft's references to the local geography of Kingston in "The Man of Stone" and "The Diary of Alonzo Typer," but those stories have little to do with that geography. We cannot really say that these stories were affected by their geography.

I do wonder whether Lovecraft as he inspected the region was in any way influenced by Washington Irving, whom he certainly respected, though the light tone of Irving's work was certainly not the tone that Lovecraft preferred. At the beginning of "Rip Van Winkle" the narrator describes the Catskills as "fairy mountains," with "magical hues and shapes" (4). In the postscript to the story he adds that it is "a region full of fable," appearing often in the Native mythologies (19).

With very little detail Knickerbocker refers to "the haunted regions of those mountains" (627) and their "enchanted regions" (629), but clearly those mountains do not belong to the mock-heroic style of that work. The mountains in both narratives are quickly dealt with; Lovecraft in his visit to New Paltz refers to "the quiet Dutch milieu so well exploited by Washington Irving" (*ET* 68), but for him as for Irving the Catskills and the Shawangunk hills are marginalized, and thus he speaks Irving's language when he says "the purple mountains loom mystically" (*ET* 67) and then turns once more to the details of Kingston, New Paltz, and Hurley. He writes in a manner fitting to "Rip Van Winkle" when he says of Hurley that "the place is delectably slow & sleepy, with true Catskill conservatism [...] tenanted by the same old families who built them" (*ET* 67).

When in Lovecraft's sub-pilgrimage he arrives at New Paltz, he reverts to the earlier language, "in the eternal shadow of the lordly & lovely Shawangunk Hills" (*ET* 68), innocent of the historical change by which the Shawangunks will become popular with moneyed rock climbers, training themselves for the Himalayas. It would not have been a change open to his sensibility. Instead, as he approaches New Paltz he rhapsodizes over "at least one old-fashioned *covered bridge*" (*ET* 69) that he sees—this, I dare say, is the bridge that is still in existence over the Wallkill, carefully preserved between Rosendale and Rifton.

New Paltz seems to have been everything he expected, very like Hurley but not slumbering. He especially appreciates the large stone house that is now the museum of the town: "under the immense sloping roof [...] a fine type of early colonial construction under Dutch influence, (though Frenchmen built it) & I examined it with the utmost thoroughness & interest" (*ET* 69), as I am sure he did. It is possible that at the end of this tour of Hurley and New Paltz he may have returned to the Strand by way of the bridge that had been built in 1922, but he never gave a clue that he had. Port Ewen, which had been founded in 1851 by the Pennsylvania Coal Company across from the Strand (www.nynjbotany.org/whudson/esopustown), never achieved a reputation of wonder or of true sleaze such as the Strand often did.

At the end of his stay in the upper Hudson valley Lovecraft turned his attention to the loss of French, which was the tongue of the French Huguenots, and Dutch: "Every effort was made to preserve the traditional piety & French ways of the forefathers, yet in the course of time the influence of the surrounding Dutch population could not help being felt [. . .] time took its revenge upon the once conquering Dutch language by pressing it to extinction as French had formerly been pressed—the latest conqueror being the all-engulfing English" (*ET* 70-71). This "engulfing" could not have been moral. It is upon this "pathos of the linguistic change" that Lovecraft concludes his meditation.

The physical evidence of this "engulfing" for Lovecraft can be seen in the fire that the British brought to Hurley; first it was a fire that the Natives brought, but now it was a war once more, "setting fire to all the edifices save those belonging to loyal subjects of our rightful sovereign" (*ET* 65). The sense of irony is alive here as Lovecraft suggests that "the political loyalty of the owner [was] the most probable" reason why the Van Steenbough house where the State Senate met was not burned (*ET* 65).

We should not be surprised that Lovecraft does miss some aspects of the city. Of great interest to him is the story of Aaron Burr, who in the Bogardus Tavern discovered the chalk drawings of a young boy upon a stable door and resolved to send the young man, John Vanderlyn, to Europe for artistic training (*ET* 66). We must keep in mind that this young man's first work of some strength some years later was the nude of Ariadne, a work that was not well received by his native city. This story, as Lovecraft tells it, is all about the perspicacity of Burr; but we have to bring to Lovecraft's account the more salient aspects of the Burr story, his duel with Alexander Hamilton in which Hamilton died and Burr's career was ruined. He was thereafter a man without a country, a fate that reminds us of Edward Everett Hale's poignant novella. The center of that work lies in the young man Philip Nolan's curse: "Damn the United States! I wish I may never hear of the United States again!" (Hale 23). As Lovecraftians we believe we have heard this story once before, not from the pen of Lovecraft but upon the lips of the Outsider. "I did not shriek, but all the fiendish ghouls that ride the night-wind shrieked for me, as in that same second there crashed down upon my mind a single and fleeting avalanche of soul-annihilating memory" (*CF* 1.271-72). This story is not a jest; it is deadly serious.

There is, however, another aspect of this city and its parasite towns that is ignored by Lovecraft, an aspect of the world that he either ignored or simply never heard of despite its powerful place in our world, at first after the Civil War and today in our multicultural world. This is the place of Sojourner Truth. Isabella was her slave name when she was born in 1797 in a rural cellar in Rifton; her house was sold for $100 in 1806 (nynjbotany.org/whudson/esopustown/), and she achieved her freedom with great difficulty in 1828 (Evers 186). During this time her only language was Low Dutch, i.e., Deutsch; shedding that language was her first step to freedom (Washington 18, 20). In time she became a powerful orator; but her freedom meant for her the freedom of all Americans, including the freedom of all women (Evers 186); thus she was more than an abolitionist before the Civil War. This demand for freedom in all its forms is one reason she remains a powerful figure for so many people. When a new library was built for New Paltz University, it was named in her honor, large photographs of her implacable, gnarly figure sitting above several of the staircases. She was illiterate, so we must learn that the letter is not the key to truth.

Lovecraft does not seem to be aware of this woman who looms above us like a fertile crack of doom. But despite this failure of imagination, two sculptures are now assumed by the two figures, the white man and the black woman, the conservative man and the progressive woman, the careful man and the outspoken woman. His statue stands firmly in place, the adult male in Providence, Rhode Island; and her statue stands as an adult in Northampton and as a young child in Port Ewen, just across the Esopus Creek from the Strand. He is gaunt, and she has been whipped. He of course does not mention her presence at all in his steps across the Rondout, for he did not believe in the freedom of the black existence; but as his own death marched upon him, the life of Sojourner Truth increased. The first plaque in her honor in Kingston was raised in 1883, before Lovecraft was born; the first in his honor was raised at the John Hay Library in 1990. We do imagine that neither would have appreciated the other, but I believe there is something of the child in both of them, and we are called upon to listen to the dark place in both.

Part Two:
Wells, Mirages, Madness, and Academe

The Brimming Wells

> "My throte is cut, un-to my nekke-boone"
> Seyde this child, "and as by wey of kinde,
> I sholde have deyed, ye, longe tyme agoon."
> (Chaucer, *The Prioress's Tale*)

I

This is a story that we know only too well out of many sources, and now we know it only too well out of various critics speaking about "The Colour out of Space," in which a well plays a nasty role. The word of the well, however, has many applications, some of them blissful, such as welcome and welfare and, yes, farewell. As a noun the word promises a well of water; this may be the most concrete meaning of the word. Many of the words as adjectives or adverbs are quite promising, though a few are threatening. Several times, depending on the usage, a word may be simply casual or intensive. I mean to examine how Lovecraft employed the word and its several possibilities. I should confess, however, that this study will not be exhaustive. I mean to deal with only a few of his weird stories, those from "The Call of Cthulhu," and those from his later work; *Webster's New Collegiate Dictionary* yields some fifty-seven different meanings, but a clever, literate mind may well discover more. I am well meaning, but I don't wish to exhaust myself or a well-read reader (*Webster's* 1330). How many of these words are liable to disgust us.

Before turning to Lovecraft, however, I want to call our attention to two moments of the world's history in the Christian Church. This is not a happy history, connected as it is to the Church's anti-

Semitism and also its several moments in the Inquisition. As James Carroll has pointed out, wells play a dramatic part in anti-Semitic stories. A fifteenth-century fresco in Arezzo "shows a man with a rope around his neck being lowered into a well" (Carroll 201). Often in a Christian court a Jew was accused and found guilty of poisoning a well, as befell twenty-seven Jews in Bohemia in 1163 (277). But the child may also be found guilty and thrown into a well. The well is a place of horror. For us the classic account of this story is Chaucer's *Prioress's Tale* as the Prioress recounts the story of Hugh of Lincoln, a little boy murdered to the glory of the *Blesséd* Virgin and his body cast into a well. No doubt this well is akin to the well into which Gardner's two sons are cast in "The Colour out of Space," his two sons at first full of so many wonderful colours.

Shakespeare, our clever classic, has an ambivalent well also, and it is not only to be found in that ambivalent comedy, *All's Well That Ends Well*. In *Macbeth* the well occurs at two crucial points, first as Macbeth considers very pointedly whether he should attack his king, and if so then how he should attack his king: "If it were done when 'tis done, then 'twere well / It were done quickly" (1.7.1-2), after this bit of impersonal casuistry the most painful well in the play is that which confronts Macduff as Ross, an embarrassed messenger, attempts not to disclose to Macduff the murder of his wife and children at the hands of Macbeth's minions:

Macduff: How does my wife?
Ross: Why, well.
Macduff: And all my children?
Ross: Well, too.
Macduff: The tyrant has not battered at their peace?
Ross: No, they were well at peace when I did leave 'em. (4.3.178-80)

This piece of dramatic irony is all the more painful through its use of the short sentences, the curt words, and the word "well" repeated three times in four lines. It is not the sort of thing that Lovecraft can miss, and neither can we his audience, as I have already demonstrated in my essay "The Blasted Heath in 'The Colour out of Space.'" These different versions of the word in Chaucer, Shakespeare, and Longfellow should also, I think, make us uncomfortable in the adults' treatment of the male child. "All is well!" sings out the watch in "Paul Revere's Ride," but he is mistaken.

Let us also notice that Milton is fond of the word. There is a crucial passage in *Paradise Lost* 9.141-229, modulating from the thoughts of Satan to the conversation of Eve and Adam; in this relatively short passage the word appears five times. The head of the Serpent, we are given to understand, is "well stor'd with subtle wiles" (l. 184); and when Eve argues that she should be able to work upon her own, Adam praises her in this line, "Well hast thou motion'd, well thy thoughts imploy'd" (l. 229), perhaps not praising her as deeply as he seems. The Serpent is already a presence in the haggling of the man and woman. However that may be, it is clear that Milton considers the word fit for epic material. In addition, he thinks the word "dwell" fit also, as in this line that points at the great mystery of the promise of the Comforter, "who shall dwell / His Spirit within them" (12.487-88). Lovecraft is not given to the doctrine of the Spirit, but he does often look to the question of human "dwelling"; and finally as we see later, the word "delve," so like and so unlike the word "well," is condemned to dig away in the sweat of Adam's brow.

How different is that early story, "Pickman's Model"! Praising his Boston studio on the North End, Pickman exclaims, "There's hardly a month that you don't read of workmen finding bricked-up arches and wells leading nowhere in this or that old place as it comes down" (*CF* 2.61). Informal as is Pickman's language, it is also potent: "I can shew you a house [Cotton Mather] lived in" (2.60). This place may not be to everyone's taste, but it is the place where Pickman discovers his perfect model. "Well, don't ask me to be too precise," the narrator says (2.64), but there it is, "the circular brick curb of what was evidently a great well in the earthen floor" (2.68). Note that this well is circular, "earthen," and "great," full of mythic power. As for the model where it at last appears, it is described in great detail, but only two aspects of that detail work well in a verbal story; early in that description is the material that makes us realize that this model is very like Goya's painting of the devouring god Saturn. More stylized is the passage that assures us this divine god "glared and gnawed and gnawed and glared" (2.69). A chiasmus is utterly appropriate to this formal moment. A few rats are casually mentioned in "The Rats in the Walls," but the only real well is the one in which the narrator is locked away in the "barred room at Hanwell" (*CF* 1.396), a famous madhouse in which he finds himself at the conclusion of the story.

II

> Sin is behovely, but all shall be well, and all manner of things shall be well. (Julian of Norwich)

The next story we shall examine, as we already have to some extent, is "The Colour out of Space," which like "Pickman's Model" contains as a part of its landscape an actual well. Lovecraft, we must admit, describes an actual farm of his time, so the farm necessarily has a "well" from which the beasts and the people drink, having brought up the water with the ancient "well-sweep" that the narrator twice meticulously mentions as he does not need to (*CF* 2.372, 374). Like the rest of the farm, this well shall be transformed. At this point in the telling of the story, however, nothing remains of the well but "the yawning black maw of [the] abandoned well" (2.369). It no longer devours, much as this well desires it, and the climb of the narrator is "welcome in contrast" (2.369) to the remnant of the farm he passes. Nevertheless, on the next page the maw of the well still "yawned deep" (2.371). We might argue, however, that the well was ready to accept "the great rock that fell out of the sky and bedded itself in the ground next to the well" (2.371). After this moment not much happens until the reader is assured that the well and the empty brown space are all that remain of these two objects, the empty hole in the earth and the kaleidoscopic rock (2.374). Neither yields to penetration nor to interpretation but only leaves death behind.

One of the effects of this demonic well is an inertia that prevents the family from understanding what is happening to them. Only Ammi from outside the family can assure that "the well water was no longer good" (2.381), but what is bad or evil about the taste of water is as indescribable as the colour of the stone. They will certainly not undertake the labor of digging another well.

The result of the inertia is that first the oldest son Thaddeus becomes mad as his mother, mad "in a way which could not be told" (2.382); but we can guess that like his mother and like his brother Merwin who had "gone out late at night with a lantern and pail for water" (2.383), Thaddeus is going to pieces. There is apparently little to bury. Perhaps the clearest comment on these deaths was that of Nahum's, "In the well—he lives in the well" (2.385), words he repeats shortly before his death (2.387).

Much of this material about the well is explored further in painful detail as the people with Ammi pull up the water of the well pail by pail, thus discovering in part Zenas and Merwin, not to be mistaken though the well is shallow, "porous and bubbling" (2.390); a deer and a dog are also to be found there, as well as a number of the bones of small animals. The men who have gathered there to investigate the deaths of the two brothers are quite nonplussed. As they consider these deaths there is a splash of something into the well, a well that was now "belching forth to the night a pale insidious beam of the same daemoniac tint" (2.391). The language that until this point has been nicely restrained now takes on another colour. "This new glow [...] appeared to shoot up from the black pit like a softened ray from a searchlight" (2.390).

The next story that calls for our attention is *The Case of Charles*

Dexter Ward, and the first detail we shall pay attention to is the plethora of names that begin with "W": the important Ward, Waite, and Willett appear early on; Ezra Weeden is important to the subplot, as are West, Whipple, and Wanton. Some of these names are historical, not a matter of choice, but surely they have an effect in a novella in which the word well appears at least twenty times in a work that is 51,000 words long; and this is not a work in which the protagonist is very well. Twice we are told that the child Ward was "wheeled" by his nurse along "the well-nigh precipitous hill" (*CF* 2.221), in a passage that suggests the young Charles is slightly ill. On the same page we learn that the older Charles is "well known" in Salem (2.265) but that he has a friend whose house is "well out toward the woods" (2.265) at a time when Charles indulges in experiments that are "a menace to the order and nervous well-being of the entire household" (2.294). He has early in the story said "farewell" (2.284) to his family, but of course he must soon return. He is then assuring his mother "that nothing had gone amiss" (2.289). His words are belied, however, by "the hideous and indescribable stench now welling out" (2.289) of his room. Even his upstairs room is treated as a well.

His language is quite different once Curwen has overtaken the world from Charles. He admits he is "not well spoke of by [his] prying neighbours" (*CF* 2.312). "You may as well know," he adds, "I have a way of learning old matters from things surer than books" (2.312). He cannot help writing, "as you too welle knowe" (2.342). The landscape is very different when Marinus Bicknell Willett climbs down into Curwen's caves and experiences the "dozens of Tartarean wells [that] poured forth their exhausted whining and yelping" (2.336). There is also "the stench from the far-away wells" (2.347) to contend with. There is of course an "unnatural well" (2.335) that has its own "kindred wells" (2.335) that may need "a vast number" to house them (2.335). These are only a few examples of the protean wells we encounter in reading this story.

III

> Eleven, twelve,
> Dig and delve. (*The Real Mother Goose* 80)

We need to pay attention to one other word, akin to "well" in its sound and perhaps in its meaning, "delve" and "delving." By the twentieth century the word has become vaguely archaic; we are more likely to find it in combination with "dig" in a *Mother Goose* collection. In Lovecraft it first takes the form of "Curwen delvings" (*CF* 2.278). But Charles is a delver also, as we see in the phrase "fellow-delvers" into the occult (2.284) to whom he alludes. He is a "dweller in the past" (2.273) whose living features now confront him. The narrator reminds the reader immediately of the "depths of forbidden lore" into which Charles "had delved" (2.285). To delve seems questionable in this world. These are strange books and "equally strange delvings" (2.287) that Charles commits himself to. In some time he admits that "his delvings had become blasphemous" (2.309), and with this admission the word drops out of Charles's vocabulary. To be a well, however, or to well out of his life as the protagonist does not do, whether he is Charles or Curwen, does not follow in this tragedy.

Let us admit then that the well from which we expect the sustenance of healthy water to spring forth will not always provide good water; nor shall that water exist that we expect. I paged through the novella *At the Mountains of Madness* very carefully, but seldom does that landscape mention a drop of water. It is cold, and very very dry. At one point the appearance of a mirage makes Dyer wonder at the nature of its "source" (*CF* 3.71). Later he feels sure that this is the source of Danforth's breakdown, the mirage of "disordered time and alien natural law" (3.94). But none of these appearances release a healing water. At only one point does an archway seem "to open on a well of illimitable emptiness" (3.83). Not every well entertains us, though the expression of the style is casual. The primordial ocean lies in the impossibly ancient past.

In "The Shadow over Innsmouth" we find the word *well* most often in conversations, as in the agent's speech, which "shewed him to be no local man" (*CF* 3.160). "Well," he says, "it's a queer kind of a town" (3.161). "Well," he adds in condescension, "there must be something like that [foreign sexuality] back of the Innsmouth people" (3.163). The grocery store boy warns the narrator against the dangers of Innsmouth: "It would be well not to make oneself too conspicuous in such neighborhoods," he says (3.177). The narrator, however, pays no attention to these dangers once he can sufficiently liquor up to Zadok Allen: "Wal, come abaout 'thutty-eight—when I was seven year' old," he launches forth (3.191), and every time he seems ready to pause he says once more, "Wal, Sir" (3.187ff). There is no stopping the man in the middle of the local obsession. This "wal," however, may be a nod to a "whale." Whaling, of course, is laborious, deadly work, so once more that which should be well is in fact horrible; it is nothing good at all.

But of course it may be nothing more than very like a whale but no more.

Some houses in Innsmouth, the narrator admits, are "well back from the water" (*CF* 3.173). A small structure that may be a factory is "a fairly well-preserved brick structure" (3.173). The door of the room in which he is imprisoned has rather oddly a "well-conditioned bolt" (3.209). When he sees the creatures later he remarks, "I knew too well what they must be—for was not the memory of that evil tiara at Newburyport still fresh?" (3.223). He is an excellent observer and narrator, but he does not see everything. "As may well be imagined, [he] gave up most of the foreplanned features of the rest of [his] tour" (3.224), only to see himself shortly in a mirror, and he knows too well what his visage in that mirror portends when he sinks into the sea. As with most of these stories, nothing is well in New England; the earth promised water, but that promise shall not be kept.

Looming at the Mountains of Madness

As Jason C. Eckhardt pointed out, Lovecraft made extensive use of Admiral Byrd's description of the aircraft he took to Antarctica and their various flights, thus substantiating the realism of the novella *At the Mountains of Madness.* Another aspect of the novella, however, goes far beyond realism, and that aspect also found its origin in Byrd as well as in other classic exploration narratives written by Scott, Shackleton, and Amundsen, gripping narratives to Lovecraft, who found in them one of the great myths of the day, the search for origins in the spot upon which the world turns. Any study of the novella needs to pay attention to those four authors because he mentions them not only a number of times in his letters (*JFM* 139 and 3.294) but also in the novella itself (*CF* 3.14, 19, 22, and 69). An examination of their narratives and Lovecraft's should uncover the relations between their treatments of reality and his treatment of a fictional world. More specifically, I want to ask what those explorers made of mirages.

There is a great variety of mirages, but each presents to the eye something that does not exist—water, ships, or buildings—in the place where it presents them. Sometimes the image is inverted, sometimes drawn out vertically, and sometimes magnified; the mirage displaces what exists. Three of the most striking mirages are the parhelion or sun-dog, in which a halo around the sun bears two or four further suns; the fata morgana, a vertical mirage of great clarity; and the looming, a variation of the fata morgana that occurs in a misty or foggy weather, magnifying an object both horizontally and vertically

("Mirage" 573). Most people recognize mirages, but the fata morgana is a different matter because it seems so real.

> Seasoned explorers, vehemently insisting on what they have seen, set down mountains and islands on their charts where there was nothing but empty sky. So convincing were these apparitions that the skepticism of other explorers (or even a member of the same expedition) was met with contempt. Expeditions sent out later to verify these new lands sometimes saw the same fata morgana, further confusing the issue. (Lopez 238)

People who are experienced in mirages learn to distrust what they see, though they recognize that every mirage, no matter how fallacious, does have its origin in something that does indeed exist, be it the mist and fog within which the rays of the sun are refracted. This point is not immediately apparent in rainbows and sun-dogs, so these phenomena are not often understood as mirages; but they would not manifest themselves were it not for the rain, mist, or fog. In addition, of course, the rainbows, sun-dogs, and other mirages would not exist were it not for the excited presence of observers.

Given the necessity of observers, let us survey the various narratives I have mentioned, the heroic accounts that appeared from the early 1900s until Lovecraft wrote his novella in February and March of 1931, and consider how those observers described the mirages they witnessed.

I

In the two volumes of *The Voyage of the 'Discovery,'* Scott remarks upon mirages eleven times but at no great length, since "extraordinary mirage effects are constantly seen" (2.188). Those he most often mentions are either mirages that belie distances, whether too near or too far, which we shall call mirages of perspective, or mirages that seem as it were to "throw up" a piece of land (2.31 and 2.77). He mentions these mirages so that later explorers will be forewarned.

Two passages stand out from the rest. In one the theme of the land that has been lifted up receives an extended treatment:

> The high, curiously shaped rocky patches seem to be suspended in mid-air; there was one a few days ago, long and flat in shape, which appeared to be so wholly unsupported that it was named 'Mahomet's Coffin,' but when the weather cleared we could see that the snow about it was really closer than the rock itself. (2.53)

Here the utilitarian nature of the comment yields to a numinous awe. In the second passage, Scott devoted more than a page to "the coloured circles of a bright double halo [. . .] intersected by one which ran about us parallel to the horizon" and to a "white fogbow, with two bright mock suns where it intersected the horizon circle" (2.35-36). His reference books assured him that no one had ever witnessed such a complex mirage, so he could only testify to the sublimity of the encounter and ask Dr. Edward Wilson to sketch the apparition, as he did in a wonderfully abstract design (2.37).

Wilson was a remarkable man, a doctor, naturalist, and artist who accompanied many of Scott's expeditions and who died with him (Simpson-Housley 96-97). His watercolors represent a muted response to the landscape and mirages; but the striking character of his work lies in its resemblance to the work of Nicholas Roerich, to whom Lovecraft's characters allude six times in his novella. Roerich, a Russian Orthodox mystic, had employed several different styles throughout his career; but it was his recent paintings of the Himalayas when he lived in the Kulu Valley—no doubt a potent name for Lovecraft (Decter 135)—paintings rampant in colors that Lovecraft had never seen, and which provided some of the inspiration for the novella (Joshi, *I Am Providence* 755, 784). After examining many of Scott's drawings, however, I believe that they also inspired Lovecraft in the realism of these references. He regarded Roerich's Tibet next to Wilson's watercolors as an authentic introduction to the world of Antarctica.

We cannot refer to Scott without referring to Amundsen, whose account deals with only one mirage at length. Returning to its base, a small expedition was confused by the sight of the tents and rushed down upon the base; Amundsen, a fairly cool personality, found himself "shaking with laughter" (1.247) at their mistake. Except for this moment he had little eye for mirages, though we can assume that he saw some. This mirage, an occasion of comedy, is comparable to several comic moments in Jules Verne's *Les Aventures du capitaine Hatteras,* which Lovecraft had probably read (*RK* 49), since he was passionately interested in polar narratives. "Toujours la refraction!" becomes a refrain of Verne's novel (273). The encyclopaedist of the expedition confesses, "Ah! les illusions d'optique! ce sont les seules illusions qui me restent, mes amis [. . .]!" (273). Both Verne and Amundsen found the mirage an occasion to laugh at human frailties. This is the only explicit reference to mirages in Amundsen's narrative; but as he bluntly remarks he did not appreciate their effects:

> The atmosphere in these regions may play the most awkward tricks. Absolutely clear as it seemed to us that evening, it nevertheless turned out later that it had been anything but clear. One must, therefore, be very careful about what one sees or does not see. In most cases it has proved that travellers in the Polar regions have been more apt to see too much than too little. (2.90-91)

He preferred the aurora, for the aurora is only what it seems, never more than it seems. The mirage always creates a language of excess, which is Lovecraft's natural language despite his persistent attempt in the novella at scientific accuracy and precision.

Shackleton's account became the classic of the genre because of his success in saving his crew; and he had a good deal to say about the mirages he and his crew experienced. His first mirage occurred in his entry into Antarctica: "Everything wears an aspect of unreality. Icebergs hang upside down in the sky; the land appears as layers of silvery or golden cloud. Cloud banks look like land, icebergs masquerade as islands [. . .], and the distant barrier to the south is thrown into view, although it really is outside our range of vision" (37). This is a precise description that does not avoid unreality and masquerade. Touching upon the classic inversions, the passage concludes, "We seem to be drifting helplessly in a strange world of unreality" (47). The next passage presents a fata morgana:

> Great white and golden cities of Oriental appearance at close intervals along these clifftops indicate distant bergs, some not previously known to us. Floating above these are wavering violet and creamy lines of still more remote bergs and pack. The lines rise and fall, tremble, dissipate, and reappear in an endless transformation scene. [. . .] Here the bergs assume, exchanging forms, first a castle, then a balloon just clear of the horizon, that changes swiftly into an immense mushroom, a mosque, or a cathedral. The principal characteristic is the vertical lengthening of the object. (67)

The persistent theme of Orientalism appears in the architecture, an urge to project the warm and exotic east joined to the theme of transformation. Yet Shackleton finds himself compelled to bracket the phenomenon that seems so driven to escape itself, as a scientific phenomenon; he does not insist that it is a mere phenomenon, yet that is the import of the passage. The last mirage, some two hundred pages later in the book, is in a very different tone. It presents the landscape as though it were full of ice-goblins, or as one of the crew-members says "dancing jimmies" (283). The mirage has lost its power to enchant.

Yet Shackleton twice meditates on the influence of the Antarctica upon the imagination of anyone enduring it for an extended period. During the antarctic winter he remarks on the "brilliantly fine weather with bright moonlight throughout. The moon's rays are wonderfully strong, making midnight seem as light as an ordinary overcast midday in temperate climes" (56), and upon the next page he naively alludes to "the friendly moon" (57). The point is that anyone living in straitened circumstances is liable "to see resemblances to human faces and living forms in the fantastic contours and massively uncouth shapes of berg and floe" (141). We may even see Cerberus (41). In an extreme landscape, where the only variety to be hoped for is a dip or rise in the temperature or a clear day or a blizzard, we create our own mirages.

Byrd is the great optimist of antarctic exploration, so his symbol is properly the aircraft, though he admits that once at an altitude of 4,300 feet it was often difficult to distinguish the land from the sky because the horizon was lost in a milky bowl. He also comments upon the difficulty of distinguishing clearly distances and heights; a man saw what he believed to be a peak and ran for it, only to discover it was "no higher than his shoulders and almost at the end of his nose" (89). For Byrd as for Amundsen the phenomenon is an occasion for comedy. Twice at no great length he describes sun-dogs (138, 279). Once he comments upon

> the strangest mountain I have ever seen. [. . .] Half-way down it ended, with a clear line of breakage, against the shimmering brilliance of daylight, as if the agency responsible for its structure had started to build it from the top, grew tired when the job was half done and left it there, like Mahomet's tomb, between earth and heaven. A mirage, I thought. (312)

Yes, a classic mirage, but the sight is merely a mirage, nothing more than a mirage, and with these words he returns to science; the allusion to Mahomet's tomb he borrows from Scott. At only one point does he seem moved by what he sees, the colors of midnight when

> green, rose, gold, red and blue commingle in delicate tones. Past the up-ended, pressure-ridden masses of ice the low-hung sun, wheeling about the horizon, casts long lilac shadows; and the more massive, towering ice forms take on the aspect of architectural magnificence, whose portals, turrets, rounded domes and cornices (of a cosmic disorder no hand could hope to imitate) diffuse a pale coloration. (71-72)

This is a passage much closer to Lovecraft's style and concerns; but the subject is not a mirage, and Byrd never suggests that it is.

Mirages may serve a variety of purposes. Scott is interested in describing them meticulously for later explorers, but twice he is moved by their numinous quality. Amundsen distrusts them; only the comedy of mistaken perspective moves him. A number of times Shackleton is moved by their numinous and aesthetic aspects; he is struck by the unreality with which a mirage surrounds him and his company, and he is often interested in their psychological implications. Though Byrd responds to the colors of Antarctica, more often he is struck by the comedy of mistaken perspectives.

II

When we turn to Lovecraft's novella its first striking aspect is that it contains many more mirages than we find in the usual accounts of antarctic exploration; yet it is a mere novella in contrast to the weighty volumes of the explorers. The narrator Dyer at first accepts the mirages as enchantments, especially "a strikingly vivid mirage-the first I had ever seen-in which distant bergs became the battlements of unimaginable cosmic castles" (*CF* 3.17). He imagines this mirage as something guarded and transcendent. Resembling the familiar fata morgana, it is the first intimation of the alien city that shall occupy the main body of the work and perhaps an intimation of the mountains that lie beyond it. The castle of the mirage seems whole; the miracle is that its massive walls do not fall. The city that Dyer and Danforth find, however, is a ruin perforated by emptiness. Also the mirage reveals Dyer's naïveté; we may sympathize with him at the same time that we hold ourselves aloof from his language. Later he experiences a mirage without explicitly announcing it: "When the vast rise loomed ahead [. . .] we knew that we had reached Beardmore Glacier, the largest valley glacier in the world, and that the frozen sea was now giving way to the frowning and mountainous coastline" (*CF* 3.21). At the end of the first section another mirage presents "distant mountains [that] floated in the sky as enchanted cities, and often the whole white world would dissolve into a gold, silver, and scarlet land of Dunsanian dreams and adventurous expectancy under the magic of the low midnight sun" (*CF* 3.23). This vision is transformed into a vision of evil in the actual mountains at the conclusion of the narrative, a good example of the fairy-tale language that permeates antarctic accounts (Simpson-Housley 93).

After these introductions to the mirage, it is useful to look at what Lake in his initial report has to say of the mountains, their "queer skyline effects-regular sections of cubes clinging to highest peaks. Whole thing marvellous in red-gold light of low sun. Like land of mystery in a dream or gateway to forbidden world of untrodden wonder" (*CF* 3.27). The next passage notes "queer skyline effects—regular sections of cubes clinging to highest peaks" (3.27), but whether this is a reference to a mirage or to an object remains unclear and thus moves us, ever so subtly, toward a main point of Lovecraft's use of the mirages: we cannot distinguish between reality and mirage. In his next report Lake compares the cubes to "the old Asian castles clinging to steep mountains in Roerich's paintings" (3.28). The architectural theme is touched upon powerfully; and if the mountains already look like cities, mediated by the paintings of Nicholas Roerich, shall it be odd if the mirages suggest cities? In the second description the mountains "hint of stupendous secrecy and potential revelation; as if these stark, nightmare spires marked the pylons of a frightful gateway into forbidden spheres of dream" (3.50). Dyer confesses, "I shuddered as the seething labyrinth of fabulous walls and towers and minarets loomed out of the troubled ice-vapours above our heads" (3.52). Despite these nightmare qualities, however, fused with exotic imagery, the mountains have regularities that suggest "primordial temple-ruins on cloudy Asian mountain-tops so subtly and strangely painted by Roerich" (3.50–51). Once more the mountains are not obstacles but gateways, architectural constructions imagined through the work of an artist-mystic.

The next mirage that occurs during the flight across the mountain Dyer treats at length, in part because he will refer to it near the end of his account. It is a "bizarre mirage" (*CF* 3.51), but that phrase does no justice to the experience. He has seen "dozens of polar mirages" before this moment, but none possesses this "wholly novel and obscure quality of menacing symbolism" that lies in "the seething labyrinth of fabulous walls and towers and minarets [which] loomed out of the troubled ice-vapours above our heads" (3.52). Like several passages about mirages this presents the paradox of a "seething" stone. This description adds "composite cones and pyramids" (3.52), which point again through the fata morgana at an Orientalism suggestive of something other than the accustomed world of these New England travelers; but when these shapes begin to, break up they assume "distorted temporary forms of even vaster hideousness" (3.53). It is no surprise that this beauty is not stable.

Shortly thereafter another mirage receives a proleptic description as Dyer speaks of their return to the ships and escape from Antarctica, "shaking clear of the thickening field ice and working up Ross Sea with the mocking mountains of Victoria Land looming westward" (*CF* 3.58). These several present participles mirror the kinetic power of the "troubled antarctic sky" (3.58). This passage out of the narrative sequence prepares the reader for the first extended description of the dead city. Dyer and Danforth try to say to themselves that what they see is merely a natural phenomenon like sites in Colorado or Arizona or perhaps a mirage such as they had seen earlier during the flight through the mountain range; but at last they have to confess that what they see is "the blasphemous city of the mirage in stark, objective, and ineluctable reality" (3.71). What they had seen earlier depended upon "the simple laws of reflection; [. . .] yet now, as we saw that real source, we thought it even more hideous and menacing than its distant image" (3.71). Reality yields to mere image. This is in part to say that they wish that what they see now was only a mirage, but also that in it the difficult categories of reality and mirage meet. The reality of the city exceeded the mirage they had seen of it earlier, and the mirage they had seen exceeded the simple laws of reflection by which it had existed. This moment shatters the categories of mirage and reality.

Shortly after this moment as they walk down from the aircraft they approach "the stupendous stone labyrinth that loomed against the opalescent west [and] felt almost as keen a sense of imminent marvels as we had felt approaching the unfathomed mountain pass four hours previously" (*CF* 3.77-8). Thus another mirage becomes associated with a past time and with an impaired memory. This point is enriched in the next instance in which the narrator asserts that the city is "a mirage in solid stone" because of its "extravagant shapes," its "terraces of every sort of provocative disproportion," and its "shafts with odd bulbous enlargements" (3.79, 80). This is a language struggling with shapes that make no sense in human experience and thereby must appeal to an oxymoron. The next paragraph attempts to express the moment in a more extended, less fragmentary expression:

> Now, outspread below us, it loomed like a dream-phantasy against a westward mist through whose northern end the low, reddish antarctic sun of early afternoon was struggling to shine; and when for a moment that sun encountered a denser obstruction and plunged the scene into temporary shadow, the effect was subtly menacing in a way I can never hope to depict. (*CF* 3.80)

This sentence begins with an unacknowledged paradox in the assertion that that which is below looms, proceeds through a careful account of the western and northern geography, and concludes in another confession of inability to account for the menace latent in the scene.

The next mirage is actually a reminiscence of "that monstrous and portentous mirage, cast by a dead city whence such skyline features had been absent for thousands and tens of thousands of years, which loomed on our ignorant eyes across the unfathomed mountains of madness as we first approached poor Lake's ill-fated camp" (*CF* 3.96). Here we find once more that odd word "loom," its suggestion of high verticality connected with the word "unfathomed" (*OED* 186 and *CF* 3.96).

The twofold description of the mountains behind which the city of the Old Ones lies has a parallel description of the immensely high mountains that start up some three hundred miles to the west. The first description depends upon a carving the Old Ones had made of these mountains that "had shot up amidst the most appalling din and chaos" (*CF* 3.108–9). After stating that the mountains must be some 40,000 feet high and giving their longitude and latitude, an appeal to the comfort of scientific data, the narrator falls back upon the private myth Lovecraft was so fond of, claiming that there may be some truth to the legends of Kadath in the Cold Waste; he had only a few years earlier written his most extensive but unpublished treatment of the myth in *The Dream-Quest of Unknown Kadath*.

This description, then, like the earlier descriptions, depends upon pictorial art and myth. The second description is more extensive and more hyperbolic; these are the "highest of earth's peaks and focus of earth's evil; harbourers of nameless horrors and Archaean secrets; shunned and prayed to by those who feared to carve their meaning; [. . .] beyond doubt the unknown archetype of that dreaded Kadath" (*CF* 3.153). This description affirms the myth and thereby undercuts the power of the pictorial art. In addition, however, it affirms the "dim, elfin line of pinnacled violet whose needle-pointed heights loomed dreamlike against the beckoning rose-colour of the western sky" (3.152), pointing at dreams, which are so important a source if intuitive knowledge in Lovecraft, and then reiterating the language and expanding it: "yet none the less sharply did their dim elfin essence jut above that remote and snowy rim, like the serrated edge of a monstrous alien planet about to rise into unaccustomed heavens" (3.153). The word "elfin" may bear too delicate connotations, but Lovecraft does in his treatment of the mirages appeal to the Irish decadence. Also, the word may be suggested by the fata morgana, which alludes to the fairy Morgana, the half-sister of King Arthur who in some stories "inhabited a submarine crystal castle" (Simpson-Housley 46). This passage modulates the language of dream by employing the language of the science-fictional sublime; but its insistence upon a radical verticality approaches the vision of a looming mirage.

III

The final mirage, if it is a mirage, occurs on the final pages of the work. Turning to look back at the city, Danforth sees something as he and Dyer near the pass, something that causes him to shriek and which obsesses him thereafter. He insists that it is a mirage, a mere mirage, and Dyer thinks it "probable," given "the churning zenith-clouds," that what he sees is a "delusion" caused by the events of the day and by the "actual though unrecognized mirage [. . .] experienced near Lake's camp the day before" (*CF* 3.156); and he further argues, scientist that he is, that "imagination, knowing how vividly distant scenes can sometimes be reflected, refracted, and magnified by such layers of restless cloud, might easily have supplied the rest" (3.157). The words "reflected, refracted, and magnified" succinctly summarize the theme of the mirage.

But Dyer's imagination has already been sensitized by another event, the climactic event of the novella, which we may also read as a mirage. This, in the depths of the city, is their encounter with the shoggoth as it rumbles past them in the tunnels that Danforth's ritualistic recitation of the stations of the subway between South Station and Harvard attempts to transform to the familiar. Several repeated elements constitute this encounter. There are the references to the thinning, curling, and thickening mist that provides them only the "half-glimpse" or "semi-vision" they have of the creature; mist is one of the components of the looming. Another component is the references to the burrows of the dead city, "morbidly polished burrows" (*CF* 3.147) that so startlingly resemble "the Boston-Cambridge tunnel that burrowed through our peaceful native soil thousands of miles away in New England" (3.149); this passage may be reminiscent of the subway tunnels the ghouls inhabit in "Pickman's Model," and given the repetition of the word "burrow" the word "peaceful" is a nice piece of irony. This element is repeated when Dyer mentions "the prodigious burrow" through which the shoggoth finds its way (3.150). If Kadath in the Cold Waste is indeed the true myth of this city at the Mountains of Madness, Lovecraft is only asserting here what he asserted at the conclusion of *The Dream-Quest of Unknown Kadath*, that there is an intimate relation between Boston and the dead city. Well-behaved Beacon Hill sits on top of a nightmare, all the more a nightmare because it is associated with the mirage.

Finally, then, let us consider the shoggoth itself as a mirage, "the great black front looming colossally out of infinite subterraneous distance" (*CF* 3.150). Dyer has already used the word "loom" seven times in his descriptions of mirages. According to Dr. Johnson the word indicates "a frame in which the weavers work their cloath," to which we might add in wonderment the loom upon which the Fates weave their futures; or "to appear at sea." *Webster's Dictionary* expands this significance: "1. To come into sight, esp. above the surface of sea or land, in enlarged, or distorted and indistinct form, often because of atmospheric conditions. 2. Hence, figuratively, to appear in an exaggerated or impressively great form." The gerund "looming" has a very specific meaning within a polar context, being "a seaman's term for the indirect and exaggerated appearance or outline of an object when it comes into view, as the outline of land on the horizon, an object seen through the mist or darkness." The verb means "to appear indistinctly; to come into view in an enlarged and indefinite form" ("Loom" *OED*). Lovecraft is playing upon a word that has become common in contemporary life, usually referring to an impending disaster, in his hand suggesting a vague threat rising and impending out of an infinite depth; but since he has used the word so frequently in connection with mirages we cannot escape the impression that the shoggoth might be a mirage.

In summary, the mirages Lovecraft presents in his novella are of two types, the fata morgana and the looming, though we must recognize that in several cases the two imageries are fused. The fata morgana is not difficult to read among his repertoire of symbols; it offers a gateway or pylon, words often repeated in the work which are of a piece with the great range of sunset terrace imagery in Lovecraft's work, evoking an adventurous expectancy, beautiful beyond belief, that may well lead to horrors (Cannon 14). The looming is more difficult to read. It is the shoggoth, "looming colossally," that finds its home even among the burrows of Boston and Cambridge; but the true horror of the shoggoth is its insidious mimicry of the creatures that made it. No doubt this is the reason for the power of John W. Campbell's "Who Goes There?" and its cinematic remakes; the shoggoth may well be among us. Lovecraft, however, has something further in mind, for he mimics the language of the Bible: "So God created man in his own image" (Gen. 1:27). The Old Ones, impersonating the god of evolution, also wrought that vaguely simian creature from which humanity has evolved; we are as it were half-brothers and half-sisters to the shoggoth. So if the shoggoth is a mirage looming over us vaguely enlarged, we are mirages also, reflected, refracted, and magnified, distortions of the shoggoths and of the makers who made us both, our fathers who died surrounded in the dead city by the obsessive images that project their history. We cannot escape these affiliations. The looming has always been upon us.

At Home in Miskatonic U.

> Gaudeamus igitur,
> iuvenes dum sumus.
> Post iucundam iuventutem,
> post molestam senectutem,
> nos habebit humus.
>
> [Therefore let us rejoice while we are young
> After the laughing youth,
> After our troubled old age,
> The grave will have us.]

Thus the first stanza of this poem that appears in so many of the poems that we joyfully and respectfully address in song as the Alma Mater in honor of the students who are now setting forth in their lives, or in honor of those no longer with us. Rather solemn, aren't they, or aren't they now, opening an essay on the theme of the H. P. Lovecraft, who never formally entered Brown University, though it stood across the street from him most of his life? Instead, it was Miskatonic University, floating just across the street as it slowly became his model of intellectual life. It is more than time, then, for us to examine the two institutions together, especially when we consider that Miskatonic University was slowly transformed within his hands as his life changed. What is a university, in any case, as Lovecraft understood the institution? "Maybe Harvard wun't be so fussy as yew be" (*CF* 2.435). To answer this challenge from Wilbur Whateley, I want to investigate material from the *Encyclopaedia Britannica* and the classic tract, *The Idea of a University,* that Cardinal Newman constructed in the midst of Ireland, wrestling with his understanding of the Catholic university that he attended as its first rector. Only with such materials in mind and having roughly examined the history of Brown University are we ready to approach the concrete evidence of Lovecraft's letters and stories.

Meanwhile, let us take note that Lovecraft did write a translation of "Gaudeamus," that quintessential college song to which we have already addressed ourselves. It is not a very good translation, as passages like this admit: "The fiend strike me blue! I'm scarce able to walk, / And damn me if I can stand upright or talk!" (*Ancient Track* 193). He wanted to be a member of the college so badly that his "college Latin" was not to be gainsaid. Let us repeat, however, Lovecraft never entered Brown or any other university.

I

Poeta pauperior omnibus poetis nichil prorsus habeo nisi quod videtis;

[I am a poor poet, poorer than all the poets for I have nothing at all but what you see] (Bernt 272)

To some extent it is futile to answer the question of how the university and its several translations came into being. Yes, we can say that something that strongly resembled the university appeared in Bologna, Salerno, Naples, Pavia, and Ravenna, from 1000 to 1200, beginning with a medical school and a law school; but this realization can only go so far. Soon the attention of the students took very different forms. Medical schools seem to have appeared early, but they would not remind us of the medical schools we have attended. The law schools depended upon the traditions of Theodosius, Justinian, and Lombardy, and the distinction between civil law and canon law. In addition, it is hardly a surprise that these various theological schools appeared under the control of reason in the hands of Thomas Aquinas.

These different ways of approaching the intellectual world are liable to create a binary world, one in which the legal construction is only too easy to manipulate. It is not surprising that out of the very clear conception of the two schools of medicine and philosophy should appear the more complex construction of the trivium (grammar, logic, and rhetoric) and the quadrivium (arithmetic, geometry, music, and astronomy). It was a fortunate construction, out of which the new schools were easily generated with a global understanding (751).

As these various comprehensions began to arise, so also the presence of the students became important to each other. The foreign student had to be dealt with; and where they were to live, whether foreign or not, became a new problem (750-51). Having to live closely together in the new dormitories and ancient inns, the students in their great numbers often rioted, a lesson they were still learning in the Colonies (Rudolph 98-99); we often face one another, citizen and student, not knowing which is which, and who is the townie? This is an experience that almost every student has had to face. But we must admit that this close living may lead to brilliant ideas.

A new kind of university appeared in the nine institutions that came into being in America before the Revolution: Harvard, William and Mary, Yale, New Jersey, King's, Philadelphia, Rhode Island, Queen's, and Dartmouth, each founded with a theological school in mind (Rudolph 3), though always to an institution that was laboring to reform itself. Having escaped from the various theologies of the old world, the colonists were eager to create their own position in the natural world. How far, however, was that possible?

The charm of Cardinal Newman's treatise, *The Idea of a University,* is that in presenting this question he replied that knowledge has no purpose, end, or use. It stands out in the world, both solitary and prolific, as anyone knows who has dedicated life to the pleasures of an eternal, liberal knowledge. Thus Newman argues that "knowledge is capable of being its own end" (130). It is more an aesthetic problem, one might argue, than an intellectual problem. To say this better, "the true and adequate end of intellectual training and of a university is not learning or acquirement, but rather is thought or reason exercised upon knowledge, or what may be called philosophy" (160). This, we may assume, is the best result of a good semester in the tutorial relationship such as Newman enjoyed at Oxford. He was later to argue perhaps, with some irony, that the goal of an education, if it has any goal, is to train a person to become a gentleman (144). It has no use in the hands of the peasant or the bourgeoisie, and so Lovecraft might argue. Where, though, was he to identify his own birth?

Keep in mind that we are interested here in the history of Brown University, which has little to do with the Anglican or Puritan world; on the other hand, it was the Baptists who founded Rhode Island and Providence a more congenial and safer place than Massachusetts from which Roger Williams had fled. At first it was a rather small institution called Rhode Island College, founded in 1764 under the impetus of the New Light movement throughout the New England clerics with a Baptist coloration (Widmer 20).

Soon throughout New England it became necessary to face the challenge and congeniality of the practical sciences. In Harvard in 1727 a professor in mathematics and natural philosophy was appointed, becoming a model for the colleges (Rudolf 222). The Lyceum of Natural History at Williams sent forth expeditions to Nova Scotia, Greenland, Florida, South America, and Honduras, experiments in natural history that no doubt became models for such expeditions as those that Miskatonic University sent to the Antarctica from 1835 to 1871 (Rudolf 227). In Brown University an undergraduate society in the sciences existed from 1818 to 1827 (Rudolf 227). In 1811 the Corporation of the Universe, through which the finances flowed, decided to construct a medical school of three professors who were to teach the *materia medica,* botany, anatomy and surgery, and chemistry. The school lasted until 1828, but it was later to appear within another form (Widmer 73-74). At the same time the classical world was taught not only through the literary world but through the architectonic world as more buildings were constructed. With its third building of Hope College the universe of the colleges grew "more Greek" (Widmer 81), as much in Providence as in the familiar world of the steep hill of East Providence.

These impulses to the study of the practical, natural sciences found another aspect in the career of Francis Wayland, who first became famous in the ideas he propounded in his book *Political Economy* (1837)—significantly, I am convinced, since this was the class in which Wingate Peaslee collapses. As things went for Wayland, within a year he was no longer the president of the university, but he remained a potent force in the reform movement throughout the United States, arguing that the classics were of benefit only to the ministry, the law, and medicine, whereas business, mechanics, and agriculture were being ignored, to which we might add physics and chemistry (Marsden 102-3). The university remained faithful to the classical curriculum, though it never gave room to any professor who wished to teach the Semitic languages as is a detail in the beginning of "The Call of Cthulhu" (*CF* 2.22), perhaps suggested by the first book in the Brown library, a *Lexicon Pentaglotton Hebraicum, Chaldaicum, Syriacum, Talmudico-Rabbinicum, & Arabinicum* (Widmer 44-45). We can well imagine this as a model for the work of George Gammell Angell, Professor Emeritus of Semitic Languages, just as we can imagine this book as a model for the *Necronomicon*. Yet today, perhaps at the expense of the classics, Brown has an intense medical curriculum in the Alpert Medical School that is now settled in Providence proper.

After a year of his rule, Wayland surprised the university by once more resigning, to emphasize the poor salaries of the staff and the degree by which the enrollments were declining. After he had brought the organization to its senses he returned to his place as the president once more, only to leave again more in 1855. He had been an imperious presence, whose work remained for several years after he left for good. It is no surprise that his name, Francis Wayland, remains in the name of Francis Wayland Thurston, the name of the dead narrator of "The Call of Cthulhu."

Thus we find ourselves now in the atmosphere of the university, but of which university, Brown or Miskatonic, we cannot be sure. The sure thing here is the book or else the books encased in the massive library, which may be the John Hay Library, holding a great amount of memorabilia dedicated to the life and death of Abraham Lincoln; or perhaps we find here hidden in its depths the frightful *Al Azif,* better known in its Greek translation as the *Necronomicon.* That is also locked away in the British Museum, the Bibliothèque Nationale, the Widener Library, the library at Arkham, and the library at Buenos Aires, to say nothing of other hidden texts (*CF* 2.407). But wherever we might be, the atmosphere of a university in the nineteenth century breathes its own Gothic space and time. Fortunately these books have not been created in the acid paper of the nineteenth century, though you would not know its source.

II

Fodere non debeo, quia sum scolaris ortus ex militibus preliandi gnaris [. . .]

[It's not my work to dig, for I am a scholar my ancestors were knights, tried in battle.] (Bernt 272)

Would Lovecraft ever have learned such lessons? During most of his life he lived barely a few blocks from the walls of Brown, advancing upon a closer house as the years passed, but never having a room in one. In one of his earliest letters he explained how, given his health, it came about that he did not attend the university. "In 1908 I should have entered Brown University, but the broken state of my health rendered the idea absurd" (*MWM* 46). How painful is that phrase, "I should have."

In a later letter he adds that he no longer visits Brown because "Once I expected to utilize [the Ladd telescope] as a regularly entered student, and some day perhaps control some of them as a faculty member. But having known them with this 'inside' attitude, I am unwilling to visit them as a casual outsider and non-university barbarian and alien" (*RK* 126). The "inside" attitude is no longer possible; but he cannot speak that "outside" language that he will invent later, to use in his story "The Outsider." The surprise in this passage is his denial of the Ladd telescope, unless we recall his loss of his telescope that now makes sense, bad sense unfortunately. He has willed his loss of the cosmos. Meanwhile, we cannot help being struck by his bitterness of this consideration. Though he was later gratefully to enter the walls of the university several times to attend various speeches and presentations, once to see Archibald MacLeish (*MWM* 375), he must have done so with a complexity of feelings. Even the celebrated T. S. Eliot presented a reading that Lovecraft felt it was his duty to accept. How can what the university accepts be bad (*ET* 232, *JVS* 126)?

A further difficulty for Lovecraft was that a number of his relatives and relatives-in-law was connected to the university; though he was proud of those relatives and of their rather traditional taste, they represented examples he could not fulfill. He would not be accepted as a faculty member. Imagine! Only his grandfather, with a library rich in weird tales in the home attic, offered an example that in time the grandson could surpass. He had to overcome these feelings, however, before he would be able to read beyond these depths of pain.

There is one further way to understand a university, the motto and seal that the university has chosen to sport, apparently as a development of the Middle Age guilds. We in our rational world need to take the history of the mottos seriously, though I don't think we ever fully understand those mottos without a click of the eye. This is a personal as well as an extra-personal matter, held beneath the aegis of the kindly Alma Mater. The first motto and seal I confronted were my own motto and seal of Indiana University, which I attended as a young boy. It is a circle that announces the obvious statement "Indianenensis Universitatis Sigillum" and the year of the university's founding, MDCCCXX. This Latin challenge is a part of the challenge offered to the rural world as a state university. But the more central part of this seal is an open book, pouring forth a radiation of palpable rays, within them at the top of the book the word LUX and beneath the book the words ET VERITAS, the rather clumsy statement "Light and Truth"; and those rays might as well be corn cobs.

The motto and seal of Harvard is quite simple, presenting a shield, not the circle that Indiana will bear. This is a shield divided into three old books which bear among them the word *Veritas,* Truth, which suggests the simplicity of truth within the peace of the trinity. On the other hand, the singularity of the flame may show forth the unity and oneness of that truth manifested by the political, Puritan authority; and to glance at that shield once more, it suggests the world of warfare into which anyone in the intellectual world shall be cast.

The motto and seal of Brown as we might expect is more complex than Harvard's. Its shield is divided into four parts, each of which bears a book, perhaps the four books of the gospel divided among them; a sun that rises over clouds above the shield bears the hope of coming into truth someday. Until then the congregation will hold all matters in tolerance. One variation of the motto bears the words *In Deo Speramus,* "In God We Hope," suggestive also of God and Erudition, so many truths to stumble through. We must take into account that Brown has a second seal, *Religio et Eruditio,* which is to say, "Religion and Erudition," a less dynamic motto than the first. It says nothing of how the relation between religion and erudition is to be handled, unless erudition is to be less powerful than religion. Perhaps that power is to be found in the hope of the first motto.

What, we ask then, would the shield, seal and motto be of Miskatonic University? On the one hand, we can be sure it shall be pious, but on the other hand, no doubt the left hand, it shall brush upon the blasphemous. Its chief colour shall be brown, divided into seven parts and reminiscent of the dark star that scatters the inertias of history. Anyone aware of the history of melancholia may dream here of Gérard de Nerval's suicide, his body swinging from a lantern in the Rue de la Vieille-Lanterne. Fifty years ago when I saw the plaque announcing his death, it was still a frightful sight, the polite plaque there in the wall.

III

Mendicare pudor est mendicare nolo; fures multa possident, non absque dolo [. . .]

[Begging is shameful, I don't want to beg, thieves own much but not without craft] (Bernt 274)

Miskatonic University first appears in the stories devoted to the career of Herbert West, bearing the rather pompous title Miskatonic University Medical School in Arkham (*CF* 1.291). Its existence as a medical school is demanded by the plot in which a medical school is called for; the two main characters are medical students, one of them narrating the adventures of his friend Herbert West and praising the "wonder and diabolism" of his friend's experiments, work defended by the theories of the well-known scientist Ernest Haeckel (1.291), but such as would make Dr. Moreau blush. More seriously, West's friend refers to the "sinister haunt" the two men enjoy (1.293), which is rather like the "grisly collection" (1.345) the two decadents gather in "The Hound." In neither case, that of West's work nor that of the two decadents, does he seem to offer anything like a tribute to science.

We learn little about the constitution of the university except that it is composed of a number of schools and colleges, one of which happened to be a medical school, no doubt one of the earliest schools. Its faculty and students distrusted West and the narrator, the man a bit more than West; and from the first story to the last he has ambivalent feelings about West that he is never able to overcome. At the time of the first story both young men were students, neither of them as most students given to see the world around them.

The reality of the university, as far as the first two small stories are concerned, is Dr. Allan Halsey, the dean of the Medical School, a gentleman "learned and benevolent" (*CF* 1.292). He represents the attitudes of the typical professor, for like the typical professor he seems "always narrow, intolerant, custom-ridden and lacking in perspective" (1.298). Though this professor suffers such sins as "Ptolemaism, Calvinism, anti-Darwinism, anti-Nietzscheism, and every sort of Sabbatarianism and sumptuary legislation" (1.299), in no great time Lovecraft consigns the dean to a madhouse; so we can only imagine the pleasure Lovecraft enjoyed in constructing this diatribe. He can say no more about the university in the Herbert West cycle, but what he has to say is detailed and bitter. It is horrible to think that knowledge is in the hands of such a man as this professor is, for he seems to betray everything that is in truth meant by the values of science.

The next appearance of the university in the stories occurs early in "The Colour out of Space," as three professors from the university, apparently from the schools of chemistry and physics, appear on Nahum Gardner's farm to ascertain the nature of the thing that has fallen there. Is it, they wonder, a meteorite, one of the earliest speculations? But every speculation needs to be surrendered.

As they move from one theory to another, the real point of this essay here is to attempt to pinpoint the nature of the three men. Ten times it seems simplest to think of them as professors, but that may be too easy. More specifically, they are called scientists, as a number of the farmers and as the surveyor who recounts the story thinks of them in the nature of their profession. From a very different angle, however, three times they are thought of as wise men and two times thought of as sages; science is left behind, and the language of the book of Matthew is taken up where the Greek μάγος is translated in the King James English as "wise man" (Matt. 2:1), no doubt an astrologer who passes attention to the heavens. It is difficult in the face of an illegible world to maintain the standards of the university, so the three scientists with their three samples remove to Arkham and leave the colours to anyone who would dare make sense of them. It has not helped to have the university come to the people.

The most striking character of this work is its repetitious use of the word "strange," especially the phrase "strange days" which appears at the beginning (*CF* 2.368), a phrase that the locals will not surrender. "There was really nothing for serious men to do in cases of wild gossip, for superstitious rustics will say and believe anything. And so through all the strange days the professors stayed away in contempt" (2.377). There is nothing that the university can do given the sense of "strangeness" that now permeates the entire valley (2.379).

The old well that lies next to the house, soaking all organic life in its deadly waters, will now become an entire reservoir, as is intimated in the "brittle monstrosity" that has the last word of the story (*CF* 2.399).

There is very little to be said of university life in "The Call of Cthulhu." Professor George Gammell Angell, Professor Emeritus of Semitic Languages in Brown University, is dead before the story begins, though his research is to have a powerful effect upon the plot. His nephew, for instance, Francis Wayland Thurston, who has rummaged about in his uncle's papers, is now also dead before the story begins. It is a shame when we consider that his parents had given him the name, Francis Wayland, in honor of the famous Brown university president and reformer.

Despite these deaths we must not regard Brown University as the center of academic despair. True, the narrator comments that "[t]he authorities at Tulane University could shed no light upon either cult or image" (*CF* 2.41); and there is also "the late William Channing

Webb, [who bears the name of the cleric William Ellery Channing] Professor of Anthropology in Princeton University" (2.32). Francis Wayland Thurston respects the academic world, but it is no use to appeal to that world. Though the dreamers and police and sailors are in the end as futile, they have come closer to the truth of the world of Cthulhu than the professors have done.

We need to know a bit more about Professor Angell, and that is to ask how he came to be a Professor Emeritus of Semitic Languages in Brown University. Or perhaps the question should be how Brown University decided that it could afford a professor of so recherché a subject as Semitic Languages. Did the financial support of that subject cause any envy within the School of Linguistics? I raise these questions only to indicate how delicate an institution a university is, and to indicate the degree to which a university depends upon the financial concerns of its Corporation. It is no surprise that oratory upon this campus carries more practical importance than we might expect (Widmer 81–82).

In the kind of study we are leading "The Dunwich Horror" gives us several difficulties. In it, however, some difficulties are solved, as should be done in a story that reaches its cataclysm at the moment when a riddle is solved. The reader, however, is not informed how that solution is achieved; this story does not follow Poe as it might have. Another way in which this story avoids Poe is that the protagonist, Dr. Armitage, has a wife, a woman who is deeply concerned for him. A reader, however, cannot care for her deeply, since she is never given a name. It is true, furthermore, that all this material does not appear until half the story is finished. Dr. Armitage is not introduced until the old Whateley dies.

We then have three men who are opposed to the phenomenon of Yog-Sothoth, three men as there had been early in the action of "The Colour out of Space," but as long as they are present in the plot, and it is true that not much is made of them; they are simply the three men. They are not the professors or the sages or the wise men. It is impossible to think of them as the biblical Magi. "In the end the three men from Arkham—old, white-bearded Dr. Armitage, stocky, iron-grey Professor Rice, and lean, youngish Professor Morgan—ascended the mountain alone" (*CF* 2.460). Armitage is at least a learned librarian: A. M. Miskatonic, Ph. D. Princeton, Litt. D. Johns Hopkins (2.433). Of the other two, one is Professor Warren Rice, his name Warren perhaps in honor of the town Warren where the first Baptist school was founded and the first Corporation men; and the other is Dr. Francis Morgan, who perhaps lost consciousness when they first confronted from the waist down the real Wilbur (2.439). This introduction of the three men, however, comes rather too late to be affected by the action of the story, action that more involves the tongues of the men of Dunwich than the men from Arkham. It is too late for them to be of any great interest to the reader.

But let us begin at the beginning. In the first chapter we learn that "some of the Whateleys and Bishops still send their eldest sons to Harvard and Miskatonic, though those sons seldom return to the mouldering gambrel roofs under which they and their ancestors were born" (*CF* 2.420). The narrator is unclear whether this story concerns these two universities or these two libraries. The truth of the matter is both; it is hard not to escape the decadence of Dunwich, and the decadence that the equivalence of the syntax hints at. Later in the story this equivalence is sharply and comically stated by Wilbur, without knowing what he says, having all the difficulties of the autodidact: "Maybe Harvard wun't be so fussy as yew be" (2.435). Wilbur is the scholar par excellence, holding in his hands during another visit to Widener "the priceless but imperfect copy of Dr. Dee's English version" (2.433) to collate with the Latin version. All that he wishes is a perfection that will enable him to allow his father, Yog-Sothoth, to break into the world as we know it. He is not interested at all in the priceless nature of the Dee volume. It is no wonder then that he locks away his Latin copy; it is perhaps a greater wonder that he did not incinerate the book.

Of course, the question of the forbidden books is rather sharp in this story, first in those handled by old Whateley and those by his grandson. The texts of certain deadly works are not available until he resolutely finds the complete edition in the Harvard Library. It tells us something of the limits of the library at Miskatonic. The mind boggles at the thought of Wilbur trying to find his way through the labyrinth of Widener without any permission or guide; perhaps it is best that he dies there.

In "The Whisperer in Darkness" we learn early the profession of the narrator, "an instructor of literature at Miskatonic University [. . .] and an enthusiastic amateur student of New England folklore" (*CF* 2.468). This is to say that in the hierarchy of the university as an instructor he is the lowest of the low and that as an amateur student he is only appreciated upon occasion. He thinks more of Henry Akeley than he thinks of himself; and not much is to be expected of him. It is interesting that though he is an instructor of literature he never quotes a line; he is much more excited by the folklore of "the *kallikanzari* of modern Greece" or the "strange, small, and terrible hidden races of troglodytes and burrowers" (2.473), which do not smack of academe.

Akeley is a very different sort of scholar. He is, as Wilmarth discovers, "the last representative on his home soil of a long, locally distinguished line of jurists, administrators, and gentlemen-agriculturists" (*CF* 2.474). There is no doubt that he immediately admires Akeley: "He had veered away from practical affairs to pure scholarship; so that he had been a notable student of mathematics, astronomy, biology, anthropology, and folklore at the University of Vermont. [. . .] From the first I saw he was a man of character, education, and intelligence, albeit a recluse with very little worldly sophistication" (2.474).

A man who has no purpose in his learning except the pleasure of this complex world, he is a good example of the man who has made best use of the universe, even mathematics; he is not obsessed in the work he devotes to the world. Cardinal Newman would happily have said of Akeley that he was not the man who approached the world as a gentleman, but nevertheless he was.

The most important nature of Miskatonic University is its devotion to the well-being of its students, led by the desperate and earnest Peaslee, whose very name suggests that in this long novella he shall not live long. He comes from Haverhill (*CF* 3.364), very near to Salem and Arkham, just as does Gilman in "The Dreams in the Witch House" (3.232). Though Gilman has a fever that may or may not be connected with very odd dreams, his life as a student appears to be very successful, leaving his professor Upham "astonished" (3.240) by his grasp of Riemannian equations. Professor Ellery, assuming the role of the wise men in "The Colour out of Space," identifies several alloys, though one "strange alloy" baffles him (3.258). Like any young student, Gilman is fond of casting around names. Though he has failed in Calculus D and Advanced General Psychology, just as Lovecraft might well have, he has high hopes of catching up. An impressive aspect of Gilman's life as a student is his ability to gather a number of various friends around him, whose names are listed towards the end of the novella: the three Polish characters, Mazurewicz, a "superstitious loomfixer" (3.252); Dombrowski the landlord, who lives important stories below; Choynski; Desrochers, a French-Canadian living beneath Gilman; and Frank Elwood, the only one of his friends who shares his interest in the mathematics of quantum mechanics and general relativity. Though foor a short time he leaves Miskatonic, he returns in the following year to graduate. We might add to this list Anastasia Wolejko, "a clod-like laundry worker" (3.263), and Mary Czanek and "her friend Pete Stowacki" (3.263), both of whom prove to be cowards as the danger becomes greater. The narrator intimates that Stowacki is happy to be rid of their child.

Also important to the life of the students are the doctors, though Gilman does not make use of such doctors as "Old Waldron" the college doctor *CF* 3.243), to whom Gilman will not pay attention, though he is quite aware that he knows Waldron will refer him to a nerve specialist. We must not ignore Dr. Malkowski, "a local practitioner who would repeat no tales where they might prove embarrassing" (3.270). At least the two hypodermics he gives Gilman seem to be a success, and he tells the truth when he announces that Gilman is "stone deaf" (3.270). These various doctors recall to us the roots of the Medical School.

One of the peculiarities of "The Dreams in the Witch House" is the extent to which it repeats details and phrases from Lovecraft's earlier works. Perhaps this is what we are to expect of a paedelogical scene. This may involve such small moments as this give-away sentence, "Dombrowski must attend to the poisoning of those rats in the walls" (*CF* 3.257). But impossible as it seemed in that earlier story to erase the army of rats, so it seems impossible here; it should be no surprise that we have a rat on almost every page, as though Lovecraft was determined to destroy the vermin at last Consider also this lengthy passage:

> a high, fantastically balustraded terrace above a boundless jungle of outlandish, incredible peaks, balanced planes, domes, minarets, horizontal discs poised on pinnacles, and numberless forms of still greater wildness—some of stone and some of metal—which glittered gorgeously in the mixed, almost blistering glare from a polychromatic sky. Behind him tiers of higher terraces towered aloft as far as he could see. The city below stretched away to the limits of vision, and he hoped that no sound would well up from it. (3.249)

What strikes me in this passage is its resemblance to the city that Danforth and Dyer see as they look down upon it; we should note, however, is that this city is as soundless as that former place—and that balustrade calls to mind in addition that city which Charles Dexter Ward had seen as a child and to which he is still susceptible.

There are other verbal patterns in this work. We have once more the "strange" word appearing on the first page, as though the author had decided to capture whatever eluded him in "The Colour out of Space." Gilman already "tries to trace a strange background of multi-dimensional reality" (*CF* 3.232). On the next page, "here he knew strange things had happened once [. . .] in the witch's room [where] the curious angles of Gilman's room had been having a strange, almost hypnotic effect" (3.235). Later on the island in the middle of the Miskatonic he cannot help but see "the strange old woman whose sinister aspect had worked itself so disastrously into his dreams" (3.246). By this time he suffers from "strange urges" (3.257) that shall in time destroy him, no doubt through the "strange and terrible alliances with beings and messengers from outside" (3.260); but all that is strange points to what is outside of us (*Webster's*). Another group of phrases to be aware of is "alien abysses of dream" (3.243), or "unknown abysses" (3.248), or "vague, twilight abysses, and of still vaster, blacker abysses beyond them—abysses in which all fixed suggestions of form were absent" (3.255). Four times yet will this language be used, when it is often associated with the violet light that signals supernatural danger. Finally I want to call our attention to the odd word "loomfixer," a description of Mazurewicz, a superstitious man who whines in prayer and who at a certain point gives Gilman his silver crucifix. The word is awkward, suggesting that the loom of all fate is lost at the same time that a great horror looms above Gilman and his friends, but Gilman in his last chat uses the chain of the crucifix to throttle the witch. Twice over, we should add, Lovecraft uses the metaphoric phrase "to well up" (3.249, 250), once more reaching out to complete the language of "The Colour out of Space" and "The Dreams in the Witch House."

"The Thing on the Doorstep" takes place "beside the darkly muttering Miskatonic" (*CF* 3.326), paying attention to a river that has not been mentioned in the past stories. The university is present here also, but in a very ambiguous fashion. Edward Derby went through it in three years, in part because his parents did not allow him to board at the university; they were afraid of it and afraid of what the university might offer him. For instance, "majoring in English and French literature" (3.327) he does well in everything except mathematics and the sciences. He does very well in the forbidden and decadent books, "though he did not tell his parents he had seen them" (3.328). He probably has very little in detail to tell his parents. Of course, he makes nothing of his education until he meets Asenath Waite, who triggers the sexuality of the material, sitting beside the Miskatonic. This moment is not love or caritas as the church or as St. Augustine understands it; for that we need to turn to the wavering Tristan chord of Wagner and other such moments in European Decadence. Still, this is "something grim, basic, pervasive, and potentially evil" in Edward Derby's eyes (3.342). Whether that something is evil, even potentially evil, I cannot so easily say; but Derby is certainly transformed by the energy of his new relationship, and this transformation is more than simply sexual. The old Derby dies in the flames of the new world.

"The Shadow out of Time" opens in a lecture hall of Miskatonic University and remains there some years. As I have already noted, Peaslee opens his new career by teaching a course that is reminiscent of the book written by Wayland, the first president of Brown University, who attempted to reform its classical curriculum. At last, since he is making nothing out of the usual curriculum, Peaslee and his faithful son go to Australia, where they hope to discover a solution to the father's amnesias. Like Thurston in "The Call of Cthulhu," Peaslee has to go to the ends of the world and the ends of time to learn the truth of our world; nothing in economics can do as much.

We meet here a theme that was present *At the Mountains of Madness,* the strong disinclination to reveal the truth of what has happened to them. Perhaps it is only librarians who feel this enigma, since they hide away the forbidden books, but they do not destroy them. This is the Loeb tradition; books that were once hidden away are now frankly revealed in risqué of Greek into Latin or English. At last we can chuckle over passages of Aristophanes, or wonder now what was so witty. Perhaps Derby dies because he can read those books.

Lovecraft's Rats and Doyle's Hound: A Study in Reason and Madness

> dea, magna dea, Cybebe, dea domina Dindymi,
> procul a mea tuos sit furor omnis, era, domo:
> alios age incitatos, alios age rabidos.
>
> [Goddess, great goddess, Cybebe, goddess and mistress of Dindymus,
> Far from my house be all your madness, Lady,
> Make others enraged, make others mad] (Catullus 63.91-93)

At the conclusion of my essay on Lovecraft's flamboyant story "The Hound" I wrote, "This story, like 'The Rats in the Walls,' concerns a supernatural, bestial destroyer, but the vision of that destroyer in 'The Hound' is more difficult to discover given the scope of the story's allusions" (*Monster of Voices* 83). One of those allusions I spent a good deal of space investigating was Sir Arthur Conan Doyle's *The Hound of the Baskervilles*. In retrospect, however, it must have seemed to some readers of the essay rather stupid of me that I did not also investigate a possible connection between Lovecraft's rats and Doyle's novel. Gavin Callaghan must have thought me especially obtuse, since he had just published his encyclopedic essay tracing the broad influence of Doyle on Lovecraft. In this essay I mean to make up for my obtuseness and pursue that connection of the hound with the rats. In the process we shall learn that we need to allow the Magna Mater into our considerations, for she will not be ignored.

When we consider the bare bones of the two stories the similarity between them must seem obvious. In England, around the time of the English Civil War, two disasters occur that leave two noble families and their dwellings damaged; this background of war is extended to the American Civil War, World War I, and the Boer War. Various legends attest to the nature of the two disasters, and both families have manuscripts that describe the disaster in detail, though the Delapore manuscript has been burned, leaving the narrator rather self-confident. Now, in the present day (circa 1888, 1901, and 1923), an heir has returned from the colonies to refurbish and re-establish the home and family. Unfortunately, the past disasters still exist as present, bestial evils that, when they strike once more, leave the two heirs maimed, whether mad or verging upon madness, or dead. Though in both cases the bestial evils seem to have been exterminated some doubt remains; a rational approach to such evils appears to be insufficient, so these heirs throw up their hands helplessly.

I

The victors and the vanquished then the storm it tossed and tore,
As hard they strove, those worn-out men, upon that surly shore;
Dead Nelson and his half-dead crew, his foes from near and far,
Were rolled together on the deep that night at Trafalgar. (Hardy 108)

Such, once we have scraped away various subplots of a romantic or a mythic nature, to which we will return, seems to be the central story of the two works, which originates in the two manuscripts. When Holmes gives his final directions to Watson at Paddington Station, he asks the good doctor "simply to report facts [. . .] and leave me to do the theorizing" (*Complete Sherlock Holmes* 817). When Watson asks what he means by facts he becomes rather vague, and when Watson later says that the landscape he meets in Devon presents "a strange jagged summit, dim and vague in the distance, like some fantastic landscape in a dream" (819), I believe we shall agree that these words may be as factual as any that Holmes originally intended or that he can expect. The simple gathering of facts will not save us from our construction of theory, from one theory after another; besides, how do we know what a fact is in depth unless it already wrestles with its theory? As Lovecraft argued, atmosphere is important and may be a guide to the truth.

Using these various remarks as a framework for our investigation, let us turn first to the two disasters as they are recounted in the manuscripts. Dr. Mortimer reads to Holmes an account written in 1742, the same year as Pope's *The New Dunciad,* giving us perhaps little trust in the account. It introduces Hugo Baskerville, "a most wild, profane, and godless man," but even more a man possessed by "a certain wanton and cruel humour" (789), who has become enamored by a yeoman's daughter and who steals her away one Michaelmas. He does her no harm at first, because he and his friends must sit down to "a long carouse as was their nightly custom" (789). For this man, apparently, woman waits upon wine and song. When she escapes he utters the Faustian bargain, to give his soul to the devil if he captures her, and then pursues her, letting loose his hounds upon her trail on the advice of one of his drunken friends. He is, however, himself pursued by a black mute hound, all the more horrifying in not letting loose the great howl as should be its nature. In the climax of this account his friends discover the hound plucking at Hugo's throat and lifting "its blazing eyes and dripping jaws" (790) upon them, sending them shrieking across the moor and dying later of shock, not presumptively before relating what they have seen. Oddly, the style of this sober manuscript shifts in tone here to a participation in the horror—"dripping jaws" indeed! The writer concludes piously, asking his sons to say nothing of this to their sister. In a patriarchal society the request is not surprising.

At this point we should turn our attention to a point that Callaghan emphasizes: both narratives picture the various beasts leaping at the jaws or throats of their victims (210-11). Why should that attack be important? Callaghan connects it with the attack on the father, and the father does deserve such an attack if we are to believe my conclusion in my essay "'The Rats in the Walls,' the Rats in the Trenches"; but I wonder whether the nature of the attack may lie in its being directed at the throat, to prevent the victim from speaking and presenting his own case. What does Hugo Baskerville have to say for himself, now that the girl is dead? Delapore's cat is leaping for his throat, but Delapore, who has now the mind of a rat or the atavistic mind of his ancestors, has already killed and partially devoured the amiable, plump Capt. Norrys. What, then, did Norrys have to say for himself, the man who initiated the action of the story by telling Delapore's son of Exham Priory and exciting his interest and then his father's? Would he plead to be forgiven for helping the Delapores take the priory off his uncle's hands? Was there not something shady about that financial deal? These questions are unanswerable, but that is my point. They and other questions like them must not be raised, neither in Doyle's world nor in Lovecraft's. The hound in the manuscript is mute, and the rats never appear in the contemporary world of that story. Twice the narrator describes the rats as an army, but they do not exercise the rodents.

The Delapore manuscript has been lost in the fire of the narrator's family plantation, but he believes he can reconstruct its message, just as he believes he can reconstruct Exham Priory, the English home of his family. Lovecraft gives readers sufficient information to believe, with perhaps too much confidence, that they can reconstruct the manuscript better than this character. Once upon a time the place of the priory became the prehistoric site of a cannibalistic ritual, long before humans became humans; and on that site other rituals, whether belonging to the Druids or to those who worshipped the Magna Mater, settled and adopted the local rite—murder and cannibalism—adapting these rituals to their home in the caverns beneath the site where the Saxons and the Normans built the priory. In the time of James I one of the sons of the family discovered his family in their rituals and killed them in a nice polite blood-bath, "father, three brothers, and two sisters" (*CF* 1.381), with no great disapproval of his neighbors or of the king, and fled to Virginia, where he became an honored albeit reclusive plantation owner. Thus matters remained until the letter and the plantation, and all the past they contained, were burned during the American Civil War, leaving the protagonist of the story ignorant, utterly ignorant, of his family and of himself. There is no reason why the rats should be mentioned in this letter, since their legend arises later than these events and the narrator believes that their story is mere legend.

The basic similarity in these two manuscripts is the admission that the two families are much too liable to outbursts of violence, in both cases treating their neighbors as much less than their equals, much less in fact than swine. To use the word repeated often in Doyle's book, both families are "masterful," regarding the people of Devon and Anchester as no more than a herd from which they can pick and choose at their pleasure. And the family of the de la Poers goes further than this, regarding their own family as prey if they do not agree that the peasantry is subhuman; violent and patricidal as Walter de la Poer's action is, there is little doubt that he acts because he has discovered the murderous intentions of his father. The true message of the manuscripts, if read aright, is that each family is liable to be murderous and they must be careful to restrain themselves—if they wish to.

One further point should be made about these stories, the degree to which one should believe them. Stapleton, the dissembling cousin of his family, sees in Sir Charles's belief in the hound an opportunity to kill him; he rationally exploits the story of the manuscript, which he does not himself believe; and the rational Holmes does not believe in it either. The original trespass, the rape of the girl, is itself a part of the legend and nothing more. The original trespass in Lovecraft's story, however, the ritual of murder and cannibalism, must be believed in; if Delapore regards it as no more than a legend he becomes liable to an eruption of his own murderous unconscious; and the story of the rats, which as we have seen is not a part of the manuscript that was burned, becomes the form of that unconscious. In this regard the two stories approach the theme of reason and madness from two very different directions.

Yet the two stories are very similar in so many ways. Let us examine the backgrounds of war, the mass murders at which the two stories gesture. In "The Rats in the Walls," as I have already argued in "'The Rats in the Walls,' the Rats in the Trenches," the patricidal and filicidal madness of the world war is played out in the sub-cellars of Exham Priory. It is, however, significant that the other two wars of the story are civil wars, which are often wars of brother against brother; and this is something of the way that Lovecraft, at one point early in the war, viewed its cataclysm. "Englishmen and Germans are blood brothers," he wrote in 1915 in his peroration to his essay "The Crime of the Century" (*CE* 5.14). Though he was to change his attitude, we should keep in mind that for him the conflict began as a civil conflict, with closely related peoples at war. Some of this material, of course, characterizes Delapore, the bland Boston business man, as a man divided; we do not expect him to become a rat.

What happens in Doyle's fiction? The English Civil War is important as background to his story. The first trespasser, Hugo Baskerville, is without doubt a Cavalier, as the lace of his formal portrait indicates; yet his face, as painted there and revealed in the face of Stapleton, a.k.a. Rodger Baskerville, is "prim, hard and stern, with a firm-set, thin-lipped mouth, and a coldly intolerant eye" (879), a description we might take as that of a Roundhead. It is a nasty, accusing face. It is a face that neither Holmes nor the reader expects. This is also a man divided against himself, who probably represents a psyche divided against itself, a division portrayed at large by the English Civil War.

Is there any other presence of war in *The Hound of the Basker-*

villes? Sir Charles Baskerville has made "large sums of money," according to the *Devon County Chronicle,* "in South African speculation"; but "[m]ore wise than those who go on until the wheel turns against them, he realized his gains and returned to England with them" (791). More frankly, Watson describes the lodge of Baskerville Hall as "the first fruits of Sir Charles's South African gold" (821). A person reading these passages in 1902 might have a complex relation to them. It was indeed a wise act to realize one's gains and return to England when you remember the very recent Boer War, from 1899 to 1901. But the story may well occur in the fall of 1888, if we are to accept Baring-Gould's chronology of the Holmes saga (2.3), though this interpretation is not asserted explicitly in the text. In any case, it would have taken Sir Charles a considerable time to amass the riches that made him not only generous throughout "the whole countryside" (791) of Devon, the riches would have enabled him to renovate the considerable pile of Baskerville Hall, as his nephew still intends at the end of the story. To do all this Sir Charles must have been rich indeed. South Africa, with its recently exploited seams of gold and diamonds, the profits of which were doubling every few years during the 1890s ("Transvaal"), was a lucrative colony which Britain was not willing to lose, even at the cost of a colonial war. This is not brother against brother, but European against European, which the Natives of South Africa had little hand in.

What did Doyle think of this situation? Though he voluntarily served as a doctor for the English forces during the war, he wrote this scathing account of his views to his mother: "Now about the Boers. [. . .] They want to spread into Bechuanaland we promptly "head" them out of that—Gold the root of all evil is found & diamond mines & the riff-raff of the world swarms down and settles & keeps on *increasingly* swarming and settling. Now can you imagine the *disgust* of those Burghers! [. . .] They would actually rather let the gold alone than work it!" (*A Life in Letters* 435). Though Sir Charles is certainly not "riff-raff," it is difficult not to believe that he has returned to England with tainted wealth through the old dispossession of the Natives.

And what are we to think of Delapore's wealth? Presumptively, after the family loses everything in the destruction of the plantation Carfax and the loss of their slaves, the wealth has its roots in his father's activity in wisely moving to the North, though Delapore would have us think that the move was made because his mother came from the North. He writes that "I grew to manhood, middle age, and ultimate wealth as a stolid Yankee" (*CF* 1.376), which is to say that most of his life was spent enjoying the excesses and clever exploitations of the Gilded Age. I believe that his career would be described in greater financial detail than in his bland words, "I merged into the greyness of Massachusetts business life" (1.376). How could he have come to England with his great plans without owning tainted wealth? Callaghan persuasively points out a similarity here between Lovecraft's story and Doyle's story "The Five Orange Pips" (212–13); but the wealth of that character lies in a plantation that does not burn down. He is not as alienated as Delapore, the would-be Englishman who is a would-be Southern gentleman and a would-be Northern magnate.

We need to notice one other detail about these heirs who are coming from the colonies to claim their home. They are doubled and redoubled, in that Sir Charles from South Africa is followed by Sir Henry from Western Canada, often talking like a man from the North-American West (810), but both are accompanied if they but knew it by their cousin Rodger from Central America. This doubling is mirrored in Stapleton's relations to his women and in the first letters of their names; he has beaten his wife Beryl, whose proper name is Beryl Baskerville, and lied to his lover Laura Lyons. Delapore is coming from Virginia and from Massachusetts, though he has been preceded by his son. He writes and talks in a studied fashion as though he were an Englishman, as Lovecraft in his life did his best to do, but Delapore is not at all an Englishman by birth. All these characters must to some extent strike the native English reader as outsiders, but they are as intimate insiders as anyone, a true Baskerville and a true de la Poer, the name that Delapore has now assumed. Exham Priory has two towers, as has Baskerville Hall.

One of their aims in their return is to renovate the home. This aim of Sir Charles is immediately taken up by his nephew, who says upon coming up to the Hall, "It's no wonder my uncle felt as if trouble were coming on him in a place like this. [. . .] I'll have a row of electric lights up here inside of six months, and you won't know it again with a thousand-candle-power Swan and Edison right here in front of the hall door" (821), as though American electricity and Saxon know-how were sufficient guard against melancholia. In the view of Watson all that is necessary after the renovating and refurnishing will be a wife, who he has no doubt will be Beryl Stapleton (840); a wife, then, is a part of the furnishings. Delapore has no wife and indicates no intention to find one. He does, however, have electricity, realized in "the electric bulbs which so cleverly counterfeited candles" (*CF* 1.383). In both cases the electric lights are an attack on the dark corners and ancient aggressions that now come to life and attack. It is as though the two men flirt with the magic world of Gothicism at the same time that they deny it—to their danger. They renovate the past at the same time as they attempt to erase it.

It is possible, however, that more than the renovation qua renovation lies at the heart of the attack on the two ancient halls. In the sixth circle of Dante's *Inferno* where the violent are punished, the violent against themselves include the spendthrifts, who are pursued by black hounds: "Dietro a loro era la selva piena / Di nere cagne, bramose e correnti, / Come veltri che uscisser di catena" [Behind them was the forest full of black / She-mastiffs, ravenous, and swift of foot / As greyhounds, who are issuing from the chain] (13.124-26). Not one hound, note, but a forest full of them. I don't think that we can gage the amount of money that Sir Charles or Sir Henry had spent or were about to spend on Baskerville Hall. Sir Charles had already spent a good deal in charity, but that is not the sort of outlay that causes us to accuse or judge a Christian gentleman; still, since so many people know of his charity, it does smell of ostentation. Much more extremely, Delapore is spending an immense amount of money on the renovation of a building from the ground up—though not, he believes, from the cellar down. If little of that money goes to anyone in the neighborhood, *tant pis;* it is their own fault because of their superstitious recalcitrance. Delapore, of course, is not pursued by black hounds; he is pursued by himself, an id manifesting itself as an army of rats. Dante would not have minded the image, though he would probably have held to his pack of black mastiffs. Bestial, instinctual rapaciousness is the point of the two stories.

After the disaster of the family plantation, a result of the institutional violence of slavery, Delapore came north to gain a wealth sufficient to buy what was left of Exham Priory after centuries of neglect, and not simply to renovate it but to rebuild it from the shell of walls that is all that remains. He has no idea of furnishing it with a wife; he need not, since he has bought a home that at one time was under the patronage of the Magna Mater; and he does not bother to overcome the animosity of the countryside with any acts of generosity. Letting "no expense deter [him]" (*CF* 1.374), he is totally focused on the priory that is to be, not upon any social connections he might make in the neighborhood. True, he becomes a friend of Capt. Norrys, the friend of his son—but Norrys is later to be his feast. He confesses that he comes of a "somewhat reserved and unsocial Virginia line" (*CF* 1.375).

II

First he relates, how sinking to the chin,
Smit with his mien, the Mud-nymphs suck'd him in. (Pope 2.331-32)

The rats in Lovecraft's story, invisible as they are, appear to resemble an army, a word that appears ten times for reasons that are clear in my earlier essay. The word "rats" appears twenty-nine times, never in the singular; of these uses, the word appears ten times in the last two pages, creating the crescendo and climax of the story. The word "vermin" appears only two times, perhaps because of its abstraction; and the word "rodent" appears seven times, always as an adjective.

The hound is only one, both in the legendry and in fact, but he has a large supporting cast. Often with great force, the word "hound" occurs several times in the novel, by my count fifty-three times; a bit less, twenty-two times in fact, half as often as "hound," we find the word "dog," most often in the purposive participle "dogging," but a number of times it appears in quite innocuous forms such as the "iron dogs" behind which a comfortable fire burns. It is not applied to the hound until the creature is dead.

And then there are the rhymes, "bog" and "fog." In the climactic fourteenth chapter the word "fog" appears ten times, and the fifteenth chapter back in London begins with a diminuendo "foggy" (892). The word "bog" appears only five times, but crucially associated with the hound and in a dramatic scene with the death of two ponies (828–29); and once in the last chapter Watson refers perhaps ineptly to the "bogy hound" (899); it is not so important as the other words.

To pursue these forms further, the hound never dogs its prey but runs and bounds after it; a dog that dogs is persistent but does not break into a run. It is as though the hound were accompanied by its own entourage of dogs and bogs and fogs, accompanied by its own shadows. When it springs upon Sir Henry out of the fog "fire burst from its open mouth," running, says Watson, "with long bounds, [. . .] leaping down the track, following hard upon the footsteps of our friend" (887). Like the rats, the hound is the incarnation of energy.

The rats are their own shadow. As a horde they move in a different manner than does the hound, yet like the hound they also pursue their prey in a rush; in one legend they are a "scampering army of obscene vermin which had burst forth from the castle" and "swept all before it" (*CF* 1.380). On the other hand, since it is quite possible that Delapore is the only rat in Exham Priory, he has some sympathy with "the hapless rats" that were trapped in sub-cellars; and in Doyle's tale, once we understand that the hound is a real hound that has been brutalized by Stapleton, a reader must have some sympathy with it also; the rats and the hound behave as they do because they are starved. Neither work believes that the animals are evil; they are so only in the manuscripts and legends that project human fears.

At the conclusion of the stories no heir is left in very good shape. Stapleton, who was certainly in line to inherit Baskerville Hall, vanishes in the Grimpen Mire and is presumptively dead. In describing the attempt Holmes and he made to find the man Watson writes, "[I]t was as if some malignant hand was tugging us down into those obscene depths, so grim and purposeful was the clutch in which it held us" (891). Here we realize the irony of the name of Stapleton's home, Merripit. These obscene depths and pits are like the caverns in Lovecraft's story. Stapleton's cousin Sir Henry has shattered nerves and the morning after the attack is delirious, with a high fever. Though we are assured that a trip around the world with Dr. Mortimer will restore him, we do not see the result, and wedding bells with Beryl are doubtful. Thus the fates of both Stapleton and Sir Henry are never narrated explicitly.

The fate of Delapore is ambiguous also. After his adventure in the caverns beneath the priory, caverns that have no bottom, he is penned in an insane asylum after suffering a madness of regression. This regression or atavism is also a theme of Doyle's novel, made explicit when Holmes demonstrates that Hugo Baskerville, the original instigator of evil in the family line, and his descendent Stapleton look remarkably alike; Stapleton is "a throwback" (879), an accusation that could be leveled at many of Lovecraft's protagonists. This theme is one reason why so much of the novel is devoted to Watson's meditations on the people who inhabited the Neolithic huts and burrows on the moor, "some unwarlike and harried race who were forced to accept that which none other would occupy" (834). It is no surprise, then, that Selden the convict is forced to hide there, himself a throwback, whose face, according to Watson, "might well have belonged to one of those old savages who dwelt in the burrows on the hillsides" (849). Callaghan has cogently argued that Doyle draws an implicit connection between Baskerville Hall and the ancient stone burrows that surround it and thus a spiritual connection between historic and prehistoric horrors, a connection that Lovecraft makes explicit (215–16).

Given how close the two stories are, we must ask why they seem to differ so much in the matter of romance. In part, of course, it is a question of genre; if there is any romance in Lovecraft's canon it is disastrous. Each of Doyle's four novels devoted to Sherlock Holmes has a romance. Two women, Beryl and Laura, are very important to the plot of *The Hound of the Baskervilles,* and Mrs. Barrymore is not unimportant, but no woman is of importance to the plot of "The Rats in the Walls." Delapore is a widower who mentions his former wife in one sentence. What has happened? The answer lies, I believe, in the indication that one of the stages of the cult of the priory was the worship of the Magna Mater, whose chariot is drawn by lions and whose worship consists of self-castration. Lovecraft is quite aware of these matters, having read enough of Virgil, Ovid, and Catullus, as has his protagonist, who shudders at the discovery of her ritual name.

But though Delapore has read the classics and Stapleton is merely an amateur naturalist, Stapleton is much more aware, much more conscious, of the various social threads he is so adroit at playing upon and of his own nature, which he is careful to suppress. Delapore has little experience of the social world or of his own unconscious and is therefore much more liable to be driven by it. As I discuss this further I want it to be clear that I am using Erich Neumann's treatment of the archetype of the Magna Mater, a symbol of the unconscious mind that bears a grudge against the conscious mind, opposed to the unconscious mind out of which it has grown because it cannot admit its dependence (147–48). This structure is apparent in the landscapes of the two stories. No home except the Neolithic burrows is built on the moor, much less on the devouring Grimpen mire; though it is rather solitary, Baskerville Hall does exist in the middle of a far-flung community. Exham Priory seems to be built securely upon a limestone cliff overlooking "a desolate valley" (27), but that superiority is fallacious since the foundation is riddled by caverns that seem to have no end.

Signs of the Magna Mater can be easily read in Doyle's story. Laura's married name is Lyons, and the hound looks to Watson "as large as a small lioness" (888); the hound that Stapleton thought to command belongs in fact to the feminine world of the Magna Mater (Neumann 170). Beryl from Costa Rica represents the foreign aspect of the Magna Mater; her worship was brought to Rome during the Republic, but she was always viewed askance, as we can see in Catullus' poem, which represents Atys as an exile. What are we to say of Mrs. Barrymore, "a large, impassive, heavy-featured woman with a stern set expression of mouth" (824)? Doesn't this description recall the appearance of late Neolithic fertility goddesses, something like the Venus of Willensdorf that Neumann presents (plate 22)? Watson notes that Mrs. Barrymore has been weeping. She has no children, but she has acted like a mother to her younger brother whom she had indulged and thus was responsible in part for the brute he became. Of his crimes only murder is specified, but the language suggests that other crimes were much worse in their ferocious, unspeakable manner; he has a whiff of Jack the Ripper about him. But outcast as he is, his maternal sister still cares for him and weeps for him, unable to control the hound that in retrospect we see as an expression of the goddess. The weeping that Watson remarks on is neither for Sir Charles nor for Sir Henry, excellent examples of the conscious world, but for her regressive brother. He is the double of Sir Henry in that he can wear the baronet's clothes and dies in his place.

Given the power of the goddess and the several similarities between the two stories that we have been tracing, what I find remarkable about "The Rats in the Walls" is the absence—some might say the suppression—of the goddess. She is mentioned, a fragment of her name in a Roman inscription is copied, Delapore shudders at the thought of Catullus' poem, and that is all until Delapore screams her name in his madness. I do not think that his scream simply records a stage in his regression, whipped through the whirlpool of his shattered self. It is an admission that he has failed in his life and that his culture has failed also, taking part with such enthusiasm in the death-wish of the world war.

What the Magna Mater commands of us we necessarily perform. To the length of self-castration? What else are we to think of the world war? I earlier argued that the army of the rats transcends personal psychosis (*Monster of Voices* 67-68). I do not believe that this is so, at least so profoundly, of *The Hound of the Baskervilles,* but it is interesting that the novel concerns several Baskervilles, not simply one; there is Hugo, who committed the original transgression; Hugo, who penned the manuscript warning his children of the curse; Rodger and his son Stapleton (under his several pseudonyms); Sir Charles, Sir Henry, and Selden, wearing the clothes of Sir Henry and thus, as far as the hound is concerned, assuming his identity. The guilt of being a Baskerville is spread wide, just as the guilt of being a de la Poer is spread wide. So the Magna Mater commands Stapleton, who has played with the materials of the unconscious, the legends of the painted hound, to flee to the center of the Grimpen Mire, a symbol of the terrible Mother, and there she devours him. She commands Delapore, because he has suppressed her in the name of reason, to regress (note how little credence he gave to his family's legends); he castrates his consciousness and becomes a slave of the unconscious, devoured by the deep caverns and mouths of his line.

This theme of self-castration cannot be ignored. According to Neumann, it arises within "a male immature in his development, who experiences himself only as male and phallic" (172). Upon occasion he captures a butterfly, but more often Stapleton is seen in the story as the failed naturalist, his phallic net trailing behind him; his wife is, as Watson puts it, the furnishing of the house, an object to be manipulated. Delapore, despite his age, is most concretely characterized by his erection of the priory. The inhibited agony of this situation is expressed in Wagner's *Parsifal* when Klingsor, who has laid a "Frevlerhand" [sinful/bold hand] upon himself (5.195), cries out at Kundry's mockery, "Furchtbare Not" [fearful need]! (5.207). What is the need that is so fearful? The answer lies in Alberich's words which almost come to echo Klingsor's, "schmählicher Not" [humiliating need]! (4.57). The castration, which seems like a capitulation to purity in the manner of the Church Father Origen, is actually a capitulation to the Magna Mater, an admission that the man cannot live a full life without an intimate, carnal relationship with a beloved. Alberich forthrightly curses love, and Klingsor renounces it; thereby they each earn a magic power that, however, proves illusory. These remarks trace the trajectory of Stapleton's and Delapore's lives. The one man dies in the Grimpen Mire; the other man abases himself to the goddess in his descent to the animal, and in this descent he is no longer a horde. He is only one weak, unintelligible rat: "*chchch*" (*CF* 1.396). These are not his last words in the story, and I am certain that he will chitter again.

No doubt the story of the hound, long after the death of Stapledon and his hound, its jaws smeared with phosphorus, will live on also, just as the peasants on the moor tell it. The peasants below the ruins of Exham Priory will tell such stories too.

Part Three: Apartments and Books

"Cool Air," the Apartment Above, and Other Stories

"Cool Air" is not a story that has the metaphoric virtues of Lovecraft's early works such as "The Outsider" or "The Picture in the House." It is a sober story that avoids their excesses, the hyperbolic style that we find in them and such other works as "Herbert West—Reanimator" or "The Hound." But it has none of the expansive quality we find in "The Call of Cthulhu," "The Dunwich Horror," or "The Shadow over Innsmouth." It falls between the stools; it is neither this nor that, it is purely what it is, and so it has few exponents.[1] I have not been one of them, so it is only now, after avoiding it for these many years, that I have decided to have a close look at it. This essay is something of an apology for a cool story; in any case, we see immediately that, though it may be a minor virtue of the tale, it is now more relevant than it once was as we read thinking of cryogenics and the possible fate of a deliquesced Walt Disney. But this is as much to say that the story is one of Lovecraft's first experiments in moving the weird tale into the broad genre of science fiction; there is a touch of the old style, worthy of "The Hound," in such broad assertions as "fiendish things were in the air" (*CF* 2.19); but later that summer Lovecraft was to write "The Call of Cthulhu" in which his transformation of the genre was complete.

---

1. S. T. Joshi, however, believes it to be "Lovecraft's most successful evocation of the horror to be found in [. . .] America's only true megalopolis" [*Subtler Magick* 109], though to describe it as the best of HPL's New York stories is perhaps to damn it with faint praise.

In looking at the story I have various goals in mind. I wish to look at the tale itself, in and of itself, but I also wish to look at it as an example of a story with a particular setting, such as we find in "The Picture in the House," "The Music of Erich Zann," and "The Dreams in the Witch House," and that we find also in Thomas Pynchon's "Entropy." Simply put, these stories present a contrast in a house between a lower story in which daily life proceeds merely as daily life does and an upper story where life proceeds in a very different fashion that we may call archetypal or ideal, depending on our preference for language. Two different atmospheres, different in vertical orientation and in narrative concerns, are at work in these stories.

I

the parching Air
Burns frore, and cold performs th'effect of Fire.
(Milton, *Paradise Lost* 2.594-95)

These stories complicate the pattern of Lovecraft's own experience, enjoying the library of his beloved grandfather, but especially that part of the library banished to the attic where the young boy found the classics of the eighteenth century that were to have such a profound influence upon his own style (*ES* 379). This is the same pattern we see in such stories as *The Princess and the Goblin* or *Lilith* by George MacDonald. In each of them the protagonist discovers that the upper stories of the homes where the action takes place have contact with spiritual powers. In the first work the Princess discovers that her grandmother lives in the top of the tower, but this is a grandmother who more than the typical fairy godmother resembles the goddess Isis, in whose robes "stellae dispersae coruscebant, earumque media semenstris luna flammeos spirabat ignes" [the scattered stars shone, and in their midst the half-moon breathed out flame of fire] (Apuleius, *Golden Ass* 11.4), fused with the figure of the Shakinah, the Wisdom that was with God in the creation, dancing before

God, often understood as a type of the Holy Spirit (Prov. 8:22-31); this grandmother has cosmic affinities that mean good by her goddaughter. Her bedroom is open to the moon and stars and her bath is full of healing. The garret in *Lilith* is more complex. Early in the book the terrified narrator compares the garret to a brain much larger than the house upon which it rests; and through a mirror it gives access to a landscape in which the main action of the narrative is played out in a more pointed fashion than *The Princess and the Goblin*, returning to us origins in Adam and Eve and Lilith. In both cases the narrow smallness of daily life is contrasted to a life that is more spacious and significant, binding together the past and present; the upper story offers a spiritual adventure in which such figures as the archetypal old wise woman find a place. This pattern is of course transformed in "Cool Air."

With these comments as a background, let us consider a preliminary analysis of "Cool Air." It begins very quietly with an unnamed narrator addressing an unnamed friend. "You ask me to explain [. . .] why I shiver more than others upon entering a cold room" (*CF* 2.11). In his account the exterior setting engages us at first. As the last of Lovecraft's stories set in New York, this story has a certain distance that the others do not and thereby achieves a greater realism. It is not simply that he has taken as its setting the brownstone on West 14th Street where his friend George Kirk lived. Most striking I think is that the time within the story is objective; the climax in which Dr. Muñoz's ammonia fails him takes place in October, not in the height of summer as we might expect. The time has no symbolic significance at all; it is such a time as one would meet in the city, profane and indifferent. At least so it seems, though October in the midst of fall does point ahead to the deep cold of winter; October may possess a capitalized name, but fall and winter are nameless.

Another aspect of this realism is Lovecraft's handling of his racist understanding of the city. The abhorrence expressed in "The Horror of Red Hook" is here nuanced. Though the landlady Mrs. Herrero is introduced as "a slatternly, almost bearded Spanish woman," she figures in the story as a sympathetic character who expresses concern for her tenants; and though the other lodgers are introduced as "mostly Spaniards a little above the coarsest and crudest grade" (*CF* 2.12), they are not at all threatening and the description has no bite to it, despite the grudging phrase, "a little above." As for Dr. Muñoz, though the narrator confesses, "I shivered as I crossed the threshold into a large apartment" (2.13), he treats the man with the utmost respect and sympathy, "a man of birth, cultivation, and discrimination" (2.14), a man "of striking intelligence and superior blood and breeding" (2.14). The racist epithets do not carry a great pejorative charge here. The worst character, whose race the narrator never identifies, is the "seedy-looking loafer" (2.19) whom the narrator hires to provide the doctor with ice in emergencies; but the man understandably flees "screaming and mad-eyed" when he sees the results of Dr. Muñoz's disintegration (2.19). As a part of this subdued style the narrator offhandedly comments that the "hot water is not too often cold," a remark that shall be important later (2.12). No one in this story is a monster unless it is the doctor himself, caught up in his project to live forever and mired at last in his disintegration.

More charged in the story is the contrast between the interior of the apartment house, especially the interior that the doctor has created for himself and the outside world. Outside is "the clangour of a metropolis" (*CF* 2.11). The apartment house itself is quiet, despite "the din of street cars," which "proved a serious annoyance" (2.12). At the conclusion the narrator insists upon "the clatter of street cars and motor trucks ascending clamorously from crowded Fourteenth Street" (2.20), a hot scene that contrasts tellingly to the cold death in the doctor's room. The narrator intends to "hibernate" in the apartment house (2.12). The verb is well chosen, since hibernation is not simply a sleep during the winter but a turning down of the activity of the organs to achieve a lower metabolism, an action that Dr. Muñoz has pursued in an extreme fashion. Both men exist in opposition to the world outside, a world of loud, vainglorious motion that nevertheless the narrator must appeal to; and thus the opposition between the inside and the outside is not clear-cut.

Three more details about the doctor need to be observed. He wears "a pince-nez" (*CF* 2.14) that shields his eyes from the outside world; visually like the narrator, aurally the doctor cannot support the glare of the outside world. The phrase, however, might suggest an aggressive tone that he uses in his war against mortality, for he is "the bitterest of sworn enemies to death" (2.14), one who must in the climax of the story "hurl defiance at the death-daemon" (2.17). He is not, however, as far as we can observe, far in the last pages of the story; nay, for the last eighteen years he conducts a hopeless siege in a body that has already been breached. One step in his disintegration occurs when "a spasm caused him to clap his hands to his eyes and rush into the bathroom" (2.18); the narrator never sees the doctor's eyes again. For the shield had become useless.

Furthermore, the better the narrator has come to know him the clearer it is that the doctor has no heart, or at least no heart beat; he jests that he will "someday teach [the narrator] to live [. . .] without any heart at all" (*CF* 2.15). Yet he does have a heart insofar as he sympathizes with the narrator and with others who have been injured, like the plumber. But he cannot help himself. Though he believes he must be as emotionless as possible, as cold as possible, to stop the advance of his death, he rages at his death; and his rage infects the rage with the narrator also. The doctor cannot die a Stoic death, the death that Lovecraft preferred.

"All day," Mrs. Herrero reports, "he take funnee-smelling baths, and he cannot get excite or warm" (*CF* 2.12). It reaches the point that the baths are "incessant" (2.17). Given his demand for a cold apartment, we suspect that these baths are cold indeed. The implication seems to be, given his baths of spices, incense, and "pungent chemicals" (2.17), that the baths form part of his hygiene to preserve his body, but we cannot escape the suggestion that he is possessed of a terrifying rage for purity. This detail may indicate a racist environment in the story which in our first reading we missed. Would the doctor have found an excuse for attending to the ancient autos de fé of Spain? Is that the secret code of purity? But there is more to a problem of purity which we shall shortly explore.

It may be important to note that the doctor does not stand alone in his effort, for a certain Dr. Torres had shared in his experiments, nursed him through his significant illness some eighteen years earlier, and died because of his efforts; the truth of the matter is that Dr. Muñoz had himself died at that time. Is Dr. Torres, then, simply an alter ego of the doctor, a man's story in which the doctor's story is truly revealed? His name means "tower" and points at the verticality that is so basic to this story and the others we shall examine. The name Muñoz, a name borne by many Spaniards,[2] means "son of Muño (a hill) or of Nuño (ninth)" ("MUÑOZ—Name Meaning & Origin"). There is some uncertainty here; and I should note that in investigating various Spanish dictionaries I found nothing to support this assertion of the web site. I am no scholar in Spanish philology (and Lovecraft was not either, unless he learned more in his years in New York), so I cannot decide the matter; but the name may be related to the Latin *mons,* which means "mountain" and is related to such words as *eminere* (to rise out), *prominere* (to stand out), and *minax* (threatening), and is cognate to the Breton *menez* (mountain) (Pokorny 1.726). It seems then likely that both Torres and Muñoz are words that point at the verticality so important to the greater story,

---

2. Luiz Muñoz Rivera was an important Puerto Rican politician, "largely responsible for the Jones Act (signed 4 March 1917), granting U.S. citizenship to Puerto Ricans" ("Luiz Muñoz Rivera"). I think it possible that this man was the source of the name for HPL, though the name was popular at the time.

the aspiration to be above the merely human.

Finally, in these preliminary remarks I wish to emphasize a detail at the end of "Cool Air" in which the narrator describes the "awful, blind hand" (*CF* 2.20) with which the doctor in his fatal deliquescence attempts to write the reason for his death. The radical mixed metaphor of the phrase "blind hand" may be reminiscent of Milton's phrase "blind mouths" in his attack upon the ignorant, shallow greed of the Anglican clergy ("Lycidas," l. 119). The hand in Lovecraft's phrase refers to the script in the doctor's note, a script that fails to communicate because of the condition of the man's physical hand, which may be understood as a synecdoche for his body, for that hand has become a claw not capable of easily dealing with the business of manipulating the pencil, and his blind body was blind, senseless from its birth. The word *blind* refers literally to the doctor's loss of sight as he dies, but it also refers to the condition of the script, which is smeared, scrawled, and nauseous. Twice the narrator says that it is a piece of paper "hideously smeared" or "stickily smeared' (2.20). There is some irony in the word "smear," since it originally referred to an anointing with oil in order to bless (*OED* "Smear"); now the oil is simply the mess that remains of the body in its mess, devoid of all sacrality. The word "scrawl" is related to "crawl," in both cases related to the inability to move the pencil across the page and to the degradation of the man and his body. Two very similar phrases in the last two paragraphs, "nauseous words" and "noisome scrawl," once more refer to the physical state of the body, its smell, but each phrase also refers to the moral state of the man who attempted to evade death.

A tacit contrast to the decrepitude of the hand lies in the cool air that early in the story "creeps" (*CF* 2.11), later "rushes" (2.13), and then "blasts" (2.14). What begins as a simple explanation for being "afraid of a draught of cool air" (2.11) concludes in an apocalyptic scene reminiscent of the judgment in "Lycidas," rendered by St. Peter upon a faithless clergy. But what is being judged, and in what way is the doctor faithless or corrupt? The answer is, I think, that he has been a sworn enemy of death, an enemy of the natural processes through which we live and die. This scene is of course replayed to its conclusion in "The Thing on the Doorstep," in which another body in deliquescence, because it is another mentality that believes in the power of the will to evade death, attempts to write and in a fury presents the narrator "a large, closely written paper impaled on the end of a long pencil" (*CF* 3.355), accompanied by "a gust of insufferably foetid wind" that "almost flung [the narrator] prostrate" (3.355). Some of the message comes through, some is willfully destroyed; but the truth of the matter is that these blind hands know not of what they write. The coherence of the body that is manifested in the importance of the hand is blown away by the sudden supernatural wind.

Let us now locate Lovecraft's story within others that deal with the same configuration of the two levels. The earliest is "The Picture in the House," in which the narrator arrives in a chilly rain at a house he had not intended to enter; it cannot be any warmer inside except for the second floor, from which the fresh blood drips through the ceiling onto the floor. From one point of view the structure seems to conform to MacDonald's, for here the difference between the lower and the higher stories appears to be a model of that developed by Plato in *The Republic,* in which the lower world, this everyday world, is a mere reflection or poor participation within the higher world, which is the true reality. Below we have the picture in the book of an African charnel house five centuries removed from the characters; above, at this instant, a real charnel house is dripping its actual warm blood in the attempt of the old man to live forever. This ideal aim lies in a secret knowledge. In "Cool Air" the higher story also obtrudes into the lower by dripping into it; in that case, however, it is the ammonia that drips down, not quite as potent or as material as blood. On the other hand, the picture does have an immediate, subtle effect upon the two characters who find themselves unaccountably moved by it.

Though Plato thought art merely a mimetic mode that clumsily imitates the actual reality, this story affirms the energy that reaches out from the picture, primitive as it is. Methexis, which does not yield to mere mimesis, bears its own power. On the other hand, what is happening on the second floor, though inspired by the picture in the book, must be quite original in New England. The old man is not using the instruments of the Congo, but the instruments that he has used time out of mind on the sheep and pigs; and what is done out of doors in the Congo the old man accomplishes in a closed room on a second floor. Living in the New World, the old man had to construct his own procedures.

"The Music of Erich Zann" is closely analogous to "Cool Air," for here once more the narrator is telling his story because of the remarkable character of the man who lives about him. And this man is as much an original, creating his own modes and procedures, under the influence of an exterior inspiration, as that of the old man and his use of the Pigafetta volume. As Peter Cannon (*H. P. Lovecraft* 150) has remarked, each of the men in the upper story, Doctor Muñoz and Erich Zann, is intensely interested in communicating his tale, but each attempt fails, in the one case because of the wind from outside the broken window and in the other case because of the narrator's decision to burn the documents. The odd detail in "The Music of Erich Zann" is that the house in which the two men live has two outsides, the daily life of a French city and a demonic storm that is the source of Erich Zann's music. It is as though the source of the ideal lies at a further remove than simply in his room. This story, however, like "The Picture in the House," affirms the power of art in the protagonist's admiration for Zann's music, even though on the night of the climax he enters the large garret "shivering with cold and fear" (*CF* 1.286). In "Cool Air" the doctor is not an artist, but the protagonist admires his cultured aspect, the way in which he has created himself, with something of the same passion as the narrator of "The Music of Erich Zann," albeit with some ambivalence because of the man's livid appearance and "coldness of touch" (*CF* 2.14). He is something of a gentleman as well as a musician.

II

> Du siehst, mein Sohn
> Zum Raum wird hier die Zeit.
>
> [You see, my son / here time becomes space].
> —Wagner, Transformation, First Act of *Parsifal*

In contrast to these three stories let us consider "The Dreams in the Witch House" and "The Dunwich Horror." The former has something of the same configuration, though the protagonist of the first work is not driven to live in the same house where a witch has lived. The house does provide cheap lodgings, as do the apartments in the other stories, but Walter Gilman—such is his fated name—actively desires to live there because of its connection with the witch Keziah Mason, and as a good mathematician because of his admiration for her art; he is not a wounded soul such as we meet in "Cool Air." The upper loft of his garret is utterly cut off from her. He only enters it through his dreams, just as through his dreams he also enters the world of multi-dimensional space, which is so much more spatial than the world below, rather like what happens in MacDonald's *Lilith*. Most of these dreams are horrific; we would use the word "nightmare" to describe them, and Lovecraft does remark on "the nightmare shape of Brown Jenkin" (*CF* 3.239). Gilman returns from this nightmare space with sunburn in a fever, drenched in cold perspiration; whatever the space he had found himself in, it "burns frore" like the atmosphere of Hell in *Paradise Lost* (2.595). Meanwhile life proceeds as it does for a student; he fails some courses and succeeds in others, believing that in some fashion the ancient history of Keziah

Mason may have something to do with his studies.[3] Moreover, he is in some confusion between the Keziah Mason he sees in his dreams and an old woman he first sees through the docks and later in the slums, persecuting him with her stare.

Now for the sake of the contrast I wish to discuss a story that in several ways is radically different from those that we have discussed so far, "The Dunwich Horror." Despite its difference, however, it highlights certain details that we have already noted. No one comes to live with Wizard Whateley, his daughter, and his grandson. No one cares to play the narrator, although their lives, studious and matricidal, are simply an everyday life; nevertheless, something has entered into the house in its upper story which they gradually enlarge until it forms a "vacant abyss" (*CF* 2.430) above their heads. By this time in their "great siege of carpentry" Wizard Whateley and his putative grandson have "knocked out all the partitions, [. . .] leaving only one vast open void between the ground story and the peaked roof" (2.429). Whatever lives there is invisible because it is unspeakable; the vision of it at the end of the story merely says that in relation with its brother Wilbur it plays out the biblical story of Jacob the trickster and his dullard brother Esau. Yog-Sothoth can do nothing but roll across buildings; his brother Wilbur is more clever, though he meets his death torn to pieces by the watchdogs of Miskatonic Library. To that extent Wilbur has the fate of Cain, fated to walk beneath the curse of God.

The metaphoric usurpation of all space that we noticed in MacDonald's *Lilith* is literal in Lovecraft's narrative. What shall we see? Does the unconscious, which never reveals itself except through its effects, devour the daily life? The unconscious, as MacDonald would have it, pervades the daily life (*Lilith* 16), though to the suffering protagonist it seems usurpation. The creature, once we obtain some

---

3. Much of the detail about his studies, his failures and his brilliance, and his sickness, may have something to do with HPL's own breakdowns and failures that prevented him from entering Brown University.

sense of what it looks like, has "great bulgin' eyes all over it" (*CF* 2.462) rather like Argos, the very emblem of the superego, at least that which Hera projects when she sets her hundreds of eyes to guard Io. Once the Dunwich Horror breaks out of the house it finds its way, almost by natural instinct, to Cold Spring Glen, no doubt the perfect place for Dr. Muñoz, from which the whippoorwills had poured on the occasion of Wizard Whateley's death. The Horror descends into the cold before it ascends to the lightning-wracked Sentinel Hill for the climactic scene of the story. It has no problem in that ascent, for "it could scale a sheer stony cliff of almost complete verticality" (2.447). Though in the later part of the story it has little resemblance to the kinds of stories we are interested in, it does not release this theme of verticality.

I wish to add another story to these exceptional witnesses, Thomas Pynchon's early story "Entropy," a story that the author has come to dislike intensely because of its careful manner. The story is built upon a stark contrast between one story and that above it. On the lower story Meatball Mulligan is celebrating the second day of a chaotic lease-breaking party. On the upper story an aesthete called Callisto, who years before had been "a young man at Princeton" (72) but is now "in the sad dying fall of middle age" (73), and his Eurasian mistress Aubade are attempting to hold the temperature of their hothouse apartment, which they never leave, while outside an early spring in February seems to be holding at a steady 37 degrees Fahrenheit.

I shall not enter into the physics or metaphysics upon which the story is based nor the allusions to Adams, Gibbs, Boltsmann, Maxwell, or Clausius, filling the same function as Planck, Heisenberg, Einstein, and de Sitter. No doubt the story is overweighted by physical argument. For us the point is that Callisto, like Dr. Muñoz, is terrified of losing control of the temperature. The world is a heat-death engine, against which he is waging a series of hopeless stratagems, "helpless in the past" (84). In the climax Mulligan rises out of the chaos of his party and takes responsibility for it, asserting a certain order, even calling a repairman to fix the refrigerator that is broken (84), while above him Aubade breaks the glass of the hothouse and opens it up to a life-giving or death-giving chaos. As Pynchon puts the matter more pointedly in his novella *The Crying of Lot 49*, we shall only live through a belief in the possibility that Maxwell's demon shall deliver us from the closed system in which we live a life-in-death existence. Callisto cannot even give life to a bird that is dying to his hands. The only sign of life in the story comes from the party below, the music and noise that ascends to disrupt the hothouse: "The architectonic purity of [Aubade's] world was constantly threatened by such hints of anarchy: gaps and excrescences and skew lines, and a tilting of planes to which she had continually to readjust lest the whole structure shiver into a disarray of discrete and meaningless signals" (73). In this appeal to geometry and a splintering shiver, what could be more Lovecraftian? But the people at the party are not in any way aware of the desperate couple above them.

We now need to look at these stories through more direct comparisons. What, for instance, are we to make of these protagonists? Most are in retreat from the world. They take up residence in rooms that shall cost less than they can afford because the outside world threatens them, sometimes actively as in the storm that forces the narrator of "The Picture on the House" to find refuge, sometimes more subtly because they have been subtly wounded. Even more, Dr. Muñoz, Erich Zann, and the old man in "The Picture on the House" are in retreat, though two of them deny their dependence on the outside world. Though he develops a fever, Walter Gilman seems a great exception, and his desire to live in that particular house may be the reason that this story seems so different from the others. The temperature is in question at all; Gilman enters spaces of a very different heat, but he had not meant to. In "Entropy," however, the man in retreat is Callisto in his upper room, fearful of the outside room as its temperature hovers at 37 degrees Fahrenheit; Aubade is also in retreat, apparently from the horrors of the French colonization in Southeast Asia.

To push this point further, we must admit that a great difference in these stories lies in the anonymity of the first-person narrators in "Cool Air," "The Picture on the House," and "The Music of Erich Zann." Each of these characters is in some way wounded or threatened. One has a bad financial situation and a bad heart, one is young and rather naïve astride his rational bicycle,[4] and one is poor and neurasthenic. They do not possess the exuberant confidence of the Whateleys or of Walter Gilman. They have no name, and no more primitive sign of weakness exists.

A striking point is that in most of these stories something is broken. In "Cool Air" the ammonia apparatus is broken so that the temperature begins to rise. In "The Picture in the House" something has broken in the upper story so that the blood begins to drip through the ceiling; that is never clarified. In any case the entire house is broken by "the titanic thunderbolt of thunderbolts; blasting that accursed house of unutterable secrets" (*CF* 1.271), which come swiftly upon the two men's recognition of the drop of blood. In "The Music of Erich Zann" the window is broken by the power of the supernatural wind. In "The Dunwich Horror" the Whateley house is broken apart as the creature within it attempts to escape into a freer life; and much of Dunwich is thereby torn to pieces. In "Entropy" a lease-breaking is the life of the party (though it is unclear whether the party celebrates

---

4. The knowing narrator of Angela Carter's story "The Lady of the House of Love" argues: "To ride a bicycle is in itself some protection against superstitious fears, since the bicycle is the product of pure reason applied to motion. [. . .] Beneficial to the health, it emits no harmful fumes and permits only the most decorous speeds. How can a bicycle ever be an implement of harm" (97). Nevertheless, in both stories, that of Carter and that of HPL, the bicycle delivers its rider to the door of an irrational, deadly creature.

the breaking of the lease or exists in order to break the lease—if the latter, the invisible landlord seems to be holding out against the madness). One of the characters has a telling account of a dispute with his wife: "She ended up throwing a *Handbook of Chemistry and Physics* at me, only it missed and went through the window, and when the glass broke I reckon something in her broke too" (75), a passage that presages the climax of the story when Aubade breaks the windows of the hothouse and holds up "her two exquisite hands which came away bleeding and glistening with sprinters" (85)—witnesses, exquisite witnesses, to the urge toward chaos, life and death. In every one of these stories something needs to be broken; anything that maintains life as it is, other than it might be, must be broken. Otherwise life and death shall not be affirmed.

Another aspect of this breakage lies in the word *shiver* with its two different but related meanings: "to shake with or as if with [. . .] cold. To quiver or vibrate, as by the force of the wind"; or "To cause to break suddenly into fragments or splinters (*American Heritage Dictionary* "shiver"). In my account of these stories we have met the word in its various meanings a number of times. Dr. Muñoz, for instance, lives in a "shivery place" (*CF* 2.15), and it is a pressing question why the narrator "shiver[s] more than others upon entering a cold room" (2.11) that leads to the story proper. It seems that the cold and the terror that cause a character to shiver operate upon two levels, one quite physical, the other symbolic—or should we at last admit that these two moments operate upon two stories? There is no escape from them. Walter Gilman almost shivers at the "seemingly unmotivated stare of the beldame" near the wharves (*CF* 3.239). When Luther Brown shivers on the occasion of the Dunwich Horror's first attack, the word seems to stand in the place of an earlier phrase, "convulsed with fright" (*CF* 2.442). Anyone who shivers, experiences horrification, the hair standing up on end. The wholeness or purity that Dr. Muñoz or Callisto attempt to attain is unacceptable.

We have some uncertainty what might be the provenance of the word *pure*. The *American Heritage Dictionary* plumps for the infinitive "to purify, cleanse" ("Peue-"), whereas the *Etymological Dictionary of Latin* prefers "clean [...], unmixed," as does the *OED*, suggesting that it is related to the Greek πῦρ, fire, to which it is cognate. I cannot decide this puzzle, though we grant that the American dictionary is more recent. Still, the notion of purification through fire is attractive, and we can see how it would lead to the meaning of "unmixed"; we shall see, moreover, that paradoxically fire does seem to be the subtext of these stories. But despite Dante's witness in the *Purgatorio* (26.92, 148), at that height neither that which purges nor that which refines changes the world.

Before proceeding in these examinations, however, we need to take up other thoughts, for the notion of purity bears certain problems with it. For what are we to make of the place that the bath occupies in Wagner's *Parsifal?* Early in the opera's first act the injured Amfortas is taking a bath in the lake, caught up in the vain hope that the special herbs in the bath will heal his wound that seems endless. In the third act Parsifal, now purified himself, laves the head of the mysterious Gundry and the wound of Amfortas. In all these acts the concept of Reinheit, "purity," takes doubly part.

This doubling of the action in the concept of purity is mirrored in another doubling that takes place in the ascension of Gurnemanz and Parsifal into the realm of the Grail; in the first action the hopes of the old man apparently fail; in the third act those hopes are fulfilled, perhaps most beautifully fulfilled, in his explanation of the joy in the Karfreitagszaubermusik [Good Friday magical music]. As we contemplate these mirrorings we may wonder at the position of the second act within these ascensions and discover them in the two repetitions of the word "keusch" [chaste]. once in the mockery of Klingsor and once more powerfully in the laughing mockery of Kundry: "Bist du keusch?" [Are you, my dear, chaste?], a mockery that reveals his self-created impotence. In addition, the mockery elicits from him much the same words twice: "Furchbare Not" [fearful need] (518, 522), echoing the same words and the same horror that once were spoken doubly by Alberich: "Schmälicher Not" and "höchster Not" [shameful need and highest need] (1427, 1511). Such is the hell of these two characters, which seems wrenched from them; such is the transformation from one height to another. The temple of the Grail does, however, look down across a valley to the world of Spain, in which the knights of the Grail may take part.

The access to the upper stories in Lovecraft's conception varies from work to work. In "The Picture in the House" this access is unproblematic; the protagonist does not attempt to go to the upper story, to which he gives no thought at all and no interest at all until the blood of the slaughter house begins to seep through the ceiling. In "The Music of Erich Zann" the narrator reminds the reader how steep the street and the apartment house are, and the musician is intensely shy about his art in the upper reaches; it is a laborious ascent. In "Cool Air" the upper air is perfectly accessible, though to the taste of the narrator rather cold, and the narrator does take the ascent into account until the cooling apparatus fails the first time and until he has an incipient heart attack; at this point he realizes that despite the cold he has a very immediate need for the doctor in the upper story. In "The Dreams in the Witch House" the loft above Gilman's garret is utterly sealed off; he does not apparently enter it and learn of its mysteries unless though his dreams, but he does dream profusely, thanks also to the aid of Keziah Mason, for he is not at all in command in his dreams as he would wish. Though the upper story seems to offer much to the questioning protagonist, he also encounters several difficulties that are increasing in this series of fictions, just as the protagonists in MacDonald's stories encounter difficulties. It is not easy to avail oneself of the knowledge that lies in the upper regions offset her and the unconscious.

Let us now be more specific about that upper chamber, which, hidden away, has much to do with the unconscious. The upper rooms of the MacDonald works, with their allusions to cosmic orders and the Holy Spirit, have much in common with the superego, the rigorous part of our unconscious that is rich and prolific in moral demands. Callisto is the spokesman for the superego, demanding that the world be saved from entropy by the paradoxical and futile construction of the hothouse, a place constructed on the principles of complete order. Callisto, parenthetically, was a nymph in the train of Artemis; Zeus seduced her and at the threat of the offended goddess set her and her son in the form of bears among the constellations. As a sign of elegant perversions and as a sign of the hermaphrodite, Callisto bears the name of a woman who is elevated to the stars and thus associated with the cosmic order, the Great Bear that never sets and that points to the pole star (Graves 1.84). On the other hand, bears are known for their hibernation, the state that the narrator of "Cool Air" yearns for, "a bearable place to hibernate" (*CF* 2.12), and Callisto through his entire story is lying in bed, but like the transformed nymph Callisto is now eternally awake and aware that she is not "keusch."

It is this aspect of the upper rooms, their connection with cosmic order, that Maurice Lévy cannot accept, believing that the way up is the same as the way down, and that therefore a step upward is simply downward into the abyss with which Lovecraft is so often preoccupied (64), as in "The Rats in the Walls" and *The Case of Charles Dexter Ward*, I would argue that the step upward is simply that, a step into the light, and that we need to read these stories with every qualification necessary, as engagements with the terrifying superego and the ideal. The system is not communicative, despite the authorities of Heraclitus and Bachelard; 2×3 does not equal 3×2, and the way up is not the same as the way down, mainly because of the dense specificity of the two paths. Thus I disagree with my earlier remarks on this thematic structure ("Landscapes, Selves" 235). Nevertheless, I think that Lévy is right in insisting that many of these upper rooms in these stories contain abysses. The question is how we shall understand these abysses and the ways in which they interact with the character of the superego.

III

> If unmelodious was the song
> It was a hearty note and strong.
> Who lists may in their mumming see
> Traces of ancient mystery.
> (Scott, *Marmion,* Introduction to Canto 6.72–75)

For O, for O, the hobby-horse is forgot. (*Hamlet* 3.2.122)

With this problem—how we are to reconcile the abyss with the superego—we return to the peculiar nature of "Cool Air" and to the possibility that it may contain, in the manner of James Hillman, a trace of mythic material. The "almost bearded" landlady Mrs. Herrero is the first character we meet (*CF* 2.12), a figure of the potent hermaphrodite of the fertility rites in the Morris-dances of England, that many scholars believe originated in Spain; this is the Maid Marian or Malkin who was played by a man ("Morris-Dance" 18.873). "Malkin," however, has come to mean more than Maid Marian, whose reputation in the ballads is not as pure as it has come to mean in our later tradition. A "malkin" is a "slut, slattern, drab, [. . .] the proper name of a female spectre or demon, [. . .] or effeminate man" (*OED* "Malkin"), Castillo and Bond "herrero," but the good landlady is a "slatternly" woman (*CF* 2.12). We should add that this figure is often called the Betty (Needham and Peck 84), and that this word has a verbal meaning: "To fuss about, like a man who busies himself with a woman's duties" (*OED* "Betty"). The Morris-dance was usually performed in May, another indication that it may have been originally in time a part of a fertility ritual; but in time its characters were liable, in an act of cross-pollination, to appear with the masked characters in the Mummers' performance, which takes place in the winter solstice and often presents a comic version of the story of St. George ("Mummers" 18.966), in which the good saint dies many times, only to rise again and in various clumsy defeats his vile, supernatural opponents.

As we survey the other figures of the Morris-dance, not many offer themselves to our inspection, unless it be the silly jokester the Hobby Horseman. This horse, distorted and elevated in the comic mode as it is, leads us to Pegasus, and we did want a story that had something to do with the vertical axis of human experience. The Greek hero Bellerophon rode Pegasus to conquer the Chimæra, a composite monster that is part lion, part goat, and part dragon, in Hesiod's account so horrific that it sports the three heads of the three beasts (*Theogony* 321-22), so horrific that Horace at the beginning of the *Ars Poetica* seems to take it as the example of what a poet should not attempt. Later Bellerophon attempted to ride the horse to Olympus in order, as Pindar intimates, to join the company of the gods in immortality (*Isth.* 7.39-47); but Zeus prevented the attempt, and the horse with better sense than its master cast him off so that he wandered the world thereafter, wretched and half-mad (Graves 1.254). This story warns against the attempt to ascend into that world which is peculiarly the gods' to escape our human, mortal state.

There is sufficient madness in Lovecraft's story. Despite the doctor's attempt to maintain his own sobriety he rages; he cannot help but rage. And his mental disturbance causes a variety of shocks in others. A young man who had safely come through the Great War suffers epilepsy when he looks at the doctor; the man the narrator had hired to maintain the doctor's supply of ice fled "mad-eyed" (*CF* 2.19); and the narrator himself began to "rage almost as violently" as the doctor (2.19). We have seen in other stories how carefully we must treat the narrations of the narrators. This narrator claims, in a break from the early realistic trend of the work, that "Fiendish things were in the air" (2.19) with no attempt to clarify their nature. Despite the sober nature of the story's opening, it debouches into hints of madness.

Let us consider Horace's version of the story, which he joins to the story of Phaethon, as so often in the form of a concise moral platitude:

> Terret ambustus Phaethon avaras
> spes, ut exemplum grave praebet ales
> Pegasus terrernum equitem gravatus
> Bellerophontem.

[Scorched Phaethon deters eager / hopes, and the winged Pegasus offers a heavy / warning weighed down by the earthly rider / Bellerophon.] (*Odes* 4.11)

The vertical axis which has so concerned us is evident in both stories, but in this case I am interested in the word *ambustus,* which signifies not only "scorched" or "burned" but also "frost-bitten" (Smith, "amburo" 41); in the height, in the domain of the gods, hot or cold, cold or hot, may seem interchangeable. But whether Olympus is hot or cold or simply a state for which we have no word, it is dangerous to a mortal. MacDonald writes stories about the glories of that domain, and within it the Princess is healed of her injuries, but even MacDonald warns against its dangers, and Bellerophon is never healed. As the crisis approaches in "Cool Air," the cold that the doctor demands in order to maintain his life in his death is utterly inimical and unbearable to mortals.

Bellerophon's mad attempt brings us to the story we should perhaps have had in mind from the beginning, the story of Prometheus. In addition to the Titan's story we should note that in Aeschylus' *Prometheus Bound* the remarkable figure of Io appears, the woman raped by Zeus whom Hera has now transformed into a cow, dancing through her pain and performed of course by a male actor; and thus this character seems to play the part of the Betty of whose importance we have already taken note. As for Prometheus, not only is he the Titan who brought down fire from Oympus to aid humanity, he is in Aeschylus' account the true founder of civilization. In *Prometheus Bound* he provides a list of the benefits he has given us, but these benefits extend beyond mere aids. In one version of the myth he is the actual creator of humanity. In the words of Goethe's poem "Prometheus" he announces to Zeus, "Hier sitz' ich, forme Menschen / Nach meinem Bilde [. . .], Und dein nicht zu achten, / Wie ich" [Here sit I, forming people / In my image [. . .] / who pay no attention to you, / like me] (46).

This Prometheus acts directly against the order established by the Olympian gods. He is not interested in order but in change and ecstatic rebellion, that rebellion desired by the general movement of *Sturm und Drang* that Goethe initiated and participated in as a young man. His punishment for ascending to Olympus and stealing fire is to be chained by the smith Hephaistos to the Caucasus Mountains, exposed to the sun, frost, and snow (Aeschylus, *Prometheus Bound* 22-25, 992-94): he must, as Milton says of hell, "burn frore." When that punishment is not sufficient, the eagle of Zeus descends to tear at his liver daily, a punishment that emphasizes he is the Outsider and none other. In stark contrast to the doctor and the musician, however, Prometheus is released from his torture and in Athens is celebrated by torch races (Burkert 171),

Dr. Muñoz, on the contrary, is a Prometheus who is not unbound but increasingly more bound into fetters, frozen fetters of his own devising, the ammonia pipes and pump that he modifies so that his room can be refrigerated to 28 degrees; the second half of his technological response to his state is his bath accompanied by spices, incense, and "the pungent chemicals" (*CF* 2.17). In the last two pages of the story, however, he leaves his fetters in the bathroom where he had so valiantly striven for his purity, a modern Amfortas, to find his way to the desk and write his final confession; this scrawl of his fetters, however, is timeworn, illegible, and hopeless. The narrator can make nothing of them. His Pegasus and his Hobby-horse are of no comfort either.

These failures are models for us in the other stories. Callisto seems bound not only to his hermetic hothouse but to his bed in the final throes of his own paranoia, which edges into the distressed madness of Bellerophon; we cannot say whether he is released by Aubade's shattering of the glass. Erich Zann is bound by his music and by his mad pen; perhaps even more he is bound to his inarticulate voice—in his case so unlike Prometheus, who in Aeschylus' rendering of the stories is remarkably articulate; and if Callisto is released by the shattered window he is only released into madness and death. Though we never see the old man in "The Picture in the House" in his upper room, we can well imagine that there he is bound to the picture that is such a tickle to him that it compels him to his butcheries. Walter Gilman discovers that he is bound to a series of revelatory nightmares through the power that Keziah Mason exerts to overcome life. Though in many ways Wilbur Whateley seems the emblem of freedom, he must bind himself into his tight clothes if he is to enjoy that freedom, so when the watchdog rips the clothes from him he dies; but his brother dies when the fetters of his invisibility are made manifest through the silly apparatus of "a powder in this long-distance sprayer" (*CF* 2.458).

We should notice that Horace's account of Phaethon and Aeschylus' account of Prometheus have something in common, the juxtaposition of hot and cold; but we should distinguish one further peculiarity about these relations: when we touch something that is cold it may seem hot, but something that is hot will never seem cold. The relation, like that of the journey up and down, is not communicative, and it thus reinforces that theme. The way up is not the same as the way down, and thus bears within itself its own fatality.

If we survey the stories from the angle of the Promethean gift, we see great differences among them. Clearly Callisto has no gift for Meatball Mulligan, though he is dictating to Aubade an apology of his life that is more intended to clarify his life to himself than to enlighten any of the *vulgus profanum*. The Whateleys have no gift for the people of Dunwich, far from it, although from their own peculiar point of view they may regard the spawn of Yog-Sothoth as a gift, one that brings home the truth of our human existence; and though Walter Gilman is a perfectly decent young man, he very much pursues knowledge for its own sake no matter the cost. The old man in "The Picture on the House" no doubt means to kill the narrator, but before that fatal moment he seems compelled to justify his own long life, happy to share the picture.

Erich Zann and Dr. Muñoz are very different from these characters. Erich Zann writes at a great pace what we assume shall be an explanation of his work for the narrator, though his notes will be flung away by the chaos outside the window that inspires them; and Dr. Muñoz writes "long documents of some sort" (*CF* 2.18) through the last weeks of his apparent life, which he requests the narrator to communicate to certain occult sages, one of them a famous French doctor "now generally thought dead" (2.18)—a request that the narrator refuses, for he destroys the documents after the doctor's death. In comparison to those documents Dr. Muñoz's treatment of the narrator's heart trouble is rather minor. So among these characters only the composer and the doctor are Promethean. Like Moses, because wisdom comes down from on high, they hope to bring down the law from the mountain, the shape of the world as it is, saying with as much irony as James Joyce contrives, "with the light of inspiration shining in his countenance and bearing in his arms the tables of the law, graven in the law of the outlaw" (*Ulysses* 7.867–69). The composer and the doctor are marginal figures in their societies, and Lovecraft has little hope that their aspirations shall aid humanity and little belief that they should.

When we consider the stories of Bellerophon and Prometheus it becomes clear that the characters in "Cool Air" fulfill these roles in a fractured manner. The single figure of the Greek myths becomes double in Lovecraft's story; that is to say, from the standpoint of the myth the narrator and the doctor are both Bellerophon with his touch of madness and Prometheus in his stubborn rebellion. Or to say it in another way, the narrator is already the wounded figure, suffering from a heart disease that the myth assures us the hero shall undergo. Dr. Muñoz in his suffering becomes bound to his own machine; he dares not escape from the instrument of his own torture, which is his noble steed, until at last he deserts it without yielding the point that the horse has thrown him, as so far he had agreed to his own fetters, and yielded to his own death. So to the question whether Dr. Muñoz is such a Promethean figure, we answer resoundingly yes, except that as we have seen Prometheus is at last released from the fire, the snow, and the eagle nibbling his liver. A part of the reason I want to deal with that figure is his involvement in the question of fire.

But also, though he does not create humanity, he is not only a doctor devoted to the physical well-being of humanity; he is a doctor who means to re-create humanity "nach meinem Bilde" (Goethe), so that he shall be at last able to endure eternal life. It is, however, at the price of the divine eagle that shall eat his liver. One puzzle remains: What are we to make of the "strange, dark place" where Dr. Torres took Dr. Muñoz when he nursed him back from death into the death he has lived for the last eighteen years (*CF* 2.16)? It is a secret that of necessity remains a secret, though we can guess at it when we realize that this is the only story Lovecraft wrote in which the bathroom plays so prominent a role, providing the bathtub in which the doctor incessantly washes himself. Next to the tub of course stands the toilet. Early in the story we learn that Mrs. Herrero's son Esteban buys food for him, a job that the narrator later accepts. Now if the doctor eats, despite the problems he has with his internal organs, we must assume that he also defecates and that, as I once remarked of the landscape in Lovecraft's dream world, "The somatic process excretes a sarkotic object" ("Landscapes, Selves" 235). Let us recall again the appearance of the shoggoth in *At the Mountains of Madness*, a transformed and transfigured black dung. The "strange, dark place" is the place where we shut ourselves in to defecate and thus produce the emblem of our mortality. It is the symbol of our great theme that Lovecraft shares with St. Paul: "Who shall deliver me from the body of this death?" (Rom. 7:24). But he does not share St. Paul's answer, and neither does the raging, broken Dr. Muñoz who has ascended to the upper story and its "strange, dark place" in order to achieve immortality. We assume that Amfortas takes part also in this unspeakable place.

Let us review this material. First, as we began, everything that happens in this story occurs in the framework of a vertical world in a lower story and an upper story. The often anonymous narrator, who represents the world as it is in the lower story, is in some fashion in retreat from that world, but he knew nothing of that upper story until the person who lives there and who hopes to triumph there invites the narrator to the ascent; there is always some difficulty involved in the ascent as well as in the descent: since the way down is the same as the way up, one is liable to be lost or maddened. Therefore, some technology is almost already involved in which both narrator and protagonist are too dependent to be represented by the figures of the hermaphrodite and Hobby-horse; Io, however, is as much in need as the ammonia pump that goes bust. The consequence of this difficulty is breakage, shivering and splintering in the face of a cold that burns, an *ébranlement* that is ecstatic but also joyless. The two phrases, "blind hand" and "burns frore," mixed metaphor and oxymoron, indicate the extent to which rationality cannot comprehend this space.

We understand thereby how the space within which this experience occurs is highly disturbing, physically and mentally; madness and harm reside there that may be experienced as a punishing superego. Zeus first has Prometheus nailed to the mountain rock through the agency of the divine blacksmith Hephaistos, the god of our human technologies, and then sends the eagle daily, so that in time the Titan learns that his immortality partakes of the mortal world in a much more intimate way than anything implied by his words, "nach meinem Bilde" or the shameful words in the "Not" of Alberich and Klingsor. Prometheus takes on the image of the mortals he meant to aid. But the range of the superego may be indicated by the upper room devoted to numbers that imply the heat-death of the universe and the upper room that is a slaughterhouse, even for doctors. No one escapes this death.

Lovecraft's Influence in Science Fiction

The Tides of His Dark Star in the Works of Arthur C. Clarke, Fritz Leiber, and Philip K. Dick

When we consider how Lovecraft was viewed by the writers who came after him we must not be misled by seeing it as purely a matter of weird fiction; several of his later stories often appealed to the conventions of science fiction. One of his last stories, "In the Walls of Eryx," is forthright science fiction. So it should be no surprise that several science fiction authors read him with interest. Arthur C. Clarke responded to Lovecraft's work, and followed his lead in feeling that humanity would be overwhelmed by the universe. Fritz Leiber was stirred by the weird aspects of Lovecraft's work, and scholars have examined that response; but Leiber was also a witty science fiction author, and we see traces of Lovecraft in *The Wanderer* and *The Big Time*. Philip K. Dick read Lovecraft with interest and explicitly felt that some Lovecraftian themes spoke to his own condition. At the conclusion of this chapter we will examine the ways in which all of these authors, no matter what their religious identity, like Lovecraft responded to the theme of the numinous.

In his autobiography Clarke devoted a chapter to his encounter with Lovecraft's late works, *At the Mountains of Madness* and "The Shadow out of Time" (Clarke, *Astounding Days* 130). At about the time he read them he confessed that, though he preferred stories with a strong basis in science, he nevertheless admired Lovecraft (McAleer 29). He had problems, however, with Lovecraft's world. Despite his admiration he spent some time detailing his fondness for tentacular invertebrates such as squids and octopuses (Clarke, *Astounding Days* 43-50); and we can trace in his work various attempts to redeem these creatures from Lovecraft's psychopathic loathing. The most striking attempt is the giant squid in *Childhood's End*, which the characters treat as a pet called Lucifer, fondly nicknamed Lucey (115). This feminine Lucey parallels the demonic appearance of the rigorously masculine Karellen in the central plot, the midwife of the novel. In 1962, in another story, Clarke imagined a race of squids with eyes "uncannily human and intelligent" (*Collected Stories* 814) that communicates through a startlingly beautiful bioluminescence. This story with its nod to the beautiful creatures of "The Shadow over Innsmouth" concludes with our horror as the narrator is cut off in mid-sentence by a gigantic squid—shades of Lovecraft's early story "Dagon." If this story by Clarke redeems a tentacular creature from Lovecraft's steady horror it is only by means of a bitter irony.

There is an even more evident trace of Lovecraft's influence upon Clarke in the Englishman's early short story "Retreat from Earth," in which the narrator, sketching a cosmic history, refers to the old ones who filled their cities "with blind, fantastic slaves" (*Collected Stories* 13); it is a naïve allusion to the protagonist race in *At the Mountains of Madness* and their creatures the shoggoths. After that story Clarke was to play his cards closer to his chest; but he often posited the existence of aliens older and more advanced than humanity. *The City and the Stars* concludes in a vision of transcendent intelligences at war at the end of the universe; but perhaps the influence is more Stapledonian than Lovecraftian, and these are intelligences that are nevertheless the product of our hands, though they transcend humanity (236-77).

It is possible to see something else that Clarke discovered in *At the Mountains of Madness* and "The Shadow out of Time," the elegiac mood that various passages of historical meditation exude in his works. He laments the extinction of alien races such as the aliens who perish for the sake of the Christmas star or the flame that bursts out of the sun. I do not think that he learned this mood from Lovecraft since it was already a part of his life, but Lovecraft confirmed him in the possibilities of this mood. It is present in the conclusion of "The Call of Cthulhu" as Francis Wayland Thurston, the author of the work, considers the death of his grand-uncle and his own imminent death. It is present in "The Colour out of Space" as in the last pages the narrator considers the almost certain danger to Ammi. It is present through much of "The Shadow over Innsmouth," only to be ironically lifted in the final paragraph. Clarke modulates this elegiac mood in another way. If *Childhood's End* concerns the plight of second-raters, as I have argued (Waugh, "Lament"), are there such second-raters in Lovecraft? Well, yes. Charles Dexter Ward counts as one such, Walter Gilman counts as such, Randolph Carter counts as such also, and so I think does Wilbur Whateley in his pathetic belief that Harvard will allow him access to the *Necronomicon*. All four are intense researchers who come to ungainly ends because they cannot control the results of their studies.

Another theme important to Lovecraft and Clarke is the immensity of the universe. Depending upon Henry Adams, Karl Pearson, and Hugh Elliot, with a nod to Lucretius (Waugh, *Monster in the Mirror* 253-57), Lovecraft believed in a complex, manifold universe which is very little available to our limited senses. It is not simply that much of the universe is too far for our instruments to attain; much of the universe is simply elsewhere, in regions where the laws of the universe as we know it do not obtain. His word for that which is unavailable, too far, too elsewhere, or too other, is the Outside, all that in effect lies beyond the flaming walls of Lucretius, limited defenses afloat in chaos. Clarke makes this statement with portentous inversions reminiscent of Lovecraft's early style in the first paragraph of his early story "The Wall of Darkness": "Many and strange are the universes that drift like bubbles in the foam upon the River of Time.

Some--a very few--move against or athwart its current; and fewer still are those that lie forever beyond its reach, knowing of the future or the past" (*Collected Stories* 104). The universe is not for us. As Karellen states simply in *Childhood's End*, "The planets you may one day possess. But the stars are not for Man" (134). If humanity is to explore the universe humanity must transform itself, so radically that it may not be possible to call the new entity human. This statement becomes a refrain in the story "Earthlight" ("[The moon] was no place for man" [*Collected Stories* 355]) and in "A Meeting with Medusa" ("[Jupiter] might never be a place for man" [*Collected Stories* 906]). This theme became all the more pressing for Clarke after his paralysis, as he delineated several crises in which characters must face a radical transformation. A tension, however, arises in this state of affairs when the reader asks how Clarke understands it. The human, by which we now understand the Overlords also, is the rational mind; that into which it must be transformed is the aesthetic, intuitive mind, to which the universe appears as a series of titanic, geometric dreams, transforming time and space, which Jeff, the young son of the protagonist, experiences before his full transformation (*Childhood's End* 163-69).

This is the situation in several of Lovecraft's stories, such as "Beyond the Wall of Sleep," "From Beyond," "The Dreams in the Witch House," and "Through the Gates of the Silver Key," each of which is characterized by a breakthrough between our universe and the Outside and by a visionary dream-state in which human categories collapse. More remarkable than these stories is "The Colour out of Space," in which the world of the Outside breaks into our world, slowly causes our natural world to decay, and then departs leaving all our questions about its nature unanswered. Since we are meditating upon this story in the context of Clarke's works we notice its resemblance to his *Rendezvous with Rama* in which an alien artifact passes through the solar system and departs, leaving once more few answers to its nature.

The nature of the influence Lovecraft exerted upon Fritz Leiber, Jr., a man in combat with several fathers, has been debated for some time, but most of this debate has concerned Leiber's horror and fantasy works. It is not surprising, however, to find traces of Lovecraft's influence in Leiber's science fiction, given the power of that influence throughout the younger man's life. This influence is at work not only in literary terms; Leiber was a lover of cats before he began to exchange epistolary confidences with Lovecraft, so we can imagine his pleasure when in *The Wanderer* he arranged a love affair between Paul and the feline Tigerishka. Perhaps he took even more pleasure in Tigerishka's mistaken belief that the cat Miaow was the intelligent species upon earth.

A central theme of *The Wanderer* is once more Lovecraft's theme of the immensity of the universe in which the human understanding is infinitesimal. This is the point that Leiber made in his 1949 essay, "A Literary Copernicus": "When [Lovecraft] had completed the body of his writings, he had firmly attached the emotion of spectral dread to such concepts as outer space, the rim of the cosmos, alien beings, unsuspected dimensions, and the conceivable universes lying outside our own space-time continuum" (51). In 1964 he repeated this judgment in one of the Change War stories: "You know, the weird and the supernatural didn't just evaporate when the world got crowded and smart and technical. They moved outward—to Luna, to Mars, to the Jovian satellites, to the black tangled forest of space and the astronomic marches and the unimaginably distant bull's-eye windows of the stars" (*Changewar* 63); and in the same year he repeated the point in *The Wanderer*: "The Earth-Moon pair, huddling by the solar fire, were almost alone in a black forest twenty million million miles across. A frighteningly lonely situation, especially if you imagined something wholly unknown stirring in the forest, creeping closer, shaking the starlight here and there as it bent the black twigs of space" (4). The infinity of worlds had been a theme that Lucretius and Bruno had proposed, but the point in Lovecraft and Leiber is that given an infinity of worlds something lies out there that humans shall never comprehend. To illustrate how Lovecraft states this apprehension Leiber cites the beginning of "The Call of Cthulhu": "We live on a placid island of ignorance in the midst of black seas of infinity, and it was not meant that we should voyage far" (*CF* 2.21). There is a difference, however, in the images Lovecraft and Leiber employ; Lovecraft places humanity on an island or a ship upon an ocean that he loathes, from which, nevertheless, we are able to see some distance; whereas Leiber twice places us in a forest, the Schwarzwald of the German imagination, within which we cannot see very far and within which a beast is ready to bound upon us at any moment.

This imagery is a restrained example of what shall be generated as the novel develops and as the different characters respond in the richness of their imaginations to the Wanderer; it looks like the yin-yang, like a dinosaur, like a duck, like a golden cock, like a mandala, like a broken egg. None of these images is final. Only Paul and Don, who have been aboard the new planet, have some inkling of its nature. The hyperspace through which it drives, however, insofar as Tigerishka can express it, taking her language from Paul's mind, is again metaphoric: "It is like quicksand you must tunnel through, or like a killing desert, waterless, which you must cross to reach a star with palms. A black, malignant seething that's to space as the unconscious is to consciousness. Alleys to which the streetlight never gets, mouthless and twisted, full of dirty death—or dark, cold, oily water under docks, roiled by great waves" (*The Wanderer* 241). There is much more of this kind of language, all attempts at the inexpressible.

The Big Time and the stories connected with it have a very different tone from *The Wanderer*, but in one theme they are very close. They refuse to answer any question about the ultimate nature of the Snakes and the Spiders, the aliens who attempt to dominate the infinity of universes with their infinity of times. In a penultimate moment of the novel the characters believe that the Emperor Spider has entered their magical space, but then learn that they have been misled by the actor in their companion Sidney. The only thing we seem to know about the Snakes and Spiders is that they do seem quite occupied with humanity. In letters and essays Lovecraft had often insisted upon the indifference of the universe towards humanity, but in his stories the alien entities seem on the contrary malevolent towards us. Cthulhu and Yog-Sothoth are neither benevolent nor indifferent. This tip towards paranoia on the part of the stories is unmistakable, but we shall have more to say of paranoia shortly.

An important aspect of the action is its interiorization, once at the beginning of the novel and once again at its conclusion. At the beginning, with more than a whiff of paranoia, Greta reminds the reader of the memories the reader has lost and of the phantom memories that persist: "Have you ever worried about your memory, because it doesn't seem to be bringing you exactly the same picture of the past from one day to the next? Have you ever been afraid that your personality was changing because of forces beyond your knowledge or control? Have you ever felt sure that sudden death was about to jump you from nowhere? . . . Have you ever thought that the whole universe might be a crazy, mixed up dream?" (*The Big Time* 6). At the second moment the wise octopus Ilhilihis suggests that all the action exists within the brain of the space, for the space in which the characters live outside the cosmos is, "after its fashion, a giant brain" (169), which is to say that the stage—and "all the world's a stage"—is itself the space of the "fourth-order beings [who] live inside and outside all minds, throughout the whole cosmos" (169). As a character asserts in one of the Change War stories, "The biggest wars are the wars of thought" (*Changewar* 22); as William Blake realized, this war in heaven is the war within the mind of the artist.

The artist is the awakened individual who lives outside the mechanical universe which is inhabited by the unawakened, mechanical individual, the zombie. This is the language that Leiber had already used in his early novel, *The Sinful Ones*, which plays out on the edge of horror and science fiction in Chicago where Greta had once lived. One of the characters in that novel probes the nature of this mechanical universe: "What's made the world this way? Have machines infected men, turning them into things like themselves? Or has man's belief in a completely materialistic universe made it just that?" (137). possibilities that Lovecraft had considered when he read Edward J. O'Brien's *The Dance of the Machines* (Waugh, *Monster in the Mirror* 265-67). In a materialistic universe human freedom comes into question. Since the zombies "are dead people whose life-lines lie in the so-called past" (15), their lives are finished; they have no ability to change. But even a zombie may at certain moments have a feeling that this life might be more than purely mechanical; the change winds blow through us all, and everyone's ego is fragile.

And so we turn to Phillip K. Dick; and in doing so we note that he and Lovecraft were not at all like one another though Dick was greatly moved by *The Case of Charles Dexter Ward* and "The Colour out of Space" (Rickman 214), and though on one occasion he gave readings of Lovecraft to his third wife's children (Sutin 101). First, Dick has a sense of humor that is basic to the interactions of his characters with themselves and with their environment; consider the extended argument between Joe Chip and his doorknob (*Ubik* 23-24). The same desperate humor takes place in *The Divine Invasion* as the Joseph of that new gospel argues with a policeman about his need to see the singer Linda Fox (194-203). Lovecraft has comedy in his letters but seldom in his fiction, and he is not given to humor; Clarke has a sophomoric sense of comedy in a number of stories, especially the collection *Tales from the White Hart,* but that comedy seldom permeates his serious work. Leiber is closer to Dick in this regard, but his dry, allusive humor partakes only on occasion of the existential bite of Dick's. In this aspect of his fiction Dick is utterly his own man; and it was not difficult for his humor to transform itself into a divine humor in the late work.

Second, we must admit that Dick is not at all concerned with the immensity of the universe. His stories occur here, within this small space of the solar system and our small, recognizable time; when he does imagine stories that take place on other planets he never loses sight of earth, in much the same way as Swift in *Gulliver's Travels* never loses sight of Britain. Dick has no interest in the worlds of different laws that Lovecraft imagines beyond our space and time; sufficient to him is the fertile shattering of our interior psyches, breaking up into various mental illnesses that Dick had personally suffered and studied. Fertile as this interior world is, however, it is often claustrophobic, an effect not to be found in Clarke or Leiber but certainly to be found in Lovecraft, perhaps most clearly in the tunnel through which the narrator of "The Nameless City" must crawl. It is present in the late work, "The Dreams in the Witch House," as the attic presses down on Walter Gilman.

In one aspect, however, the worlds that Dick portrays are immense, as this passage makes us realize: "Eventually everything within the building would merge, would be faceless and identical, mere pudding-like kipple piled to the ceiling of each apartment. And, after that, the uncared-for building itself would settle into shapelessness, buried under the ubiquity of the dust. By then, naturally, he himself would be dead, another interesting event to anticipate as he stood here in his stricken living room alone with the lungless, all-penetrating, masterful world-silence" (*Do Androids Dream of Electric Sheep?* 20). Kipple had been preceded by gubbish in *Martian Time-Slip*, but whether Dick has a word for it or not this intimate, intense experience of entropy is typical of his work. Nothing is orderly or clean; it is a world that would seem to be very unlike what we find in Lovecraft's work.

We would be very wrong to believe this, however. The order of

Miskatonic University is invaded by Wilbur Whateley, leaving a horrible mess on the library floor; Providence is invaded by Joseph Curwen, who at the end of the story is no more than "a thin coating of fine bluish-grey dust" (*CF* 2.366); Arkham is invaded by the thing on the doorstep with disgusting results; the "trim white Nahum Gardner house" (*CF* 2.371) is reduced to dust by a colour that is of no detectable order though the odor it leaves is unmistakable; and this is to say nothing of Innsmouth, an entire town reduced to a nasty decay. This is as intimate and intense a disorder as anything we find in Dick.

Little wonder, then, that Dick's characters suffer a severe fragility of the ego. The various psychological ills he suffered led to the rich psychic material that his characters suffered. Autism, schizophrenia, depression, compulsive-obsessive neurosis, paranoia: it is a dense display in which the America of the '50s, '60s, and '70s saw itself. More generally, in his works we are taken through a varied exhibition of the mind's fragilities, often painful, sometimes exhilarating. He undertakes one aspect of the Modernists' program, the investigation of the inner life. But his world of psychic dysfunction is not more immediate; Dick is fond of indirect discourse, not of stream of consciousness. His text is much more objective than the Modernists' if it were not for the incessant pressure of psychic pain, focused by his humor; no doubt several readers would have liked to have escaped this tomb world, "the immutable cause-and-effect world of the demonic" (*Three Stigmata* 71), very like the machine world Leiber depicted, but Dick's growing popularity demonstrates that his readers recognize this world as their world. In their eyes we are all ill, and no doubt our society is also. Kicking and screaming he brought us into truth.

Did Lovecraft bring us into truth? I am reminded of Henry Anthony Wilcox in "The Call of Cthulhu," the delicate aesthete living in the Fleur-de-Lys Building immediately across from the First Baptist Church. Surely the geography indicates something divided in the young man's mind between the presumptive rationality of the church, pitifully dependent upon the word, upon Christ as the word and upon the biblical word, and the irrationality of decadent art. Revealed in dreams for which the young man's decadence has prepared him, the truth for that young man is Cthulhu, the ultimate bricolage monster.

We hesitate to call Lovecraft paranoid, though it is fitting and proper to call Dick paranoid since he easily admitted it—but surely not the Lovecraft we discover in his genial letters. There are of course the letters of racist raving, but to recognize the breadth of his paranoia we need to listen to the testimony of his stories in which the protagonists live in a growing expectancy that something—they know not what—is waiting to betray and destroy them. Delapore in "The Rats in the Walls" leaps to mind, whose paranoia escalates into madness; and Walter Gilman is also a case in point as he begins to fear that "somebody was constantly persuading him to do something terrible which he could not do" (*CF* 3.243).

In conclusion, we need to specify a theme which is definitely shared by Clarke, Leiber, and Dick and which they share with Lovecraft, a taste for the numinous moment and a need to express it. This taste is closely related to the theme of the universes and the theme of the fragility of the ego—it is *we* who are too slight and too incoherent to bear the complexity of the world we live in, and it is *that* which always overcomes us. We have no chance to establish a relationship with that world but in acknowledgement and awe. Let us consider this awe in the framework of these three authors as they deal with moments of numinous encounter. As the models of this encounter I will take two from the Bible, when Jacob wrestles with the angel and when Elijah listens to "a still, small voice" (Gen. 32:24-30; 1 Kings 19:12). I am rejecting moments of thunder and lightning and instant decision, the moments of Moses on Sinai or of Job in the face of the whirlwind, for moments of a difficult, dynamic wrestling with the numinous that occurs within a deep, personal silence.

Clarke is insistent upon the scientific basis of his stories, and in this regard he is the closest of the three to Lovecraft. Yet a number of his stories touch upon what he once called "reverent awe" (*Collected Stories* 442). Though he will always plump for a scientific explanation, one of his characters insists that this explanation will not destroy awe and that on Jupiter he feels as though he lives "in some magical realm between myth and reality" (*Collected Stories* 917). Clarke's best known short stories, "The Nine Billion Names of God" and "The Star," have a quiet relationship with each other. The one has a background in Tibetan Buddhism, the other a background in Christianity. The punch of the first story depends upon its last sentence: "Overhead, without any fuss, the stars were going out" (*Collected Stories* 422). The tone is quiet, restrained parlor-talk, though the title does offer a grandiose subject; the other title is restrained, though it refers to the most basic icon of science fiction, the star, but its conclusion is restrained and anguished; each story wrestles with destruction, in the one case the destruction of the universe, in the other case the destruction of a civilization that dies in order to light the way to Bethlehem. The one seems comic at the beginning and through most of the narration until the gathering twilight of the conclusion; the other maintains its restrained anguish from its beginning until its end. Each seems to depend upon the existence of a divinity, whether Buddhist or Christian, but each wrestles with that divinity.

Leiber does not promise so much, though he comes to this problem of the numinous from two distinct directions. In the aesthetic direction he learned the Shakespearean style at an early age, and later in life he paid close attention to the style of his work; and in the other direction we take note of his career as an Episcopal priest, a short career for which he seems to apologize but which he cannot quite shrug off with the Mouser's disbelief nor with the parody of that career in "The Bazaar of the Bizarre." Leiber is a skeptical being, with all the energy that worldview implies; but he is very aware of the human awe towards which that skepticism is directed. In *The Wanderer* one numinous encounter is the orgiastic moment when Sally claims that at the top of the roller coaster, at its climax, in the middle of her own sexual climax she will make the stars move, and she does—the gravitational squiggle of stars as the Wanderer approaches earth! This moment has nothing to do with a still, small voice but perhaps everything to do with the dynamic encounter; and this moment receives its parallel between Paul and Tigerishka. Every moment, however, within the narrative that produces a new metaphor for the Wanderer records another numinous encounter. In *The Big Time* it is tempting to accept the conversation between Greta and Ilhilihis as the numinous moment of the novel, but it is perhaps too explanatory of the symbolic language. More immediate is Kaby's narrative, "I could feel a Change Gale blowing, working changes deep inside me, aches and pains that were a stranger's. Half my memories were doubled, half my lifeline crooked and twisted" (63). She is of course a devotee of the Triple Goddess. But perhaps the action is too swift for a numinous moment to occur; or perhaps the point is that the numinous moment is always occurring within the war in heaven. The word "change," incidentally, is perhaps cognate to "crooked" (*OED*).

In Dick this skepticism is profound. Of the three authors he is the one most interested in institutional religions, having flirted several times with Episcopalianism. He enjoyed a friendship with Bishop Pike, himself something of a speculative heretic, a friendship that led to Dick's writing *The Transmigration of Timothy Archer*. In several novels he played fast and loose with the Christian myth, most obviously in *The Three Stigmata of Palmer Eldritch* and *The Divine Invasion*. At the end of his life in the *Valis* manuscripts he fulfilled the charge of a Christian mystic, still in argument with God. For all his joking persistence, he was very much in touch with the Japanese concept of wu, which he employs in *The Man in the High Castle* as Mr. Tagomi strives to achieve a numinous detachment through nothing more than a pin, an asymmetric silver squiggle (225–30), and only achieves the discovery of an alternate history in which kipple is the sign of a world that has not enjoyed Japanese order; Robert Blake had similar difficulties with the Trapezohedron in Lovecraft's "The Haunter of the Dark." Of a different order is the suggestion in *The Three Stigmata of Palmer Eldridge*, offered in several different versions, that Eldridge in his several avatars is actually an alien entity that, though it is not god, might as well be--shades of the entity that inhabits Ephraim Waite, at his death his daughter Asenath, and that intends to inhabit Edward Derby.

What is it then in Lovecraft that attracted these three so different authors? This man who was definitely an atheist although he allowed that skepticism was a more honest position, how did he excite them and allow them to approach the numinous experience? Destructions of the universe or of earth or severe distortions of them; solemn assertions of human nothingness; a wild assertion of the irrational in the face of his epistolary rationality; the awareness of the conflict of forces utterly outside the human ken; a paranoia that is only too perceptive; a claustrophobia that realizes itself everywhere; a sense of things falling apart; and in his best stories a pervasive sense of "the fixt mass whose sides the ages are" (*AT* 79). What was there not to like? There is no doubt that these narratives in various fashions contain within their recognition of the numinous a tragic attitude; and I would argue that this recognition becomes an assurance of the seriousness of the undertaking. Clarke, Leiber, and Dick had learned from Lovecraft that this business of writing stories was very serious indeed and laid upon the author a basic obligation. You must write well or die.

Lovecraft Dallies with the Nobel Prize

We discover new books and new authors through quite a variety of paths: we stumble upon one in a bookstore; we take the recommendation of a friend or of a teacher; we take the assurance of a newspaper or of a blog that the book is high in its list; we realize that the style of this book is in the air; we pay attention to a Swedish committee that has chosen this author for this year. Did Lovecraft, I wonder, read a book outside of his usual fare? Did he pay any attention to the Swedish committee? Was he caught up in the new movement, "perhaps the oldest prize that strikes us as fully contemporary, as being less a historical artifact than a part of our own moment" (English 28)?

I did find the question intriguing, though I must admit that I followed the trail of the Nobel Prize only so far; we are aware now that the taste of the committee is something that appeals to us only so far. I was not moved to read Sully Prudhomme, and I am still not moved. I agree with Baudelaire's witticism, occasioned by his opinion of George Sand: "La femme Sand est le Prudhomme de l'immoralité" (1214). The first winner of the prize, Prudhomme was chosen instead of Tolstoy; on the other hand, with this essay in mind, I was moved to read Selma Lagerlöf, the Swedish winner in 1909, and Sigrid Undset, the Norwegian winner in 1928, both of them quite brilliant novelists in their different ways. Lovecraft probably did not read them, but shortly before his death he was smart enough to recognize their stature next to that of Romain Rolland and Thomas Mann (*CLM* 210). What I wish to do in this essay is to consider the novelists, poets, and playwrights of the Nobel Prize that Lovecraft paid attention to, whether he read them or not, and to ask what he might have seen in them. We will study these materials as long as the committee lived, which is as long as Lovecraft did; with his death in 1937 it was as though the committee had also changed in its state. This is a chancy pursuit, but that is after all what literature is about, even when the work is as difficult as can be imagined.

It does not harm our question to be aware of the Swedish Academy that every year is attempting to find "the most outstanding work of an idealistic tendency" (Österling 85). This is the kind of work that Alfred Nobel asked for in his will, but I am afraid that we are now liable to laugh at this language and its effects. What did he mean by idealistic tendency? Well, he probably had in mind Percy Bysshe Shelley, whom he admired, so we should have in mind the poetry and utopian worlds that Shelley was creating, especially in the prophetic pity that he expressed so powerfully in *Prometheus Unbound* 1.625-31 (Österling 86) and that his wife was to express in *Frankenstein,* though that novel was probably beneath the regard of the Academy. This idealistic tendency no doubt had a strong moral, political, religious, and social direction that Nobel hoped his prize would underline. Making Prudhomme the first choice of the committee emphasized this aspect; in doing so the committee took the safe, most obvious direction. Tolstoy they thought was much too speculative a moralist, and so they continued to think until he died in 1910; it is a choice that now strikes us as rather ridiculous, and throughout this essay I mean to call our attention to mistakes and difficulties like this.

* * *

Salve, Umbria verde, e tu del puro fronte
nume Clitumno! Sento in cuor l'antica
patria e aleggiarmi su l'accesa fronte
gl'itali iddii.

[Hale, green Umbria, and you with your pure brow, / God Clitumno, I feel in the old / fatherland to rest upon my burning brow / the Italian Gods.] (Carducci 833)

Considering the early winners of the Nobel Prize for Literature in 1906, I step aside from the attraction of the poet Frédéric Mistral and his poems of the Provençal that the committee chose early on, to choose instead Giosué Carducci, who concluded his long career with the collection *Odi Barbare*. These poems are foreign, barbary, barbaric, because he is using metrical forms of Latin, which the German poets Klopstock and van Platen (and we might add Goethe) had used before him. When Carducci uses the Sapphic stanza he gestures not only toward the erotic themes of Catullus and Horace, he is gesturing also toward the imperial and political themes that Horace had faced and used. At the end of the *Risorgimento,* when Carducci's poems joined the cause of Italian freedom, he turned to the ancient of days, as we can see in the "Alle Fonti del Clitumno," in which the theme of his childhood in Umbria joined the history of Virgil's presence in the *Eclogues* as well as alluding to the presence of the pagan and Christian temples standing next to the fountains. This is a verse complexly at work in the numen. Forgive me—the god could do no good.

On the other hand, Carducci could write a very different poem in contrast to the Sapphic stanza with which he praises the Clitumno. I have in mind here in Alcaics a poem that has no mystery about it. It is, as it says, "Alla stazione, in una mattina d'autunno," shortly bearing away the beloved Lidia in the train. The weather is raining, the sky leaden, the locomotive a monster. The poem ends in a profound despair, such as Leopardi might have addressed. It had taken some time for him to become a profound figure.

> Meglio a chi'il senso smarri de l'essere,
> meglio quest'ombra, questa caligine:
> io voglio io voglio adagiarmi
> in un tedio che duri infinito.

[Better whoever has lost the essence, / better that shadow, that fog: / I want, I want to rest / in an exhaustion that lasts forever.] (907)

What, then, would the reclusive, sixteen-year old Lovecraft have read in the elderly Carducci, if the young boy had learned Italian? The secret, I believe, was an open secret in the open use Carducci made of the pagan, classical world. It was not simply that he referred often to that world. No, he had turned away from it and its frequent use of the rhymed quatrain, which in the Italian language was so easy, to the difficult world of unrhymed quatrains in which the metrical count lay in the counted syllables. A reader might have believed that through the Sapphic and Alcaic stanzas one smelled the classical world of Euripides and Horace; of course we should keep in mind that the Romans learned by sweat and tears the difficulties of a meter that was not to be learned as a mother tongue. How much more difficult it was for a Roman and Italian poet. He was truly writing an *odi barbari*!

***

From the horrible to the commonplace is but a step. (Kipling, "The Phantom 'Rickshaw" 75)

For they're hangin' Danny Deever, you can hear the Dead March play, The regiments in 'ollow square—they're hang'n him today. (Kipling, *Verse* 451)

Our first person of interest then, after Carducci, is Rudyard Kipling, who received the prize in 1907, when Lovecraft was barely seventeen years old; Lovecraft had, however, a firm opinion of the man whom he could "only tolerate," one other of his "pet detestations" (*RK* 122). He had not changed his opinion much when in 1927 he damns Kipling next to Stevenson; on the other hand, in a few months Kipling may not be so bad, since he lived in Brattleboro, Vermont, in the heart of New England. The truth is that Kipling has an immense ability to be found in his Cockney poems of the *Barrack-Room Ballads*, which Lovecraft felt "was an immeasurably healthy influence in breaking the spell" of the Decadents; his *Jungle Books* and *Kim*, which cannot permit him to lose his love of detail, the great splash of color as Kim and his lama walk through the Indian landscape; and finally his skill in short stories, many of which deal with the life of the Indian imperialists, and some of which, as Lovecraft admitted, deal with the weird: "virtually all of the world's first-rate authors (for example—Henry James, Rudyard Kipling, Edith Wharton [. . .]) , have at one time or another written weird material)" (*CLM* 314). The Swedish committee had good reason to choose Kipling's "power of observation, originality of imagination, virility of ideas and remarkable talent for narration" (Sohlman and Schück 108). In his day few could match Kipling's varied narrative abundance. *Kim* is the great example of this abundance, whether the action takes place in the plains or the hills. "It is a great and terrible world" (39), says Kim's old lama.

Choosing from this abundance is not difficult for our purposes, however, since we have Lovecraft in mind. "The Phantom 'Rickshaw" is an excellent weird tale that opens on an everyday account of a young man who has difficulties with two ladies, one of whom is a married woman unable to control her obsessive feelings for him. When she dies upon his attachment to the other young lady, her spirit in her rickshaw begins to haunt him, so intensely now that on the last pages of the semi-comic world it is very much colonial Bombay that is closing upon the tragic world. Kipling is aware that all must bow to the tragic, even the colonials. How could Lovecraft have ignored such a story?

* * *

Then the beautiful Marianne leaned down and kissed Gösta Berling. She didn't know why; she had to. He extended his arms around her head and held her tight. She kissed him again and again. (Lagerlöf 70)

In 1909, two years after Kipling had received the prize, the committee chose a very different writer, Selma Lagerlöf, a Swedish novelist who had written only a few stories and novels when she produced a very striking novel; at the time, we should note, she was the first woman to be chosen for the honor of the Nobel Prize. As for Lovecraft, he did not notice a Scandinavian author who was a woman until February 1937, when near death he wrote an epistolary list of great novelists (*CLM* 210).

The Lagerlöf novel is *The Saga of Gösta Berling,* named for the minister who in the first chapter is defrocked from his pulpit, throughout the rest of the novel trying and not trying to find his way into the church again, and from chapter to chapter seeming a very different man, often assuming the color of the people who surround him, just as they also may be changing, tall or short, old or young, humdrum or a poet. He is often attempting to marry this or that beautiful woman; at the Christmas ball many women find it almost impossible to kiss. That disastrous kiss turns to a tragedy when the drunken father of a young lady locks her out of the house to freeze to death—and that is hardly a quarter of the way through this very disturbing book. There is still much room for the panorama of a style modeled on Carlyle's *French Revolution* (Lagerlöf xii–xiii), much room for metaphysical horror, for several love stories, or for an oblique ghost story that remains unaccountably creepy; I feel sure that Lovecraft would have found that startling. Meanwhile we should note that there is not much room for a plot or for directed action. Only style and landscape and a light ironic touch are of importance.

This description of the novel by another of the characters may be misleading, for another of the characters, Sintram, a mill owner, appears (27), like so many of the other characters, a chameleon. Often they may think him rather nasty; at other times they may think him the Devil incarnate; and he would have happily fulfilled that role. Whatever he may be, through him a moral edge in the novel is not to be denied; it is not merely something lovely at the end of the *fin de siècle,* and the harm and pain of the novel is not something that is put on. It is no surprise, then, that within one paragraph Lagerlöf can appeal with ease to Olympus, Yggdrasil, Valhalla, King Arthur, Jupiter, and King Charles the Twelfth (33). In contrast to Lagerlöf we do not discover in Lovecraft any metaphysical whisper; when we read him carefully, his gods in *The Dream-Quest of Unknown Kadath* do not surprise us as creatures of the physical universe, physical and nothing less. He would not have approved of this aspect of Lagerlöf. He would, however, have found something rich in her style that was even richer than he would have found in Dunsany, something rather like the early Lovecraft would have approved.

* * *

> My song has put off her adornments. She has no pride of dress and decoration. Ornaments would mar our union; they would come between thee and me; their jingling would drown thy whispers. (Tagore 6)

Rabindranath Tagore was the great surprise in 1913, for only one person on the committee could understand the language of his original poetry; the rest was Tagore's own translation, which I admit in 1962 I found merely pietistic; but in the original, which I later heard read by an actual Hindu reader, it was truly ravishing. Thus I learned that all poetry must be heard in the original to be properly judged. In the meantime I needed to learn German and French and Italian if I was truly to understand Goethe or Baudelaire or Dante. It was an important lesson. Returning to Tagore, I realize that written in the background of the Rig Veda and the Upanishads as well as to be found in the immense popularity of his other lyrics, plays, and stories, the decision the Nobel committee made of selecting the *Gitanjali* for the prize made very good sense; it is an individual love cycle in which the beloved is a woman, just as is the point of the Song of Solomon, and that which lies beyond the Buddhist maya. The cycle as such is marvelously inventive, but I doubt that Lovecraft ever mentioned it and probably never saw it, despite Yeats's enthusiastic reading of it and the Irishman's introduction.

Imagine then this poem recited to the strings of the sitar by a musician who has respect for the poem:

> I dive down into the depth of the ocean of forms, hoping to gain the perfect pearl of the formless.
> No more sailing from harbor to harbor with this my weather-beaten boat. The days are long passed when my sport was to be tossed on waves.
> And now I am eager to die into the deathless.
> Into the audience hall by the fathomless abyss swells up the music of toneless strings I shall take this harp of my life.
> I shall tune it to the notes of fore ever, and, when it has sobbed out its last / utterance, lay down my silent harp at the feet of the silent. (91-92)

* * *

> Le grondement du fleuve monte derrière la maison. La pluie bat les carreaux depuis le commencement du jour. Une buée d'eau ruisselle sur la vitre au coin fêlé [. . .] Et le grondement du fleuve, et le mer bruissente chantèrent avec lui:
> —Tu renaîtras. Repose! (Rolland 3, 1593)

> Once upon a time and a very good time it was there was a moocow coming along the road and this moocow that was coming down along the road met a nicens little boy named baby tuckoo. (Joyce, *A Portrait* 3)

> riverrun, past Eve and Adams [. . .] A way, a lone a last a loved a long the (Joyce, *Finnegans Wake* 1, 628)

In 1916 Romain Rolland received the prize ostensibly for his large, complex novel *Jean-Christophe,* which opens in the nursery of the baby Jean and closes years later on the composition of his death; it is possible of course that the committee had given Rolland the prize for his intense antiwar labors through the first two years of the war. Having admitted that possibility, we grant that the work is a very striking attempt to create a symbolic novel, with Beethoven and Wagner very much in mind, using the materials of music. Especially useful in reading the book are the *thèmes conducteurs* (March 66) of the river, its waves and tides, the bells, the faces, the hero, the island and the city (56-73). What is remarkable about the novel is the extent to which it is an internal meditation wrestling with Europe, its great values and its diseases. Perhaps most striking is his interpretation of Spinoza, which sees in every phenomenon a manifestation of poles, the river flowing between its two banks, and a manifestation of the naturans and the naturata, as Rolland would see the matter (*Die Ethik* 72-74). Without pressing the point, this is the landscape of *Finnegans Wake*.

Considering the complex intellectualism of the novel, it is startling how far its reputation extended. Rolland's name was mentioned along with many other topics early in Sinclair Lewis's novel *Main Street* (10). Lovecraft may not have read Rolland, but he knew the man's name and recommended it with a list of others in a very late letter (*CLM* 182), just as he knew the name of James Joyce, who never received the prize.

I mention Joyce once more because Lovecraft did in fact talk about the Irishman a number of times in his letters. The first time in 1924 is simply because of the book's reputation for smut (*SL* 1.283). The second time he mentions Joyce much more seriously, along with Eliot, Hart Crane, Virginia Woolf, Marcel Proust, and others as examples of the Modernist movement. They are to his mind artists who are straining their materials and methods; they are not good artists, yet they will have a strong influence upon the future artists (*SR* 133). A few months later in a satire excited by the work of Proust we read:

> Here *Joyce* appears with Odyssey demure,
> His Prose a Sunk-Pile, and his Mind a Sewer (*AT* 187)

The comedy is not bad, and not too good either: the reference to the *Odyssey* shows that Lovecraft has taken the trouble to learn something of the structure of Joyce's novel. In 1930, in the middle of a discussion of the various ways that sex may be handled in a work of art, Lovecraft has described Dreiser, Hemingway, and Joyce as artists who deal in "impersonal and serious descriptions of erotic scenes, relationships, motivations, and consequences in real life" (*MWM* 250). However he is treating Joyce now, it is in full seriousness. He may think Joyce is morbid, but he is "an indispensable figure in the expression and interpretation of Western Europe between 1850 and 1930" (*MWM* 266). Nevertheless, "Joyce is hardly worth reading unless one be a specialist in the history of literary form" (*JVS* 27). By 1932 he has read extracts from *Ulysses* and "Anna Livia Plurabelle," but none of these persuades him to read any more; he still thinks Joyce is too extreme, though he does believe "there is no more powerful or penetrant writer living than Joyce when he is not pursuing his theory" (*JVS* 89). All this may explain why Joyce never received the Nobel Prize, though he is the writer that inescapably haunts all literature, whether European or South or North American. He is not yet to be found on *Main Street* or for that matter to be met by *Babbitt*. Nevertheless, when they let go a bit, Babbitt would surely have enjoyed Lovecraft at the organ of the First Baptist Church playing "Yes, We Have No Bananas" (*MWM* 506-7). Perhaps incidentally, the name of the Shunned House, a name not to be uttered unless in a letter, was Babbitt (Faig 156).

* * *

Her loins arched, her head throw back, and, as it were, dragged down by the weight of her heavy red hair, her eyes swimming with voluptuousness, eager, languishing, compliant, she would have made Cleopatra herself grow pale with envy. (France 246)

This passage from "The Procurator of Judaea" gives a good sense of Anatole France, who received the Nobel Prize in 1921, and of his narrative world: compliant and often sensuous, but also distant and ironic. The irony lies here in these two speakers, elderly gentlemen of the Roman empire, discussing how they might have behaved in times part, as one of them confesses to the other in the last paragraph that he has no memory of a man who was probably brought before him: "Jesus? [. . .] Jesus—of Nazareth? I cannot call him to mind" (France 246). France is neat, noncommittal, often quite erudite in the historic materials that he has gathered. In this story, for instance, the backdrop that is not important to the actual story offers the reader ten pages of material telling a story of the bureaucratic world of the Empire, with mildly snide remarks concerning men who have long since passed away. France has a very good ear for these men.

We should admit that he has other works in which he deals with very different kinds of men, though in Crainquebille it certainly has a number of magistrates and gendarmes. The main character is a costermonger of dubious vegetables and fruits who is taken into custody by the police because he insistently, ignorantly insists on saying "Mort aux vaches!" In a cold night the warm prison gives him a good home, but he learns that not every gendarme will be insulted. It is a comedy that edges upon being a satire of society. This is France's great strength, moving from one style.

We cannot say that this is a control of language that Lovecraft is comfortable in, but this poor idiot who cannot hold his tongue does look ahead to Zadok Allen, the profound drunk who knows the truth of Innsmouth. Lovecraft writes to a friend, "I believe you would really enjoy talking Cabell and Machen and Anatole France with her" (*SL* 1.254). Lovecraft has a casual language with his friend to whom he is sending this letter and this young woman.

III. APARTMENTS AND BOOKS

* * *

> Hearts with one purpose alone
> Through summer and winter seem
> Enchanted to a stone
> To trouble the living stream. (Yeats 181)

> Minnaloushe creeps through the grass,
> Alone, important and wise,
> And lifts to the changing moon
> His changing eyes. (Yeats 168)

The committee recognized the agony of the new statehood of the Irish when it recognized the poems that Yeats had been writing for some forty years, a recognition that Lovecraft took a part in, as we shall see in some detail; in a public act he had been made a senator of the Irish Free State. Thus this first quatrain taken from the painful "Easter, 1916." The second quatrain is from the playful "Minnaloushe," in which the cat changes and the human creature changes according to the time of the moon.

In "Among School Children" he had wryly accepted his new public life, "A sixty-year-old smiling public man" (216). As far as the world of poetry was concerned in England, Ireland, and the United States, any poet after Yeats must reckon on him. To mention only a few names, Dylan Thomas, Hart Crane, John Berryman, and Theodore Roethke felt his late work powerfully (Ellmann 240).

Lovecraft's first mention of the Irish poet is a comparison in March 1924 to the Anglo-Irish poet and fantasist Lord Dunsany. This is a comparison that he does not wish to pursue, though he admits he likes Dunsany better for not appealing to "ponderous profundities" (*SL* 1.333). His next mention is in 1927, when he laments that New England does not have the power to create a New England Renaissance as occurred in Ireland. Yeats is then mentioned in a list of Irish authors such as A.E. and Synge; it is a conventional list that does not admit Joyce (*MWM* 454). In 1929, however, he has no difficulties:

Yeats is "the greatest poet alive today" (*ET* 54). Later, in another of his lists, he refers to Yeats and Synge as "queer fellows" (*MWM* 335)—no argument there, I should think. In 1932 in the midst of a discussion of poetry, he reiterates his argument that Yeats is no doubt the greatest Anglo-Irish poet (*JVS* 114). There is, however, a difficulty that seems implied when he mentions a story that has a dialect—this from a writer who has often used dialect. Now he says "it sounds theatrical & literary—like some old-world picture by Hardy or Synge or Yeats—& and I can't seem to make it fit into old New England" (*JVS* 211). Late in 1936 Lovecraft was still connecting Yeats with the "incontestably superior minds & personalities" such as Albert Einstein, Romain Rolland, Bertrand Russell, and Thomas Mann (*CLM* 182). It is interesting that practically all these names were those who had received the Nobel Prize.

The difficulty that we meet with almost the entirety of this ongoing endeavor is that we are left with no distinction that Lovecraft draws in all the long career that Yeats pursues. This is the difficulty that almost anyone faces in dealing with Yeats. Stylistically the thirty-year-old poet writing of fairies and red rose is very different from the poet ranting about Parnell. The love poetry vibrates between the divine and the carnal. Towers and gyres (you must draw the geometries), Maud Gonne and Lady Gregory are the ladies who helped him onto the stage. But what does Lovecraft find here that is useful?

First, we should notice that Lovecraft did enjoy the world of the eighteenth century; Yeats admired the aristocracy of that time, which like the aristocrats of America was shortly to vanish. Indeed, it may take a while, but the Lowells knew that they would vanish at last. This political tension finds its place also in poetry; Lovecraft is an expert in the heroic couplet, which Yeats can play with as long it is the Romantic couplet, and he is an expert from his youth to his age in the difficult septometer that Michael Drayton employed. Still, I believe it was the early Yeats besotted with fairies that Lovecraft found most engaging. Madam Blavatsky did not sing to him at all.

* * *

> The Devil: Wagner once drifted into Life Force worship, and invented a Superman called Siegfried. But he came to his senses afterwards. So when they met here, Nietzsche denounced him as a renegade; and Wagner wrote a pamphlet to prove that Nietzsche was a Jew; and / it ended in Nietzsche's going off to heave in a huff. And a good riddance too. (Shaw, *Man and Superman,* Act III, 174-75)

In 1925 George Bernard Shaw received the Nobel Prize, as seemed only proper for a dramatist who had recently created the play *Saint Joan;* on the other hand, here was a playwright who had created through a thirty-year career an attack on things as they are. And what was one to make of the recent cycle of plays *Back to Methuselah* with its span of thousands of years? Whatever we make of it, Lovecraft enjoyed it greatly; it spoke his language, especially when both he and Shaw spoke the language of Ernst Haeckel in his attacks on the anthropocentric dogma (Haeckel 11-13), on the problems of Lamarck and Neovitalism (233-35), and on the problems of Kantian teleology (255-60, 270-74). Joshi has discussed the extent to which Lovecraft admired Haeckel (*I Am Providence* 316ff.). No doubt Lovecraft found it interesting to recognize the extent to which he could play the game of Shaw and Haeckel. We must not, however, ignore the fact that he received the comedy as a gift from Sonia Greene, whom he was shortly to marry. It is nevertheless difficult to say whether he was obliged out of politeness to read the cycle; it did take him more than a month to read it. It is certainly a difficult text; but having read the book, he came out of the experience with praise for Shaw, a praise that was not to lessen through the years.

On the other hand, he could not have ignored the fact that though the cycle was definitely interested in evolution, it is not a Darwinian evolution that concerned him. Three times he refers to the language of creative evolution, once in the prose explication and twice in the second play of the cycle, "The Gospel of the Brothers Barnabas." First he asserts that "all scientific opinion worth counting has been converging rapidly upon Creative Evolution" (78). This is God, the force behind evolution, that shall drive us ahead in its sharp intention (80). That is all very well, but it is the language of Henri Bergson that Shaw finds so useful and that Lovecraft and Darwin find so objectionable. Lovecraft writes that "Vitalism is a pleasing fad, but it cannot overcome the evidence for determinism" (*Letters to Alfred Galpin* 116). On the other hand, he does not believe that Shaw is

> so great a man as Swift; he is too much preoccupy'd with trivial questions of society; and doth not perceive to the full the tragedy of existence. He is too humorous—the truly great pass beyond humour, and retain only a terrible admixture of infinite disgust and soul-rending pity. (*Letters to Alfred Galpin* 116)

This is one of those moments in Lovecraft that aesthetics yields to morality.

Leaving aside these matters, there is the question of the prize and the reputation. At first Shaw considered not accepting the prize, but in the end he did accept it, dedicating it to the memory of Strindberg, which no doubt the Swedish author would have accepted, given the intensity with which the irascible man had pursued the prize until his death. Such plays as *Miss Julie, The Dance of Death, A Dream Play,* and *The Ghost Sonata* had already transformed the stage (Sohlmann and Schück 121).

* * *

Le philosophe doit aller plus loin de le savant. Faisant table rase de ce qui n'est qu'un symbole imaginative, il verra le monde materiel se résoudre en un simple flux, une continuité d'écoulement, un devenir. Et il se préparera ainsi à retrouver la durée réele là où il est plus utile encore de la retrouver, dans la domaine de la vie et de la conscience.

[The philosopher must go further than the scientist. Making a tabula rasa of everything that is an imaginative symbol, he will see the material world melt into a simple flux, a continuity of flowing, a becoming. And he will be prepared to see real duration where it is most useful to find it once more in the realm of life and consciousness.] (Bergson, *L'Évolution créatrice/Creative Evolution* 368, 401)

We had only to wait for two years before the committee in 1927 awarded the prize to Henri Bergson, whom Lovecraft despised, no doubt in part because of Bergson's striking confidence in progress; at least so it seemed through several passages in *Creative Evolution,* a title that seemed optimistic to many readers, as Bergson seems so early in his classic: "Il n'est pas douteux que la vie, en son ensemble, soit une évolution, c'est-à-dire une transformation incessante" [There is no doubt that life as whole is an evolution, that is, an unceasing transformation] (232, 252).

"L'essentiel est la continuité de progress qui se poursuit indèfiniment, progress invisible sur lequel chaque organisme visible chevauche pendant le court intervalle de temps qu'il lui est donné de vivre" [The essential thing is the *continuous progress* indefinitely pursued, an invisible progress, on which each visible organism rides during the short interval of time given it to live] (32, 32). But it has no choice in the matter. "Nous choisissons en réalité sans cesse, et sans cesse aussi nous abandonnons beaucoup de chose" [We choose in reality without ceasing; without ceasing, also, we abandon many things"] (101, 111). This ambivalence is shown later in the theme of finality, which is present in creative evolution, that transcends finality (244-45). This finality is difficult to express because the word traditionally points to the *telos,* that conclusion that orders the chaos and energy of our lives. "Le cadre de la finalité est donc trop étroit pour la vie dans son intégralité" ["The category of finality is therefore," he confesses, "too narrow for life in its entirety"] (225, 241).

It is no surprise, then, that this book of philosophy has several conclusions:

> Le courant passe donc, traversant les générations humaines, se subdivisant en individus: cette subdivision était dessinée en lui vaguement, mais elle ne se fût pas accusée sans la matière. Ainsi se créent sans cesse des âmes, qui cependant, en un certain sens, préexistaient. Elles ne sont pas autre chose que les ruisselets entre lesquels se partage le grand fleuve de la vie, coulant à travers le corps de l'humanité.
>
> [On flows the current, running through human generations, subdividing itself into individuals. This subdivision was vaguely indicated in it, but could not have been made clear without matter. Thus souls are continually being created, which, nevertheless, in a certain sense pre-existed. They are nothing else than the little rills into which the great river of life divides itself, flowing through the body of humanity] (270, 294)

"O tell me all about Anna Livia! I want to hear all about Anna Livia" (*Finnegans Wake* 196.12-17). No doubt people in the English-speaking world are liable to put the matter like this; we return to Rolland and his riverine motions in this manner, with a difference; and in these dividing currents we return to the rhythms of *Back to Methuselah*. We see here why Shaw wrote so massive a cycle, as much as we understand why Lovecraft must have despised here Bergson's optimistic attitude. He must have read Shaw with some distance; and if he read Bergson, which I doubt, he read the French author with utter disdain. This man full of Darwin could not have done otherwise.

※ ※ ※

The sun was shining but it had rained hard during the night so the streams were splashing and singing everywhere on the hillsides, and wisps of fog drifted below the mountain slopes. (Sigrid Undset, *Kristin Lavransdatter* 7)

Ekki var margt um í samförum Þeira Geirmundar ok Þuriðar. Var svá af beggja Þeira is hendi. Þrjá vetr var Geirmundr með Óláfi, áðr hann fýstist í brott ok lýsti Þuríðr myndi eftir vera ok svá dóttir Þeira, er Gróa hét. Sú mær var Þá vetrgömul. En fé vill Geirmundr eke eftir leggja.

[The marriage beween Geirmund and Thurid was not really very happy, and they were both to blame for that. For three years Geirmund stayed at court with Olaf, but then he wanted to get away and announced that he was going to leave Thurid there with their daughter Groa, who was a year old. He refused though to leave any money behind.] (*Laxdaela Saga* 81)

Despite Shaw and Bergson tragedy is about to return. Nineteen years are to pass after Selma Lagerlöf before another Scandinavian author is to appear in 1928, a Norwegian novelist who is best known for her austere trilogy, *Kristin Lavransdatter*. Sigrid Undset is, however, a very different sort of author. Where Selma Lagerlöf is so frequently ecstatic and comic, Undset is careful; a careless reader might think her dispassionate. Writing an historical novel that presents Norway in the fourteenth century, she follows the passionate life of a young woman through some forty years, determined to address that woman's everyday world. One aspect of that world, an aspect that grows greater as the three novels proceed, is the religious aspect. It is no less and no more than something that the characters must deal with, but it does seem rather like the world with which a novelist like Zola grapples. There are witches in this society, but they were best recognized through their knowledge of the herbs (Undset 41ff.); they are not at all daemonic. At the conclusion of the trilogy Kristin, now more than fifty years old, joins a convent and shortly thereafter dies of the plague. The description of the effects of the disease is quite horrific but no more so than to be found in the pages of Camus. But Undset is reading much of the past literature in order to maintain the proper balance. "Veðr var got ok sól upp komin" [The weather was good and the sun was risen] (*Njáls Saga* 147) carefully sets the ground against which a horrible slaughter occurs, an effect that Undset often strives to cast.

Much of the landscape, as is to be expected, is the land of the Norwegian mountains in summer and in winter, but this landscape, given the fact that the characters of the novel deal with it day in and day out, does not suggest as a reader might expect the land of the sublime. Skis rattle and are put in the corner, just as the mountains are put away. Given the firmness with which Undset treats the psychology of her characters, she does not need the mountains or the storms to build the book's aesthetic effect.

As we have said, this is more a question of a similar world view than of an influence; along with Undset he is moving into the dark modern age, of which the wreck of the *Titanic,* the 1918 influenza, and the crash and the depression that followed are emblematic. In this new state unknown forces represent fate in the works of Undset, who read the style of the sagas so carefully.

* * *

Es war recht still im Saale geworden. Der Augenblick war grotesk, ungeheuerlich und spannend--der Augenblick von Mario's Seligkeit.

[It became utterly still in the hall. The moment was grotesque, weird and tense—the moment of Mario's bliss.] (Mann, "Mario und der Zauberer" 710)

There is a certain embarrassment that the committee suffered in granting Thomas Mann the prize in 1929. *Der Zauberberg* had been published in 1924, but the committee seems to have ignored this complex diagnosis of Europe. It was *Buddenbrooks,* published in 1901, that they noticed and awarded the prize, more worthy when we consider how thoroughly he is given to moments of the daemonic in the magician at the climax of "Mario und der Zauberer," the madman in the middle of München in "Gladius Dei," such figures as Tony in the last paragraph of *Buddenbrooks,* Naphta at the climax of *Der Zauberberg,* and Adrian Leverkühn in the climax of *Doktor Faustus,* more broadly the landscape of "Der Tod in Venedig." Two chapters have room in the spacious *Zauberberg,* whether it be "Totentanz" or "Walpurgisnacht." Having said so much, I must admit that Mann's imagination is more spooky than we can quite account for, unless we turn our minds to Lovecraft. But first let us consider the early novel.

There is much that one can learn from *Buddenbrooks.* First of all, it is a well-made novel, a narrative in which every detail is connected to every other. It is only gradually, I believe, that a reader learns how important the young girl Tony is to the full pattern of the work; but at the conclusion it is a different Tony who speaks for the family. "As schoolgirl, wife, divorcée, mother-in-law, and bereaved daughter and sister, from start to finish of the novel, she is driven by a sense of her own importance which she derives from the one source: the family" (Ridley 35). At the end of the book it is not Tony, however, but the dwarf Sesemi Weichbrodt who assumes the role of the prophet, insisting in the last sentence of the novel that the Buddenbrocks shall live forever: "Sie stand da, eine Siegerin in dem guten Streite, den sie während der Zeit ihres Lebens gegen die Anfechtungen von seiten ihrer Lehrerinnenvernunft geführt hatte, bucklig, winzig und bebend vor Überzeugung, eine kleine, strafende, begeisterte Prophetin" [She stood there, a victorious woman in the good fight that she conducted throughout her life against the attacks of reason, hunchbacked, tiny, and shaking from conviction, a small, punitive, inspired prophet] (670). Insistent and demented, the studied music of this sentence is overwhelming and comic. It is easy to look forward to the deadly comedy of *Der Zauberberg.*

Lovecraft Dallies with the Nobel Prize

* * *

> To George F. Babbitt, as to most prosperous citizens of Zenith, his motor car was poetry and tragedy, love and heroism. The office was his pirate ship but the car his perilous excursion ashore.
>
> Among the tremendous crises of each day none was more dramatic than starting the engine. (Lewis, *Babbitt* 24)

Sinclair Lewis was a very busy author, accustomed to writing a three-hundred-page novel every two years, so he was not overwhelmed when in 1930 he was to receive the Nobel Prize for *Babbitt* and for the novel of *Main Street* that had preceded it. Its humors must have been a relief to the committee after the complexities of Mann's work. Indeed, the committee pointed out in Lewis's novels "his ability to create, with wit and humour, new types of people" (Sohlmann and Schück 123). *Babbitt* is not a well-made novel; its sprawl is nevertheless important to its themes, for horrid as this world is, the novel insists on its horrors. But despite these horrors the main character often dreams of an ideal world whose existence condemns the actual world with which he must contend. The main weapon he has is exaggeration. Everything in this world is more puffed than we would find in our usual world, even the world of commerce that provides this style. "Perilous excursion," "tremendous crises," "none was more dramatic"—no paragraph slips by the eye of the author without receiving a lurid brush from this style. Lewis must have had great fun as he wrote this novel.

Lovecraft felt strongly that he would have chosen Dreiser for the award that year, just as others might have chosen O'Neill, Cabell, Cather, or Wilder (*ET* 166). Nevertheless, he agrees that Lewis wrote novels "sound in craftsmanship"; then, as he warmed to these remarks, he wrote: "he has punctured the pitiful shams & inanities of conventional American life as few others have; & certainly deserves a prize for social service, whether or not he merits one for sheer artistic craftsmanship" (236). We may doubt, however, that the committee cared for sheer artistry.

Incidentally, Lovecraft paid close attention to College Hill in Providence upon which many of his stories occur and where he lived most of his life. But if we ask where Lewis found the name of Babbitt, we have no further to ask than the name of the house in which Lovecraft found his shunned house (*Letters to Family and Family Friends* 1.188). But say what you will, Babbitt is a very silly name to bear. Only in a steady pace does a reader learn how sad this business man's life is sure to be. He has no life to escape from.

* * *

Si dovrebbe poter comandare alla luna un bel ragion decorative . . . Giova, a noi, giova, la luna. Io per me, ne sento il bisogno, e mi ci perdo spesso a giardarla dalla mia finestra. Chi può credere, a giardarla, che lo sappia, che ottocent'anni siano passati e che io, seduto alla finestra non possa essere davvero Enrico IV che guarda la luna, come un pover'uomo qualunque? Ma guardate, guardate che magnifico quadro notturno: l'Imperatore tra I suoi fidi consiglieri . . . Non ci provate gusto?

[If it were possible to command a decorative ray from the moon . . . As for me, I feel the need of it and I often lose myself watching it from my window. Who can believe to look at it that in truth it is Henry the Fourth who watches the moon like some poor wretch? But look, look at this magnificent nocturnal frame: The Emperor among his peers. Don't you love it?] (Pirandello 201)

There he stands on a stage, wearing a Van Dyke beard that is strongly reminiscent of Mephistopheles. In 1934 many people were surprised that the recipient of the award was the Italian playwright Luigi Pirandello, best known to us no doubt as the author of *Six Characters in Search of an Author,* which received a raucous reception on its premiere (1921). Not concerned by those audiences, he went on to such plays as *Right You Are* (*if you think you are*) or the apparently historical drama *Henry IV.* He was the author of forty plays, some in Sicilian, as well as poetry, novels, and short stories. Early on in his career he was trained in Romance philology (Caputi 20) and wrote his dissertation in Bonn on the dialogue of his native town, following the trail of many Italian authors of his time who turned their backs on the Italian of the Renaissance and scorned the tradition of Florence. America had its own difficulties in this regard, possessed of so many dialects.

This particularity of the language is inextricably joined to his sense of the tragic, welded to the problematic presence of the soul in the face of Freud (Österling 128). His characters often earn their masks—as do marionettes, if we imagine them producing an evening of Orestes when

> the paper sky of the little theater develops a tear. What would happen. [. . .] His eyes would go there, to that tear, through which, now, all sorts of cosmic wrongs would invade the scene, and he would feel his arms drop. Orestes, that is to say, would become Hamlet. The whole difference, [. . .] between between ancient and modern tragedy consists in this, believe me: in a hole in the paper sky. (Pirandello, cited in Caputi 49)

In this fable we see Pirandello's insistence on the presence of *umorismo* in the drama. Look again, however, at the epithet from *Enrico IV* to see how the grotesqueness of the situation is mixed with nostalgia.

It should be no surprise that Lovecraft would have respected the fable, though he may not have cared for the marionettes. He would have certainly followed so many characters who wrote according to the global word of the dialects. I have in mind such characters as Zadok Allen and Wilbur Whateley, who only come alive with those words in his mouth. We need to have more tongues as these, cast in the old dialects of Provence.

Within the framework of his training in German idealism, Pirandello came to argue that history "was a smear of fragmentary myths and fables, an embalmed, denatured reduction of events never grasped in their entirety in their own time and largely created anew in the present" (Caputi 34). The danger of the language in Italy is that Petrarca began the tradition of words, a rhetoric that convinced the culture that words were superior to things (Caputi 20-23).

* * *

"Oh, Shendoah, I long to hear you
A-way, my rolling river.
Oh, Shenandoah, I can't get near you
Way-ay, I'm bound away
Across the wide Missouri.

"Oh, Shenandoah, I love your daughter
A-way, my rolling river." (O'Neill, *Plays* 1.43)

Once more looking at an author through Lovecraft's eyes, we must remember that he was quite fond of the theater, but the dramatist he was most fond of was Eugene O'Neill, who received the prize in 1935, two years before Lovecraft's death. We should also confess that O'Neill had not yet written his masterpiece, *A Long Day's Journey into Night,* or his ensemble triumph, the bleak jest *The Iceman Cometh;* before his reception he had already deserved so much that it is difficult to characterize the body of his work and difficult to characterize his life. When I had first begun to read him the common thought had been that he owed his approach to Strindberg, but it is impossible to say that, considering the cycle of his sailors' lives; against those naturalist plays we would have to notice how often in many different ways he paid close attention to the Greek themes and style. The truth of the matter is that he could not help himself from experimenting with the stage, trying to discover the truth of our lives there.

In 1934 it was clear that the committee had selected O'Neill on the basis of his recent, massive trilogy *Mourning Becomes Electra,* a work inspired by the Greek *Oresteia* trilogy, comprising the plays *Agamemnon, The Libation-Bearers,* and *The Eumenides,* which in

O'Neill's hands become *Homecoming, The Hunted,* and *The Haunted* (there are ghosts galore in that play). Very few other poets would have accepted this challenge from Aeschylus, though it is not odd that we should have called to mind *Prometheus Bound,* that test case of "an idealistic tendency," but with all the labor involved we cannot be surprised by a trilogy that takes place shortly after the War between the States, responding to a national guilt that is not yet purged. At the conclusion of the plays, as Seth picks up once more the song "Oh, Shenandoah, I can't get near you / Way-ay, I'm bound away," Lavinia Mannon stops him with these words, "I'm not bound away—not now, Seth. I'm bound here—to the Mannon dead" (*Plays* 2.178). Edmund in *A Long Day's Journey into Night* would agree: "The fog was where I wanted to be [. . .]. I didn't meet a soul. Everything looked and sounded unreal. Nothing was what it is. That's what I wanted—to be alone with myself in another world where truth is untrue and life can hide from itself" (131). O'Neill would be in agreement with Pirandello.

* * *

> And Jean's nae mair my wife
> Than whiskey is at times,
> Or munelicht or a thistle
> Or kittle thochts or rhymes.
>
> He's no a man ava,
> And lacks a proper pride,
>   Gin less than aa the warld
>   Can ser him for a bride! . . . (MacDiarmid 46)

No one is more difficult or more pugnacious than the Scotsman Hugh MacDiarmid in the midst of writing *A Drunk Man Looks at the Thistle,* first published in 1926 in Scotland. One aspect of his difficulty lies in his decision to write in Broad Scots, which leaves Burns far behind. That is our argument: that in the process of the Nobel committee so much of great merit becomes lost—but not without a fight.

> Surely much moved, even by chance conjunction,
> All declamatory emotion scoring,
> Explications forming upon a process
>   Metric makes gnomic. (Hill 854)

I am concluding our inspection of these books with Hugh MacDiarmid's epic meditation *A Drunk Man Looks at the Thistle* and also with the *Complete Poems* of Geoffrey Hill, in part because neither of those authors ever received the Nobel Prize after years of speculation. Both were dead first. Whether the poet was Welsh or Irish or Scots, the honor of the prize was to be granted to Seamus Heaney, whose lucid verse was devoted to the great difficulties of growing up in Northern Ireland. In reading him we are often reminded of Yeats, but Heaney is much more down-to-earth than the elder poet who became a senator—as did Carducci at the opening of the century. Hill, after growing up in the navel of England, became an academic figure in Cambridge, Leeds, Boston, and Oxford. Dare we say that he is as difficult as Joyce? Hill's poetry is sensuous, intellectual, difficult, and allusive, often devoted to the horrors of the last century in the two world wars, but also reaching into the American Civil War and the War of the Roses. Atrocity is Hill's inescapable theme: but like Tolstoy and Joyce and Lovecraft he likes to pick a fight.

The particular reason, however, that I have for turning to Hill is that one of the groups of poems that he wrote late in life bore the title *Odi Barbare,* the same title as the collection of the late poems of Carducci. He does know what he is doing, for the second page, once more in a Sapphic stanza, addresses itself to Carducci, as I repeat once more (Hill 854). Allusive as he so often was, Hill was always careful to grip the hands of his poets, as obsessive in writing his Sapphics as Lovecraft was in writing his heroic couplets.

Let's then take the hand of MacDiarmid (who never received the prize).

Part Four:
Apologies and Defenses

An Apology in Kadath

An apology is a tricksy rhetorical moment, whether in Greek or Roman or English. We receive it from the Greek poet Stesichorus, who wrote a poem in which he played fast and loose with the figure of Helen, the daughter of Zeus, blaming her for the deaths those warriors died at Troy fighting for her. Blinded by the power of this semi-divine, Stesichorus wrote a palinode to the first poem, singing a song both old and new in which he confessed that he had made a mistake in attacking her in his poem—and thus at once he regained his sight (Stesichorus 12–18). Since then the second Helen, her shadow, has assumed an important role in Western culture, whether it be in Euripides' play *Helen,* in which she did not go to Troy but in the clouds to Egypt, leaving behind only her shadow, or in the second part of Goethe's *Faust,* in which once more she is a shadow, albeit quite substantial; and the figure of Stesichorus has his own model as the poet who has made a dire mistake, only his words are shadows. And indeed, don't we make a fertile mistake when we project these shadows in our dreams!

With these accounts in mind I felt that I should write a palinode to conclude this collection of essays, the new prelude that Stesichorus sang, to my treatment of Lovecraft through the years. This will not necessarily be a defense of what I wrote previously; but the nature of the defense now attaches itself to the apology. That defense of all that I have written, however, is much too large a challenge; I do not wish to become the dog that has returned to its own vomit. As a small version of that challenge I decided to look again at *The Dream-Quest of*

Unknown Kadath. In the past I have not written any essays devoted to that work, no doubt because I was something of a snob about Lovecraft's early imitations of Lord Dunsany, contrasting its sugar-coated prose to the power and iron structure of his weird fiction; I confess, I found it very difficult to accept the dream world that he was slowly constructing. Further, paging through the first book again I noticed that in one of its essays it was necessary that Keats should face "The Awful Rainbow" once more, as also should Leopardi and Baudelaire. Needless to say, given the nature of *The Dream-Quest*, there will be a good deal of spillage, twisting and turning ahead of us; and I will deal in shadows through becoming a shadow, just as did Stesichorus.

I

Helen: "Ich schwinde hin und werde selbst mir ein Idol" [I waste away, and become an idol to myself] (Goethe, *Faust* 8879)

The Dream-Quest of the Unknown Kadath begins with the character Randolph Carter, who has already appeared in three short works. He is almost waking for the third time from the same dream in which from a "high terrace" (*CF* 2.98) he surveys a breathtaking sunset city laid out before him; but alas for the third time he is "snatched away" (2.298) by a force he can hardly articulate. The only hope he has is to sleep in a light dream and from there to undertake his quest. But we need to describe this city before we undertake his quest. The city is obviously rich, glowing like gold in the sunset light, the perspective from which he always views it, frozen in time, never open to human activity; it does have fountains rich in sprays of water for gardens. It seems as challenging an object as Keats's "Ode on a Grecian Urn," a poem that seems frozen in time both as an object and as a scene. Its graven priests are ready to perform a sacrifice, "emptied of this folk, this pious morn" (Keats, *Poems* 373). If Lovecraft has any sacrifice in mind, however, it is hidden away, though in his dreams he shall undertake many sacrifices that shall be performed. That might be easy enough, since on a closer look we realize that the Lovecraft's city is in two parts, the older section "on steep northward slopes [with] tiers of red roofs and old peaked gables harbouring little lanes of grassy cobbles" (*CF* 2.98). That word "harbor" may not be as innocent as we often believe (*OED* "Harbour: often with some notion of lurking or concealment"). In four paragraphs the narrator will refer to these "cryptical hill lanes" (2.100). Let us consider this stanza from Baudelaire's "Rêve Parisien," one of his many poems that summon forth an intricate city: "Et sur ces mouvantes merveilles / Planait (terrible nouveauté)! / Tout pour l'œil, rien pour les oreilles! / Un silence d'éternité" (174). Horrifying, a silence that is inescapable but of which I am thoroughly aware. Carter, however, is swept away from his frozen, golden silence, so intense that three times he receives a profound temptation in this city that behaves like a flirt, almost awake to the daily world that he is happy to leave behind—if only he can.

Unlike Baudelaire, however, he does not seem ambivalent about this city. Nevertheless I do wonder why in a city of "walls, temples, colonnades, and arched bridges" (*CF* 2.98) there is no mention of a hotel. True, such an obvious commercial sight is not to be seen in Baudelaire's cities. Whether this is Boston or Providence, the hotels in the center of the city are very obvious. When Lovecraft traveled he preferred to bed down with friends; if that wasn't possible he preferred such places as the YMCA. He did not have a fat purse, but he might also have felt that hotels were dangerous. The hotel in Innsmouth proved to be a very dangerous spot. Perhaps most importantly, he was aware that his father, a commercial traveler, collapsed in a hotel far from home and never recovered (Joshi, *I Am Providence* 21). There were many reasons Lovecraft had for avoiding hotels if possible and for expunging them from his ideal city.

But this is no familiar city. It is "a fever of the gods" (*CF* 2.98), and much more will be said about the gods as the dreams grow larger.

Somehow the city is connected with memories, "the pain of lost things" (2.99), which later dreams will hide away but we should think of those losses as latent for they will be revealed in the conclusion of this work. Meanwhile these "tyrannous gods" hold him in "bondage" (2.99), unable to walk down to the city, though he painfully wishes that he could. Mystery hangs about the city "as clouds about a fabulous unvisited mountain" (2.98), a mountain that he shall climb when he is deeper in dream. At last then for a fourth attempt he decides to seek for the "unknown Kadath," that by which the fated heart dies (Κήρ, Liddell and Scott 376), without realizing that he has now entered with a sacrifice into a fourth dream. The quest has begun.

After all these attempts to learn whether it is possible to approach Kadath, Carter first finds his way to the bearded priests of the pillar of flame by descending the seventy steps in a light slumber to the cavern of flame; and then, having learned all that he could, he descends "seven hundred steps to the Gate of Deeper Slumber" (*CF* 2.101). This must be a mighty achievement if Freud is right in thinking "steps, ladders or staircases, or, as the case may be, walking up or down them, are representations of the sexual act" (390). Ah, that is a dream! Since we are now in a state of deeper slumber, not only by seventy steps but by seven hundred steps more and never hamstrung, we need to be alert to whatever it may be that the reader undergoes in this new state. Most obviously we are deeply into a myth of the chthonic powers, opening this world to a resurrection; but there are many more ways to understand it. Through these two stanzas from Baudelaire's poem "L'Irrémédiable" ("The Incurable"), we confront a gulf and the great-eyed beasts that slither through it:

> Un damné descendant sans lampe,
> Au bord d'un gouffre dont l'odeur
> Trahit l'humide profondeur,
> D'éternels escaliers sans rampe,

Où veillent des monstres visqueux
Dont les larges yeux de phosphore
Font une nuit plus noire encore
Et ne rendent visible qu'eux. (151)

[A damned man descends without a lamp / At the edge of a gulf that stinks / Of a humid depth / of eternal stairs with no ramp, // Where slimy monsters wake / With large, phosphorous eyes / That make the night blacker yet / And make them visible.]

I will not count how often Lovecraft's protagonists descend these abysses with little hope of return. As Carter approaches his first stand in his dream he meets the two priests Nasht and Kaman-Thah and we meet our first challenge—what are we to make of their alien names, which Lovecraft called "sinister" (*CE* 5.223)—what are we to make of the many names sprinkled throughout the text? Perhaps these two priests gnash their teeth; perhaps Kaman suggests the Cayman Islands where alligators and other monsters breed, another toothsome thought. Nothing helps us but the sound and look of the three words; in other cases the word in question may be a portmanteau word, shadows of Lewis Carroll and James Joyce. Every time we face such words, it is a radical moment in which we find ourselves, as Keats would say, soul-making, guessing at whatever meaning they might represent, as Keats and Hillman challenge us; but enough of that in time.

I do not mean to tease out a meaning from every one of these exotic words that Lovecraft presents us with, but we should not ignore them, just as we cannot ignore "the hidden gods of dream" or the Great Ones (*CF* 2.99); or any of the other gods that we shall face, as it were looking over the shoulder of Carter as he deals with these occult numens, such as on the next page we read of "the gigantic ultimate gods, the blind, voiceless [and] mindless Other Gods" (2.100-1). This is a new version of the ancient theomachia. And incidentally, we may be tempted to reverse Thah for Hath, which often appears in *The Quest* as "-ath," as in wrath or as in the proverbial lament that overlooks the defeat of Saul, "Tell it not in Gath" (2 Sam. 1:20). Kadath, incidentally, has the shape of Kaddish, the Hebrew prayer for the dead. This meditation is pressing when we consider that the gesture of this syllable is to be found in the heart of Nyarlathotep.

Having descended to the Gate of Deeper Slumber, Carter confronts the zoogs (perhaps dogs, creatures that we should find only in a zoo) and is able with no difficulty to speak their fluttering language, through which Carter could do a good deal, especially contact "the great King Kuranes" (*CF* 2.102), the crowned man whom he knows under another name. That is all very well, but Carter does not approach Kuranes yet. Suffice it that we learn of the zoogs that though they have strength it is not very great. They have "a slight taste for meat" (2.101), as do many denizens of the dream world, but this odd phrase does not mean they do not extend it to a cannibal sacrifice, as do the other beings in the pits of this magical space, the bholes, ghouls, gugs, ghasts, and night-gaunts whom we shall meet later, no doubt related to meditative gargoyles. To return to the zoogs, it is possible that they are related to the Little Formless Fears in O'Neill's *The Emperor Jones,* which Lovecraft had seen in 1922; they are very small creatures that without speaking a word terrify Jones on the run (*SL* 1.173). Lovecraft's zoogs are impossible to deal with.

In this forest it is not surprising that the light is no more than "dim-litten" (*CF* 2.102). In other places the light is "pale-litten" (2.203), twice "red-litten" (2.116, 175), and once strikingly "green-litten" (2.179). But these words are not the only examples of archaic language in *The Dream-Quest.* Carter is taught "how to spring when the rest sprang" (2.119). Later the cats "sprang from every hearth and housetop" (2.145). In a very different moment at the climax of the narrative "worlds sprang flaming into life" (2.212). Very different is the word "strown," describing "a sky that was black and star-strown even though the sun shone scorchingly in it" (2.114), as the sky truly appears from outer space. Lovecraft is very fond of these words that shadow a relative color in this mindland next to its dreamland.

Other words like these demonstrate the extent to which Lovecraft made use of archaisms, giving some sense of how greatly the reality of daily life is transformed in the dream world. The word "shew," which occurs fairly often in many of Lovecraft's stories to give a sense of archaic English diction, occurs here twenty-three times. The words "gaunt" and "haunt" occur together as I count them some thirty-one times, in part because the night-gaunt, Lovecraft's *bête noire* as a child, appears often in the story, but not so frightful in the climax. "Loom" occurs twenty-five times, almost always within an ominous context; and "well," which I have examined in the chapter "Wells" in this collection, occurs in *The Dream Quest* some forty-three times. Each of these words to a greater or lesser degree seems meant to tangle the simple narration. Like the treatment of these words once more, I consider the ten or eleven words made of such materials as -ath, like Kadath; in addition, consider such words as Nyarlathotep, Shub-Niggurath, Yog-Sothoth, shifting to -oth and Shoggoth, so important to Lovecraft's mythology.

As we play with words, Carter is finding his way to Ulthar, where for half the year Kuranes rules. The splendid city of Celephaïs in Ooth-Nargai "beyond the Tanarian Hills" (*CF* 2.129) [cf. the Tanana river and Tananarive city] attracts his attention, "where the rushing Skai flows [from] the slopes of Lerion, and Hatheg and Nir and Ulthar dot the plain" (2.103). Carter admires this city, especially the bridge over the Skai built with a living sacrifice, touching casually on a theme to which we will often return; it seems that almost every cult that greets Carter practices living sacrifice. This passage, from Celephaïs to Ulthar, comes from Lovecraft's short stories. Though the description of the first city seems approving of it, Lovecraft may have had in mind the high priest Caiaphas, who was central in the trial of Jesus; the rhythm of his name is very like this word, Celephaïs, he gave the city. The high priest Caiaphas, not asleep at all, argued that it was expedient that one man should die for the nation (John 11:49–53).

Ulthar may be a portmanteau of Ulan Bator and Ultima Thule, both of these traditionally at the center of a most distant place. A wise patriarch called Atal, "three centuries old," discusses with him "the Other Gods from Outside, whom it is better not to discuss" (*CF* 2.105); the rhythm of his name may come from Attila the fatherly Hun, who sacked Rome. Not satisfied with the paltry information Atal offers, Carter gives the old man several drinks from the gourd of moon-wine he had received from the zoogs, causing him to babble of the great mountain Ngranek, like a black neck, on the island Oriab, hinting bibulously that the Great Ones had in the past married "the daughters of men" (*CF* 2.106). Shades of Genesis 6! Atal has so much more to say, just as Zadok Allen did when he had drunk more than enough, but Carter is very taken by the idea that something of those Great Ones is still present in their human descendants that can tell him where to find his own dream city, the true point of his quest. So barely has he initiated his quest on the word of an old drunkard he turns in another direction.

As he leaves the temple he realizes that he does not hear the accustomed "suppressed fluttering" (*CF* 2.107) of the zoogs that have followed him. In its place the "complacent cats of Ulthar are licking their chops" (2.107). So Carter accepts this surprising sacrifice and the small black kitten that adopts him. Ulthar is not as innocent as it may have seemed at first; and the sated cats depart, perhaps for "those cryptical realms" known only to cats "on the moon's dark side" (2.108). The next day he joins a caravan moving south towards the sinister city of Dylath-Leen, "a great city" that has a bad reputation (2.107). I would parse the name as a long death dying, loath and lean, accepting once more Lovecraft's frequent use of "lath-" as a derivation from the Greek *lanthano*, "to escape notice," "to overlook or to forget," and the root of Lethe (Liddell and Scott 406). Carter had to wait some three days before a boat would arrive from Baharna, a rather ornate barn, that would bear him to the island Oriab, in the

Orient, where the mountain rises.

Unfortunately, the merchants on a galley that has just arrived are wide-mouthed, two-horned, and flat-footed, with "stout black slaves from Parg across the river" (*CF* 2.110). Consider Samuel Johnson's dictionary ("Park: a piece of ground enclosed and stored with wild beasts of chase"). One of these merchants, a slant-eyed man, attaches himself to Carter, and he will often return to be at Carter's side—is he then an ugly double that Carter cannot confess? He offers a drink to a merchant who promises him a secret lore, but Carter passes out at the "least sip" (2.111) he takes of a wine the creature offers him. The boat that they are now on passes the shores of "Zar, abode of forgotten dreams; the spires of infamous Thalarion, that daemon-city [. . .] where the eidolon Lathi reigns and lets the world pass by; the charnel gardens of Xura, [. . .] and the harbor of Sona-Nyl, blessed land of fancy" (2.112). This is a mouthful of names: Czar is imperial, Thalamus is a bed leading to dreams, an *eidolon* is a phantom or dream such as the second Helen, known from Euripides to Goethe. *Lath* is to overlook or to forget, xero and X-ray are piercing in their strengths, and the son is a sun of the Nile, perhaps a secret name of Memnon.

Without stopping, the vessel steers toward the Basalt Pillars of the West, very like the Pillars of Hercules, beyond which some say lies the alluring Cathuria where people are purified, but which the wise say is "a monstrous cataract wherein the oceans of earth's dreamland drop wholly to abysmal nothingness" where "Azathoth gnaws hungrily" (*CF* 2.156) to the dance of the Other Gods; Thalamus is a bed which no doubt invites us to dream. But Carter sees something a step more awful, "the nameless larvae of the Other Gods, and like them [. . .] blind and without mind" (2.113), as horrifying as the blind nightmare of blind Gloucester who complains: "As flies to wanton boys, are we to th' gods, / They kill us for their sport" (*King Lear* 4.1.31–32). There is no innocence or order to this state. This is perhaps the only moment in the quest when "Carter felt the terrors of nightmare as earth fell away and the great boat shot silent and comet-like into planetary space" (2.113).

Fortunately the vessel turns from these visions and steers for the dark side of the moon, "its fields of grotesque whitish fungi [and] the oily waves of a sluggish sea" (*CF* 2.114). "No fully human person, save perhaps the dreamer Snireth-Ko" (2.114), could have ever seen that landscape. What a peculiar assertion! It is difficult to encounter anyone who is fully human, much less such a person who sneers snidely, though he is K. O. Further ahead Carter sees "great grayish-white slippery things which could expand and contract at will" (2.115), toadlike with no eyes, absolutely detestable to Carter's mind, which strike me quite possibly as shoggoths, though Carter is too innocent to suggest that—his dream comprehends more than he does. The vessel with this sight comes to land, and Carter finds himself imprisoned in darkness, refusing anything to eat, since he is certain that they are tempting him with cannibal fare.

When he is released from his timeless prison he finds himself saved by a phalanx of cats, among them "the very little kitten" (*CF* 2.119) he had made friends with in Dylath-Leen, where the army of cats now returns him in his old room, which he had left barely a week ago. So he finds himself, "before he fully realised what had happened" (2.120). This language hints that this is a planetary dream, a dream within a dream, of the other side of the moon, where according to Ariosto we find all that is lost on earth; the cats, "black, gray, and white; yellow, tiger, and mixed; common, Persian, and Manx; Thibetan, Angora, and Egyptian," etc. (2.118) take important part in both oneiric levels. Perhaps strengthened, Carter now takes up his quest once more to the port of Baharna, perhaps with a nod to the exotic Bahaism, on the orient island of Oriab.

II

"Because it's there [. . .]. / I suppose we go to Mount Everest, granted the opportunity, because—in a word—we can't help it." Mallory, cited in Davis 465-66)

The action on board this boat is very quiet. At first they sail eastward for two days, then turn south. Though he asks the captain many questions about the mountain Ngranek, the man would not say "just what a night-gaunt might be like, since such cattle are known to haunt most persistently the dreams of those who think too often of them" (*CF* 2.121). Would such dreams be more dreams within dreams? Is this what Carter sees in "the pleasant fishing towns" that have "old dreaming wharves and beaches where nets lay drying" (2.121). The style is more concrete, subdued, and immediate than the insistent, nudging style that Lovecraft had used earlier. A paragraph is devoted to a drowned city where "dolphins sported" and "porpoises revelled clumsily" (2.121), a charming passage, followed by a paragraph about a city by the shore where in the moonlight Carter saw "an odd high monolith, [. . .] a sailor in the silk robes of Oriab, head downward and without any eyes" (2.122) bound to it. Carter is glad when a rising breeze takes the ship onward. When they come to the harbor of Oriab "the twin beacons Thon and Thal [thunder and] gleamed a welcome" (2.122). When the ship arrives in Oriab Carter accepts the captain's invitation to stay with him in his house on the shore of "the inland lake of Yath," which may be mindful of Dunsany's "Idle Days on the Yann." Carter spends his time laying "his plans for the ascent of Ngranek, and correlat[ing] all that he had learned" (2.123). Lovecraft carries this sober style through the entire venture of climbing Ngranek until the night-gaunts snatch away Carter, tickling him. It is a somber, detailed style that we find in every account of the attempt in 1924 to climb Everest, which culminated in the deaths of Mallory and

Irvine; it was not possible, writing of mountain-climbing in 1926, to escape the impact of that tragic event.

The climb is not so difficult at first. "The [prismatic] magah birds sang blithely as they flashed their seven colours in the sun" (*CF* 2.124), rather as though they were rainbows. There is a solemn touch of pathos in the phrase extended in this passage, "so in the end all of them [the exiles from the hills at the base of the mountain] went down to the sea [. . .] teaching their sons the old art of image-making which to this day they carry on," a short, brilliant outline of the genesis of art (2.125; cf. Ps. 107:23).

"All this time the great gaunt side of Ngranek was looming up higher and higher as Carter approached it" (*CF* 2.125), and at his approach the slope of this base becomes steeper. As he nears the true side of the mountain a forest gives way before him and the "anaemic shrubs" (2.126) that he would like to take handholds of become fewer until "great patches of bare rock" (2.127) crop out. His climb is hopeless when he comes upon a ledge that seems to turn around the side of the mountain just as he wished. He is ready to believe in the nightgaunts that until this moment he had thought merely fabulous. "Poised in windy insecurity miles above earth" (2.128), he begins to understand why climbers before him feared this hidden side of the mountain and approached "the snow uncounted thousands of feet above, and below it a great beetling crag" (2.129), when he realized that he faced "the carved and polished features of a god" (2.129), the very face he had wished to see.

Lit by the gathering sunset, the most dangerous rocks to hang on, this stern and haughty face seemed to pour forth divinity: "those long narrow eyes and long-lobed ears and that thin nose and pointed chin, all spoke of a race that is not of men but of gods" (*CF* 2.129). But he had no need to search further for that face was "the kin of such as he had seen often in the taverns of the seaport Celephaïs which lies in Ooth-Nargai" (2.129), under the rule of King Kuranes. "So to Celephaïs he must go" (2.130), he decides, "back to Dylath-Leen and up the Skai to the bridge by Nir, and again into the enchanted wood of the zoogs, whence the way would bend northward [. . .] by Oukranos to the gilded spires of Thran, [. . .] over the Cerenerian Sea" (2.130); it's not too far. No doubt the dreamer in Carter dreams this geography into existence, but before he can climb down from the mountain the night-gaunts snatch him away for the tremendous tickling they are best known for. The most significant detail in this itinerary is the enchanted wood of the zoogs, where once his quest began. Unspoken is the suggestion that all that lies behind him was a dream within a dream. This gives him all the time in the world to contemplate the celebration of Celephaïs, the great egg of Ooth-Nargai by which one swears an oath, Oukranos the muscular river that is second cousin to Oceanos, Thran as Thrang, and the Cerenerian Sea. But Carter has no time for these details as the night-gaunts bear him through a cave in Ngranek down to the non-Euclidean space of the Peaks of Thok, soon to be joined by bholes and ghouls. Here the voiceless creatures leave Carter, in the pit of the earth, but they shall return for a long passage in which the sleeper seems deeply disturbed though never on the edge of waking.

Carter is not in so bad a situation as it might seem. He knows "from a certain source" that he is "in the vale of Pnath" (2.132), which I am sure shows a path natheless for a person who "had a very singular link" (2.133) with the ghouls who could let down a ladder for him; this singular person turns out to be none other than the quondam painter Richard Pickman. Carter has little time to consider this surprising turn of events, not that one truly considers events, when he sends out "that meeping cry which is the call of the ghoul" (2.133), summoning the ladder and climbing, nastily pursued by a "loathsome and overfed" bhole (2.134). At last he comes to the end of the ladder in a plain surrounded by ghouls, but with Pickman on his side he is not afraid of them, "probably nearer the waking world than at any other time since he had gone down the seven hundred steps" (2.135) at the beginning of his quest.

With some solemnity there sits his friend on a tombstone, much deteriorated from the Pickman he had known, "its human origin [. . .] already obscure" (*CF* 2.135). Nevertheless—or should we say "natheless," arguing that all things are decayed in this chthonic underworld of the dream—Carter confides his quest with his friend, but Pickman warns him that great difficulties lie between him and his world, like "the web-footed wamps [and] the terrible kingdom of the gugs" (2.135). He argues that Carter should either plan to "leave the abyss at Sarkomand, that deserted city [. . .] guarded by winged diorite lions [. . .], or to return through a churchyard to the waking world and begin the quest anew" (2.136). Carter, however, finds both of these possibilities distasteful and persuades Pickman to guide him "inside the great wall of the gugs' kingdom [. . .] and reach the central tower with the sign of Koth upon it, which has the stairs leading up to that stone trap-door" (2.136) in the enchanted wood of the zoogs. I have commented upon this passage previously, claiming that in this mythic underworld "the somatic process [that] excretes a sarkotic object" (Waugh, "Landscapes, Selves" 235). Thus it is in this underworld that the dreamer creates "the sarkos, the body of flesh that is in command but badly sewn together, rather than soma, the body of wholeness and fitness" (235). This nastiness is combined with the sign of Koth, which suggests Kot: dirt, filth, [. . .] droppings, dung; excrement, faeces. Pokorny suggests quâd, 'stercus' (2.484).

A further point needs to be made about this passage, that shortly after Lovecraft has finished *The Dream-Quest of the Unknown Kadath* he turned to writing *The Case of Charles Dexter Ward,* in which the reversal of the words and symbols was very important as the ascending and descending nodes: imagine the omega inverted Ω, wholeness undone by unwholeness. The principle of inversion in the work of weird fantasy finds its proper place in the work of weird reality.

III

Mein Schlaf ist Träumen,
Mein Träumen Sinnen,
Mein Sinnen Walten des Wissens.

[My sleep is dreaming, / my dreaming sense, / my sense the ruler of knowledge.] (Wagner, *Siegfried* 3.1.2021-23)

The gugs are the chief antagonists in this level of dreams. Once they "made strange sacrifices to the Other Gods" (*CF* 2.135), disturbing the earth's gods so badly that they banished the gugs to this level, restricting "their diet to the ghasts, those repulsive beings which die in the light, and which live in the vaults of Zin [. . .] where gugs hunt ghasts in the dark" (2.176), the place of archetypal darkness. It is easiest to claim that this is the darkness of sin, but the German word *Sinn* bears such meanings as feeling, intellect, mind, meaning, consciousness, and opinion—a great range of possible meanings as we can see from these few words, whether subject or object (*New Cassell's* 430). It is all very like the generation of thought in *geheim* and *geheimlich, geheuer* and *ungeheuer*. The vaults of Zin resemble the pits of unconsciousness, an extension of mind or a Gordian knot that we must cut through rather than unknot.

Before Pickman and Carter sally forth, the ghoul advises Carter to disguise himself as a ghoul, shaven and shorn, "wallowing naked in the mould [. . .] and loping in the usual way" (*CF* 2.136), doing his doubling best to get the right smell of it. This is very important, since they will pass the cemetery of the ghasts who "try to come out when the gugs sleep" (2.137), especially since ghasts will eat ghouls as readily as gugs. Ghouls, however, look forward to their own luau, "for a buried gug will feed a community for almost a year" (2.137). This passage is rather like the tone of *A Modest Proposal,* a polite gentleman doing his best to please us.

This politesse is left behind, however, when a group of ghasts gather to attack a gug big as a barrel, "nipping and tearing" at him (*CF* 2.139) and slowly backing the great feed into a cavern. The quickest of Carter's ghouls leads him onward through the monolithic towers, a city made for the giant gugs. At last they come to "a tower even vaster than the rest, above whose colossal doorway was fixed a monstrous symbol, [. . .] the central tower with the sign of Koth, and those huge stone steps" (2.140) that lead to the upper dreamland and the enchanted wood, through which he would come to Celephaïs, a hurried shining light. At last they come upon the stone trap-door that they lift and Carter steps out on "the blessed soil of the upper dreamland [. . .], a haven and a delight after the gulfs he had now left behind" (2.142–43), an emotion that Lovecraft has created. It is a moving moment when he then "sought a forest pool and cleansed himself of the mud of nether earth" (2.143). After this baptism he undertakes his quest once more.

He stops in his tracks, however, because he hears the zoogs in a hollow tree planning a series of attacks upon the cats. The entire countryside, from Ulthar to the river Skai, an alphabet list of armored cats is on the move "from every hearth and housetop [. . .] and the sight of shapely, wholesome cats was indeed good for his eyes after the things he had seen and walked with in the abyss" (*CF* 2.145). Even his own friends were there, including "a brisk young fellow who proved to be none other than the very little kitten in the inn where Carter had fed it with a saucer of rich cream" (2.145) in an earlier life. The time since then has again passed swiftly.

It does not take long for the cats to deal with the doglike zoogs, so with a sense of justification Carter the "pilgrim" (*CF* 2.148) undertakes his quest once more, passing through the demesne of the king Ilek-Vad, often walking "close to the bank of Oukranos" (2.148) and remembering the "quaint lumbering buopoths" (2.148), fearful oxen, of his former dreams. In the evening he arrives in the city of Thran, where he admires the thousand spires made from a single solid piece, "by what means no man knows" (2.148). Here no gate is forbidden except the southern gate, unless Carter told the sentry three dreams beyond belief; presumptively tells these dreams and gains from the south a new life. In the new direction he learns at old taverns, "seamen he had known in myriad other dreams" (2.149), coming from their country, cold Inganok, in the north, strongly resembling the look of the gods. Jason C. Eckhardt suggests that Inganok is based upon such Algonquin place-names as Sagadahoc, Naugatuck, and Monadnock ("The Cosmic Yankee" 92). With this aperçu the best sense I can make of Inganok is Chingachgook, the last of the Mohicans, a desperate putting together of an ancient tradition, or perhaps some ink in a nook. The next day Carter buys a place on board a ship going to Celephaïs, the next step in his quest.

The galleon now forces its way through "the perfumed jungles of Kled" (*CF* 2.150), rather like the jungles of Angkor-Wat in Cambodia; Kle or Kled, a key or the key. After the river begins to broaden the ship comes to the city of Hlanith, much given to trade and barter, very like the waking world; Hlanith is perhaps cognate to other lanith words of secret moments. After some time the ship sails out once more "over the sunset sea" (2.151).

In two days the peak of the Aran mountain loomed up ahead, at its base the gingko-trees, announcing the land of Ooth-Nargai, the cloud-city of Serannian where "time has no power to tarnish or destroy" (*CF* 2.152), and the city of Celephaïs. Carter has achieved the first stage of his journey, and once more he meets a friendly cat that introduces him to where Kuranes may be found, given the changes in the city. Born in Cornwall, Kuranes does his best to live in the time of Queen Anne. Carter finds him in his library, "looking out on his little seacoast village and wishing that his old nurse would come in and scold him because he was not ready for that hateful lawn-party at the vicar's, with the carriage ready and his mother nearly out of patience" (2.155). Which is worse then, dead as a beggar in Lovecraft's story

"Celephaïs" in which Kuranes originally dreamed this pocket landscape, or this sterile life of his nurse and his mother, the only point in the narrative when women appear in this "most farraginous chronicle" (Joyce, *Ulysses* 345)? It was all "worn out, and monotonous for want of linkage with anything firm in his feelings and memories" (2.156).

Carter is waiting once more for a ship that will bear him north, but once it arrives he waits for another week before the dark ship takes sail. The world to the south grows perceptibly smaller. The ship does stop at six ports where the ship trades in onyx, an important gem for the further north. On the twentieth day a jagged rock rises, "the first land glimpsed since Aran's snowy peak had dwindled behind the ship" (*CF* 2.159), a portentous sign that everyone on the ship fears. As for Carter, "he dreamed terrible dreams within dreams in the small hours" (2.160). As formerly, he recognizes a new stage.

IV

> Burningly it came on me all at once,
>   This was the place! those two hills on the right,
>   Crouched like two bulls locked horn in horn in fight;
> While to the left, a tall, scalped mountain . . . (Browning 288)

As another sign of this stage, they land at Inganok city where he recognizes the skill of men carving the head of a god "with that same skill displayed in the monstrous face on distant Ngranek" (*CF* 2.160). In one of the taverns he sees "a squat form [. . .] unmistakably that of the old slant-eyed merchant" (2.162) he had seen in Dylath-Leen, here trading eggs that are rumored to be those of the shantak-bird. His captain showed him the various temples of the city, where "always to the east [. . .] rose the gaunt grey sides of those topless and impassible peaks across which hideous Leng was said to lie" (2.162); the plateau apparently here receives the intensive, Lelag-Leng. Rumor is the stuff of trade, and for rumor the captain leads Carter to the famous temple of the Veiled King's palace. Nothing is real in this part of the city, so Carter determines to hire a yak and find his way now further north.

At the village of Urg (urge or [erg], energy) the traders rest and the great caravan roads turn west to Selarn, or to Salem, to the solarium; but still Carter with energy holds north: "all the while the great gaunt sides of the impassible mountains towered afar off at his right, and the farther he went, the worse tales he heard of them" (*CF* 2.166). He paused when "he thought he saw approaching the camp that squat and evasive old merchant with slanting eyes" (2.166). As we know, sometimes our paranoia is for real. He enters a space of "bats or urhags or less mentionable presences haunting the endless blackness" (2.168), a blackness that could generate anything. But an urhag, the archetype of old women, or still the haunt of Helen? What are we to make of the word? No doubt this is the cruel language that Stesichorus used in his first ode to Helen.

In the fallen darkness of the dream Carter and his yak come to the peak of his endeavor, but tearing out of his hands the creature bursts away; and now he can see the plateau and something more that lies before him: "All in a great half circle they squatted there atop the world like wolves or ghouls, [surely different from those with whom he had played in a different dream] crowned with clouds and mists and guarding the secrets of the north for ever" (*CF* 2.169). He did not, though, have long to consider this landscape before he looked behind where "the squat slant-eyed trader of evil legend [. . .], grinning astride a lank yak and leading on a noxious horde of leering shantaks, to whose wings still clung the rime and nitre of the nether pits" (2.170), a nasty concoction of consonants, but now so distorting that we meet shantaks in the place of shanti, shanti, shanti, very like shanks or shanties. Taking the place of the night-gaunts, they are much more evil, leering and mocking, than those amiable ticklers.

In this flight they pass over the city of Sarkomand, which shall now be mentioned more often. After this flight the merchant lead

Carter into a windowless monastery, its walls lit by a small clay lamp, showing walls of scenes "older than history" (2.173) in which the toad-like creatures came down from the moon and conquered the people of Leng. Carter, however, pays them back by shoving the merchant into the well "which rumour holds to reach down to the hellish Vaults of Zin" (2.176). He is rather paid back himself, however, as the candle flickers out and he slips, shooting down a hole that receives him much as a well would have. When he comes to a stop he discovers that he is in the ruins "that were in truth primordial Sarkomand" (2.177), the seal of mere flesh. Indeed, there is no doubt, as the narrator insists, that stretching before him lay "the great corpse-like width of fabled Sarkomand with its black broken pillars and crumbling sphinx-crowned gates [. . .] and monstrous winged lions" (2.182).

Recognizing the typical *meep, meep* of his friends the ghouls, whom he had directed to Sarkomand, now in the hands of the moon-beasts, he descends another spiral staircase to bring help from the ghouls, since Pickman is once more in charge, and night-gaunts. That is as far as Carter can go, once more ascending those stairs, though we must grant that he is practical in this decision. Nevertheless, when it looked as though the alliance of the ghouls and gaunts was about to fall apart, he did successfully instruct them in the use of the banked oars of the galleon in which the moon-beasts had arrived. Now they are ready to attack the beasts.

The battle that follows is told in great detail, but in a rather statuesque style. The detail that we read earlier in the battle of the cats and ghouls is absent here; it is important that it strains back and forth around the great jagged rocky island that Carter had noticed earlier, an island that has no name, causing Carter to suffer nightmares within nightmares. Much of the ensuing battle is an attempt on both sides to take control of this awful place. In this wreckage Carter now assumes the role of a nurse, though that is difficult, since his patients are hardly human. Furthermore, certain "submarine lurkers" (*CF* 2.191) stand by to devour anything that happens to fall their way. What seems so orderly, given the polite style, is not orderly at all. We may well wonder whether Lovecraft is influenced here by descriptions of the Great War, this battle is so extended. "Over a fourth," the scrupulous narrator reports, "had been lost in the day's battles" (2.192). This procedure is so much better than "the old ghoulish custom of killing and eating one's own wounded" (2.192). While reading this passage every reader should remember that we read it as the dreamer, so we have partaken of those feasts in the past.

And now Carter, the dreamer of deep sleep, as about to gain his goal, since "the final journey [is] either to the marvelous sunset city itself, in case the gods proved favourable, or back to the earthward Gate of Deeper Slumber in the enchanted wood" (*CF* 2.194). Whichever it may be, he rides a shantak, accompanied by the ghouls and night-gaunts. And soon he is accompanied also by the mitred, two-headed, carved mountains that protect the plateau of Leng, and this double head is doubled in the constellation of a pshent; no doubt we recall that the two priests also wear pshents, which were worn by pharaohs as symbol of their rule in both the lower and the upper kingdoms. At this point readers are reminded that "in the land of dream dimensions have strange properties" (2.199). It may be well to consider once more "the hellish Vaults of Zin where gugs hunt ghasts in the dark" (2.176). "A force not of earth" (2.199-200) grips Carter's army and hurtles it north through "the atomless aether" (2.200) that is pre-Einsteinian in its power, "where the cryptical moon and the mad planets reel" (2.200).

Here a mountain unknown to the human race, whether human or ghoul, "loomed before them" (*CF* 2.200), and "vaster and vaster loomed the tenebrous towers of the knighted castle" (*CF* 2.201) into which they are hurled. Carter realizes that he will not find the gods, whether of earth or of the Great Ones or the Other Gods, none of them such as he expected. Someone or something must speak for them.

"Then the Lord answered Job out of the whirlwind, and said, Who is this that darkeneth counsel by words without knowledge" (Job 38:1-2). The book of Job is unfortunately the most difficult book of the Bible, but I would argue that the long oration of Nyarlathotep, a new man unseen or overlooked, is difficult also, speaking as a "dark god or fallen archangel" (*CF* 2.204). Though I do not think Lovecraft is a counter of paragraphs, these paragraphs leading to the palace after being looking down on a great desert are the words of a tempter or tester; forty is one of the potent numbers, a promise of revelation after great hardships. We need to hold onto our assurances while we listen to "the mild music of Lethean streams" (2.204) in Nyarlathotep's argument. But there is so much to forget.

In the first six paragraphs Nyarlathotep introduces the history of the Great Ones, whom he seems to despise, since they have allowed themselves to be seduced by the art of Carter's city, and of the Other Gods whom he finds more interesting, coming from outer space. "Thus the earth has no longer any gods that are gods" (*CF* 2.205).

The next four paragraphs are a remarkable peroration in honor of New England, though the seventh paragraph opens in the threatening words, "I spare you and charge you to serve my will" (*CF* 2.206), words set aside in the praise of Boston, Salem, and Marblehead, Providence, Kingsport, and "Arkham, [. . .] with its moss-grown gambrel and the rocky rolling meadows behind it" (2.207). This mixture of nonfiction and a bit of fiction supports Nyarlathotep's insistence that the dreamer Carter is the only man who has brought the entire body of those states into existence, and thus he is the only man who can speak to the gods. What really counts, according to Nyarlathotep, is Carter's recognition that his ideal city rises through the city and nation he was born to: "These, Randolph Carter, are your city; for they are yourself" (2.207). Five paragraphs now present the cosmic framework of the "stars of eternal night" (2.207), as represented by Vega and Antares, shining through Carter's Beacon Hill window

(401). He insists that Carter should climb on his shantak once more and steer by those stars to his sunset city, where he will drive out "the recreant Great Ones" (2.208), though they will find that task difficult. This section concludes in two careless paragraphs with the admission that the Other Gods are "good gods to shun" (403).

"*Hei! Aa-shanta 'nygh!*" [Ho! A!-shanti or shantak enough], the speaker sings out. "You are off! Send back earth's gods to their haunts on unknown Kadath" (*CF* 2.209). This short passage, with its ironic nod to *The Waste Land,* concludes the argument of the crawling chaos that outlines the mystique of the materialistic world. He will have more to say, but for now the narrative glides to Carter's ride on the shantak, devoting six paragraphs to it, and this change in narration may suggest how remarkable the first seventeen paragraphs are.

In the three paragraphs that follow Carter pays attention to the monsters of the deep, "[the] great polypous horrors [that] slid darkly past"(*CF* 2.209) until dawn breaks and the shantak flies faster and faster, though Carter is now in the same danger to which Icarus fell. As he faces that danger he considers more closely "the sardonic caution of the daemon legate" (2.210), that word *sardonic* most often applied to the ruins of Sarkomand. The following five paragraphs describe the race all the more, "unswerving and obedient" (2.210), that "pawed and groped and groped and pawed," uncovering "the nameless larvae of the Other Gods, that are like them blind and without mind" (2.210-11), described in the beginning of the next paragraph as "onward unswerving and relentless" (2.211), "onward–onward–through the screaming, cackling and blackly populous gulfs" (2.211). The style is certainly over-the-top now, almost senseless in its use of a chiasmus and a rhyme and a repetition.

The next paragraph is rendered in Nyarlathotep's voice, but gives this in the voice of Carter, summing up his yearning for Boston, its Commons and the Charles, the home he loves; once more in the twenty-fifth paragraph the words "onward–onward" (*CF* 2.212) begin the paragraph, but concludes in the words "turn—turn—blackness on every side, but Randolph Carter could turn" (2.212) in a turning that means home. So in the next paragraph he leaps from the back of the shantak and begins to fall through the universe, "born anew" (2.212) through matter and light. "And comets, suns, and worlds sprang flaming into life" (2.212).

The final three paragraphs are all afterword, but not unimportant. "There were gods and presences and wills; beauty and evil, and the shrieking of noxious night robbed of its prey" (*CF* 2.212). The passage may be clumsy, but it is an earnest attempt to reconcile aesthetics and morality. At least it expresses the wish that they could be reconciled, as might happen in deep sleep, beyond the Cerenerian Sea, so like the Sea of Cyrene, near Libya. Does the plausible geographic allusion suggest that the sleep is passing? It's been a long sleep—but I am dubious whether he has indeed at last come awake.

V

That was the prick of the spindle to me that gave me the keys to dreamland. (Joyce, *Finnegans Wake* 615.27-28)

Let us look now at the geography of this dream more broadly. When I do so, what most strikes me is "the central tower with the sign of Koth" (*CF* 2.140), not difficult to understand backwards as Thok. But though I read that clearly, I am liable to miss the point that these two words suggest our humanity. When I step back, I see that the two mountains of the narrative, Ngranek and the mitre-heads, are balanced one to another as the rivers Okeanos and Skai, ocean and sky that run between them. How like this is to the geography we uncover to the truth in *Finnegans Wake!* Early in that work "the humptyhillhead of humself promptly sends an unquiring one well to the west in quest of his tumptytumtoes" (3.20-21). In *Ulysses* every chapter was dedicated to a human organ, and now in the *Wake* "the Human Form Divine"

(Blake, "A Divine Image," l. 3) was in some detail laid out upon a map of eastern Ireland; the phallus stood high in the Wellington monument. Joyce found this detail not difficult, since Howth Hill is known as Howth Head. The river Liffey runs through the center of Dublin between the Celts and the Vikings, just as Oukranos runs through the center of Carter's personal dreamland. Should we ask for more detail there is the first proposition of Euclid that behaves as a map to the rere of Anna Livia Plurabelle (*Finnegans Wake* 293-300).

Before we pursue any further this comparison let us note that both Joyce and Lovecraft were fascinated by dreams. Joyce had an early fascination, but he was not by any means a Freudian, just as in later life he was fascinated by Jung but he was not a Jungian, especially where his daughter was concerned (Ellmann 85). In 1916 he kept a dream book, just as Lovecraft copied several of his dreams into his commonplace book. As Joyce began to work on *Finnegans Wake* he would often spend some time interpreting his own dreams as well as pressing his friends to offer up their dreams.

If dreams are so important to both of these authors, we should note that Joyce has a dream within a dream that once in the *Wake* the narrative turns to a dream within a dream as the action turns with this dream to the last chapters of the book; of course there are several moments, practically page by page, in which the narrative is almost aware that the sleeper will wake. In the same way Lovecraft has at least two moments when Carter is on the verge of waking and other moments when he wakes to sleep again. And the book to which both men, Irishman and New Englander, will be attracted is *The Thousand and One Nights,* which in its narration is no doubt best read at night (Boysen 580-81n412). In an early letter Lovecraft confesses to his friend Frank Belknap Long his fascination with the Oriental world from which he filched Abdul Alhazred to be the author of the *Necronomicon.* There is no escaping these nights, "since in this scherzarade of one's thousand one nightinesses that sword of certainty which would indendifide the body never falls" (*Finnegans Wake* 51.4-6). Who can say no to such naughtiness, though a certain identity is impossible?

True, a reader may object, Joyce did not read Lovecraft; but Lovecraft did read extracts from *Ulysses,* passages long enough to convince him that "it represents the intensive development—the concentration or exaggeration—of a literary principle which will greatly affect future writing, but which defeats its own ends of normally-proportioned portrayal when isolated & intensified to this extreme degree" (*JVS* 89). "The same is true," Lovecraft adds, "of Joyce's later 'Anna Livia Plurabelle'" (*JVS* 89). We cannot imagine how large those extracts were that he read; in any case, as is clear from his account of his reading, he did not throw the book against the wall.

So when I now reconsider Lovecraft's *Dream-Quest of Unknown Kadath,* which is so often dense in names, I very much have the human shape in mind as I turn to the beginning where Carter stood, its head and neck and the creatures, zoogs, ghouls, bholes, gugs, and ghasts, their ceaseless battle a symbol of the mental war of the gigantic and the small that are eating one another alive; and the gods, the gods of the earth, the Great Ones who care for this side of reality and the Outside Gods who inhabit what is outside our universe and its laws, outside like the dark, permeating matter over which we bother our minds now; its torso, composed of the rivers Skai and the sky reaching up to the universal world, the sky, and Oukranos and its Southern Sea and other great oceans, its pleasant meadows and cities, Celephaïs, Ooth-Nargai, Olathoë, and at the base of its spine, Dylath-Leen; and its arms and legs, Ngranek and Kadath. Its head is composed of its mind, the two eyes in the central area, Nasht and Kaman-Thah who speak for the individual, and the feminine power revealed "in the cavern of flame" (308), imagery suggested by H. Rider Haggard's *She.* As for the legs and wings, Carter does a good deal of walking, which happens often in this kind of genre; and despite his wishes he is swept away to the pale light of the moon, and later to the pale light of the onyx palace.

There is more to be said of this shape, for there are moments of significant difference. Ngranek is one long phallic mountain, protected by the fearful night-gaunts, the other side of the plateau protected by the shantaks. The onyx palace of the gods in Kadath is protected by something unimaginable: "all in a great half circle they squatted, those dog-like mountains carven into monstrous watching statues" (*CF* 2.169). Very like the mountain Ngranek, carved into a face that is a "menace against mankind" (2.169), and very unlike also, wearing peaks that look like mitres, a mockery of the distant earth's gods. It may seem a strain, but we do ask whether the mountain of Ngranek to the south is balanced by this mountainous half-circle to the north, the phallic to the omphalos, each of these symbols directly pointing toward the center and the city of Sarkomand, an order of the flesh; Sarcophage, a stone coffin, a devouring of flesh; Samarcand, a city of central Asia; and Sagamore, an old wise man (Cooper 33). So many possible, dense meanings.

It makes good sense, I think, to pay attention to the moment in which the central voice falls. We are not surprised by this; we are always falling in this world, falling in love and falling asleep. The third paragraph of the *Wake* opens "The fall [the hundred lettered thunder] of a once wallstrait oldpard is retaled early in bed and later on life down throughall christian minstrelsy" (3.15-19). Tim Finnegan falls from his ladder, and so does everyone else. We have already been introduced to Sir Tristam, whose tale with Isolde has not yet been "retaled" (3.20), but it shall be. For now let us consider Augustine's understanding of the lapsus that we all suffer, through which we truly become that which we were meant to be. The Cartesian sense of the ego becomes "Si fallor, sum" (Matthews 152). Cogito is all very well, but the mistake, with its echoes of Eden and Babel, lies closer to the authentic bone. I am convinced now, however, that Matthews in his translation of the "fallor" commits a mistake that seems to be accidental. *Deferrari,* in his translation of Aquinas's Latin, would have us try to deceive, trick, dupe, cheat, or disappoint (386); another translation would produce an attempt to elude or betray (Tucker 90). This is close to the language of the snake or the language of the aggressive magician. Consider now the argument of Augustine, with a slight improvement:

> If I am mistaken, I am. [fallor, sum] [or] If I am hidden, I am.
> If I am not mistaken, I am. [non fallor, sum] If I am not hidden, I am.
> Either I am mistaken or I am not mistaken. Either I hide, or I do not hide.
> Ergo, I am. Therefore I am (hidden as I am).
> If I am not hidden, I am. (Matthews 152-56)

The difficulty is that whatever I lose in existence, I gain in my loss of being, with a deeper insight into my hidden *Trägheit* and *Nachträglichkeit* that loses me in an inert traumas and betrayals that gain in substance (Waugh, *Monster in the Mirror* 258-62). Whom do I betray? It is an intimate *fallor,* mistake as in a lapsus linguae. It is as though the tongue were bound against an impossible freedom. Everyone is betrayed, but above all my self; it's a fractured being that I am dragging through life to the grave, and all the more for a mere lapse of the tongue that seems like nothing. We are following the compulsions of Tim Finnegan and his family in his deep dreams; or Randolph Carter in his deep dreams.

An Apology for John Keats et Alii

Keats could have warned us. Truth be told, he did.

I

So let us now turn back from Augustine without leaving him behind, turning to Keats, who was always, I must confess, first and last in my intellectual and emotional world, the poet to whom I have had to return so often throughout my life, always with these lines from "In drear nighted December" in mind: in three stanzas these are the crucial lines: "The feel of not to feel it, / When there is none to heal it, / Nor numbed sense to steel it, / Was never said in rhyme" (*Poems* 221). These awkward, maladroit lines in clumsy repetitions did not please Richard Woodhouse, one of Keats's friends, who suggested that the line "To know the change and feel it" (221n) was more acceptable for a lyric, as is the implied erotic pain of the "gentle girl and boy" (221). It removes the blunt repetition and the adscription of knowledge. Woodhouse wrote more bluntly to a mutual friend:

> I have tried unsuccessfully to admire the 3d stanza of "Drear knighted Decr" as much as the 2 first.—I plead guilty, even before I am accused, of an utter abhorrence of the word "feel" for feeling substantively—But Keats seems fond of it. and will ingraft it "in aeternum" on our language—Be it so [. . .] (Keats, *Letters* 1.64)

One cannot help the suspicion that "feel" in this usage stands in the place of the Cockneyism that later the critics would lambast Keats for in his treatment of the language in *Endymion.* The only comfort for this "drear nighted" condition is a language from home. Otherwise

Apollo, the god of poets, would not be praised. In fact, Keats was no longer appealing to Apollo, who by implication is frozen, infertile, and forgotten. If the poet felt the need to call on divinity, it was now more often to be the lying thief Hermes, as we shall see when we turn our attention to *Lamia* and Keats's two labors on his late subject, *Hyperion*.

Besides epics, lyrics, and popular songs, Keats wrote several verse epistles, a genre popular in his day, so he was probably not anxious about writing a new one to his friend John Hamilton Reynolds, who was ill; it does fulfill the necessary formality and intimacy, very much constructed with the friend to whom it is addressed, sensitive and intelligent. At first, though, the poet it seems can only begin with platitudes. The poem, however, comes alive first when he confesses that he, the poet, has "a mysterious tale / And cannot speak it" (86–87). What a peculiar reticence. Then, after he adds that the evening is lovely, something of the worse follows:

> but I saw
> Too far into the sea; where every maw
> The greater on the less feeds evermore:
> But I saw too distinct into the core
> Of an eternal fierce destruction. (244)

The language is factual and firm; its couplets are no longer the swooning, enjambed lines he had learned from his patron Hunt and grown sick of in *Endymion*. The simplicity of terror is better worked in the earlier description of the painting, "The sacrifice goes on; the pontiff knife / Gloams in the sun, The milk-white heifer lows, / The pipes go shrilly, the libation flows" (242). This vision is not too distant from the later lines in "Ode on a Grecian Urn" that ask innocuously, "Who are these coming to the sacrifice?" Who are these that have emptied the city? (373). The answer, I believe, is that we are the sacrifice. Once more, this poem does not seem written under the hand of

Apollo. Perhaps it is too true when his ode to Apollo takes place in the dying west (34–36).

I conclude this short survey of terror in Keats with this description of Lamia in her transformation, touched by Hermes; her body is like "[the lava that] ravishes the mead, / Spoilt all her silver mail, and golden brede; / Made gloom of all her frecklings, streaks and bars, / Eclipsed her crescents, and licked up her stars" (456). Nothing but pain and ugliness remains. The contrast between the wit and control of the lines and the factual horror of the cosmic ruin strikes home—if she retains or owns a reality behind the cosmic world of this ruin. But the woman will leave the skin of the snake behind and flee into the mask of the woman.

Both of these poems became further important when we brought Leopardi next to the Englishman in the lines of sexual destruction and cosmic destruction that opens his complex poem, "La ginestra":

> Qui su l'arida schiena
> Del formidabil' monte,
> Sterminator Vesevo,
> La qual null'altro allegra arbor né fiore,
> Tuoi cespi solitari intorno spargi,
> Odorata ginestra,
> Contenta dei deserti. (ll. 1–7)

[Here on the arid ridge / of the formidable mountain, / the destroyer Vesuvius, / which neither a tree nor a flower can make happy, / you sprinkle your solitary leaves, / perfumed broom, / contented in the deserts.]

This is a poem in which two powers are addressed; but the weakest, moral power, despite its intense beauty shall always lose. The other power, a formidable destroyer, is a sublime thug, possessed of no moral or sublime gesture. Nevertheless, this power believes deeply in progress and it never looks away—that is its brand name.

Turn wherever the reader would choose, the power of the ocean or the power of the volcano, the state of things leaves us open to destruction, "E l'infinita vanità dell tutto" [and the infinite emptiness of all things] (l. 16), especially the emptiness of the beloved which the rest of this broken poem has ascribed. This second poem, "A se stesso," wrestles with his own hopelessness in the face of the beloved's indifference:

> Or poserai per sempre,
> Stanco mio cor. Perì l'inganno estremo,
> Ch' eterno io mi credei. Perì. Ben sento,
> In noi di cari inganno,
> Non che la speme, il desidero è spento. (ll. 1-5)

[Now rest forever, / my tired heart. The last illusion has perished, / that I thought eternal. Perished. Well I feel, / what we have of dear illusions, / Not only hope, desire is exhausted.]

This is the first of three stanzas, composed of broken lines, fourteen or fifteen caesuras in sixteen lines; this is unlike anything Leopardi had written earlier. Anyone who has read these poems, "La ginestra" or "A se stesso," has become familiar with the cosmic, indifferent state of the universe that Lovecraft shall soon open to his readers and his friends. Both of these fragments are affirmed by the metaphoric imagery of the desert.

And Baudelaire? We have already paid attention to the gulf into which the poet descends eternally. He certainly has poems in which the sublime indifference of nature is centered. I have in mind his exemplary sonnet, "Le Gouffre" that begins:

> Pascal avait son gouffre, avec lui se mouvant.
> Hélas! Tout est l'abîme,—action, désir, rêve,
> Parole! Et sur mon poil qui tout droit se relève
> Mainte fois de la Peur je sens passer le vent.
>
> Eh haut, en bas, partout la profondeur, la grève,
> Le silence, l'espace affreux et captivant . . .

Sur le fond de mes nuits Dieu de son doigt savant
Dessine un cauchemar multiforme et sans trêve.

J'ai peur du sommeil comme on a peur d'un grand trou,
Tout plein de vague horreur, menant on ne sait où;
Je ne vois qu'infini par toutes les fenêtres,

Et mon esprit, toujour du vertige hanté,
Jalouse du néant l'insensibilité,
—Ah! ne jamais sortir des Nombres et des Etres!" (244)

[Pascal has his pit that is moving with him, / Alas! All is abyss,— action, desire, dream, / word! Et on my skin that lifts up straight up / I feel the wind of Fear pass by. // Above, below, everywhere the pit of executions / the silence, the terrifying space, captivating ... / at the bottom of my dreams God with his knowing finger / designs a multiform nightmare, with no rest. // I fear my sleep the way a person fears a cave, / full of vague horror, leading we know not where, / through every window I see nothing but infinity, // and my spirit, haunted by vertigo, / desires the nothingness of insensibility. / Alas! Never to escape Numbers and Beings!][1]

Nothing is so fated in the modern age than the abstractions of numbers and philosophy, out of which now the Dasein peers. No doubt Pascal would agree that this perception would affect the misery of the human condition. Remarkable as that poem is, however, the poem "Les Sept Vieillards" conveys a greater anxiety, addressing the city; but of a greater difference in his poetry are the poems that take place in the city, "Fourmillante cité, cité pleine de rêves, / Où le spectre en plein jour racchroche le passant!" [Swarming city, city full of dreams, / where the specter in full day solicits the passerby"] (159). Lovecraft and his friends took to this new world with a great fervor, leaving behind the secret horrors of even so agreeable a city as Providence.

---

1. Here we find that typical imagery of the abyss of which HPL is so fond.

II

> This castle has a pleasant seat: the air
> Nimbly and sweetly recommends itself
> Unto our gentle senses. (*Macbeth* 1.6.1-3)

Now let us conclude with Keats more thoroughly. One of the reasons he is so important as a poet is that in his twenty-five years he wrestled with himself as a poet and a short person who was more than a poet. Three times he worked at creating a model for our human life, each time looking at it from a different angle, so open to this labor that he argues the definitive process, which limits and cuts, is very different from the creative world which amplifies, extends and connects (Hillman 30-31n). To employ this symbolic compound word that Keats and others have used, this is soul-making, an exploration of the social, sensual, moral, and spiritual worlds (Keats, *Letters* 2.102). In the process of making myself, I am beginning to understand that my labor will have no end, especially if I stumble a few times.

Having gone so far, there are other ways we may choose for following Keats's ideas in selfhood. "they are very shallow people who take everything literal A Man's life of any worth is a continual allegory—and very few eyes can see the Mystery of his life—a life like the scriptures, figurative—which such people can no more make out than they can the hebrew scripture" (*Letters* 2.67). We should remember that allegories and figuras are embedded in a layered history, but Keats seem to be moving beyond the traditional structure of four layers. But for the sake of the poem, we wish to see the myths of the classical world in motion, dynamic and expansive—as Hillman would say, amplified and extended, already bearing with us the myth let free. This is perfect description of what I do when I read Lovecraft seriously. The mystery of his life does take some time to understand his reading in this way; often we find ourselves called upon to take the mystery of his work, to realize that the story is something more than simple and untouched.

But to return to my understanding of Keats, this time I find myself especially touched by this passage in *Hyperion* in the encounter between the poet, Saturn, and Thea, the wife of Hyperion:

> O aching time! O moments big as years!
> All as ye pass swell out the monstrous truth,
> And press it so upon our weary griefs,
> That unbelief has not a space to breathe. (1.64-67)

Just as in Leopardi's "La ginestra" there was that horrifying contrast drawn between the great and the small, the volcano and the flower, so here we find this contrast and disjunction drawn between the years and the moments. A few lines further on the contrast is drawn between her painful silence and "his palsied tongue" (1.93). Such a contrast is drawn in a remarkable passage of Virgil's *Georgics:* "angustum formica terens iter, et bibit ingens / arcus" [an ant cuts its narrow way, and it drinks from the great / rainbow] (1.380-81). This may seem a purely natural scene unless we recall the conclusion of the *Aeneid* as Iris, the rainbow messenger of the gods, announces the death of Dido (4.693-705): "omnis et una / dilapsus calor atque in uentos uita recessit" [all at once / her color departs and her life recedes] (4.704-5). This death, summoned by the pity of the goddess Juno, is especially moving in that phrase, dilapsus calor. We meet here the two rainbows, the natural and the numinous, Newton's and Keats's.

In moving from the laborious world of *Hyperion* to the questioning world of *The Fall of Hyperion,* we enter upon a world that is even more incomplete, distant and removed. This new stage of otherness offers no life amenable to the state of the poet:

> Then saw I a wan face,
> Not pin'd by human sorrows, but bright blanch'd
> By an immortal sickness which kills not;
> It works a constant change, which happy death
> Can put no end to; deathwards progressing

> To no death was that visage; it had pass'd
> The lily and the snow; and beyond these
> I must not think now, though I saw that face—
> But for her eyes I should have fled away.
> They held me back, with a benignant light [. . .] (1.256-65)

If it were not for the richness of the language we should have noticed early in our encounters with Keats that these lines are under the rule of a dialectic movement. Moneta is rich in an admonition, a word that bears with it an interior, mental aspect, a command to consider and remember through a "menos," a spirit; and so we come round to Moneta once more (*Webster's* "admonish" and "mental"), Moneta looks down upon the poet with eyes that give and take away: it "works" a "constant change" with "no end." Though it is "deathwards progressing," just as happens throughout the mortal world, "to no death was that visage," lying of the other side of "The lily and the snow," or beyond the physical world of the visage and the face. This dialectic motion is further sustained by a series of oxymorons, "bright blanch'd," "constant change," "immortal sickness," and doubtless the "benignant light" of Moneta's eyes. Though it is a language that affirms death, it is also a language that brings us back, one which we cannot cease from enduring.

What, then, did Lovecraft make of these authors? In 1929 he thought of Baudelaire and Keats as two of a kind of the aesthete-pagan tradition (*ET* 26). Not long thereafter he spoke of Keats as one of a kind: "Four the soul & substance of poetry, there is no richer source than Keats. Join his spirit & fire to the simple language of straightforward conversation, & you have the utter apex of poetic possibility" (*SL* 2.336). This intense response you do not find that often unless for someone like Poe. A year later he joins the names of Keats and Herschel in two lines of Chapman's Homer upon the discovery of Pluto (*ET* 139). Shortly afterwards he asks "what John Keats has to say about the intimations of hidden, tremulous strangeness & beauty therein" (*JFM* 237). Much more than scholars, Keats has a true experience of Hellenism because he is "a single-track dreamer" (3.252). Nevertheless, he cannot help himself when he measures Keats and Jack the Ripper on the cosmic scale (*SL* 3.311–12). Thus he is driven to speak of "your prattling little Keatses & Baudelaires" (*SL* 3.314) when weighed against Newton or Einstein—and we know what Keats thought of the rainbow that Newton measured according to his prism and the hole in the window. Still, I am pleased to see Keats and Baudelaire treated together; in 1936 Lovecraft still joins Keats to Baudelaire, and he still thinks the two of them as important as Poe, Spinoza, and Shakespeare (*CLM* 183). Lovecraft's judgment of Keats and Baudelaire seems quite steady through the years, open to the universe of cosmic indifferentism, except that Keats still faces the world with his sense of tragedy intact. To that degree he and Leopardi may differ from the monstrous world of Baudelaire and Lovecraft.

Works Cited

The American Heritage Dictionary of the English Language. Ed. Anne H. Soukhanov. 3rd ed. Boston: Houghton Mifflin, 1992.

Amundsen, Roald. *The South Pole: An Account of the Norwegian Antarctic Expedition in the "Fram," 1910-1912.* Tr. A. G. Chater. London: Murray, 1912. 2 vols.

Baring-Gould, William S., ed. *The Annotated Sherlock Holmes.* New York: Wings. Books, 1992. 2 vols.

Baudelaire, Charles. *Œuvres completes.* Ed. Y.-G. Le Dantec. Paris: Librairi Gallimard, 1954.

Bergson, Henri. *Creative Evolution.* Tr. Arthur Mitchell. New York: Random House, 1944.

———. *L'Évolution créatrice.* Paris: Presses Universitaires de France, 1943.

Bernt, Günther, ed. and tr. *Carmina Burana.* Stuttgart: Philpp Reclam, 1992.

Blake, William. *Complete Writings.* Ed. Geoffrey Keynes. London: Oxford University Press, 1974.

Boysen, Benjamin. *The Ethics of Love: An Essay on James Joyce.* Viborg: University Press of Southern Denmark. 2003.

Browning, Robert. *The Complete Poetic and Dramatic Works.* Ed. Horace E. Scudder. Boston: Houghton Mifflin, 1895.

Burkert, Walter. *Greek Religion: Archaic and Classical.* Tr. John Raftan. Cambridge, MA: Harvard University Press, 1985.

Burroughs, Edgar Rice. *A Princess of Mars*. New York: Ballantine, 1963.

Byrd, Richard Evelyn. *Little America: Aerial Exploration in the Antarctic: The Flight to the South Pole*. New York: G. P. Putnam's Sons, 1930.

Callaghan, Gavin. "Elementary, My Dear Lovecraft: H. P. Lovecraft and Sherlock Holmes." *Lovecraft Annual* No. 6 (2012): 199-229.

Cannon, Peter. *H. P. Lovecraft*. Boston: Twayne, 1989.

———. *"Sunset Terrace Imagery in Lovecraft" and Other Essays*. West Warwick, RI: Necronomicon Press, 1990.

Caputi, Anthony. *Pirandello and the Crisis of Modern Consciousness*. Urbana: University of Illinois Press, 1988.

Carducci, Giusuè. *Poesie: 1850-1900*. Bologna: Nicola Zanichelli, 1911.

Carroll, James. *Constantine's Sword: The Church and the Jews, A History*. Boston: Mariner Books, 2001.

Carter, Angela. *The Bloody Chamber and Other Stories*. New York: Penguin, 1981.

Clarke, Arthur C. *Astounding Days: A Science Fictional Autobiography*. New York: Bantam Books, 1990.

———. *Childhood's End*. San Diego: Harcourt Brace, 1953.

———. *The City and the Stars*. New York: Harbrace Paperbound Library, 1967.

———. *The Collected Stories of Arthur C. Clarke*. New York: Tor, 2000.

Cooper, James Fenimore. *The Last of the Mohicans: A Narrative of 1757*. Albany: State University of New York Press, 1983.

Deferrari, Roy J. *A Latin-English Dictionary of St. Thomas Aquinas: Based on* The Summa Theologica *and Selected Passages of His Other Writings*. Boston: The Daughters of St. Paul, 1986.

Dante Alighieri. *La Divina Commedia.* Ed. Ann. C. H. Grandgent and Charles Singleton., Cambridge, MA: Harvard University Press, 1972.

———. *La Divina Commedia.* In *Tutte le opera.* Ed. Edward Moore. 3rd ed. London: Oxford, 1904.

———. *The Divine Comedy.* Tr. Henry Wadsworth Longfellow. Boston: Houghton, Mifflin, 1884.

Davis, Wade. *Into the Silence: The Great War, Mallory, and the Conquest of Everest.* New York: Alfred A. Knopf, 2011.

Decter, Jacqueline. *Messenger of Beauty: The Life and Visionary Art of Nicholas Roerich.* Rochester, VT: Park Street Press, 1997.

Dick, Philip K. *The Divine Invasion.* New York: Timescape, 1982.

———. Do Androids Dream of Electric Sheep? New York: Ballantine, 1982.

———. The Man in the High Castle. New York: Vintage, 1992.

———. *The Three Stigmata of Palmer Eldridge.* New York: Vintage, 1991.

———. *Ubik.* New York: Vintage, 1991.

Doyle, Sir Arthur Conan. *The Complete Sherlock Holmes.* Preface by Christopher Morley. Garden City, NY: Garden City Books, 1953.

———. *A Life in Letters.* Ed. Jon Lellenberg, Daniel Stashower, and Charles Foley. New York: Penguin Press, 2007.

Eckhardt, Jason C. "Behind the Mountains of Madness: Lovecraft and the Antarctic in 1930." *Lovecraft Studies* No. 14 (Spring 1987): 31–38.

———. "The Cosmic Yankee." In Schultz and Joshi 77–100.

Ellmann, Richard. *Yeats: The Man and the Masks.* New York: E. P. Dutton, 1958.

The Encyclopaedia Britannica. 11th ed. Edinburgh: A. & C. Black, 1910–1911.

English, James F. *The Economy of Prestige: Prizes, Awards, and the Circulation of Cultural Value.* Cambridge, MA: Harvard University Press, 2005.

The English Bible: The New Testament and the Apocrypha. Ed. Gerald Hammond and Austin Busch. New York: Norton, 2012.

The English Bible: The Old Testament. Ed. Herbert Marks. New York: Norton, 2012.

Euripides. *Helen,* Trs. and ed. Arthur S. Way. London: William Heinemann/Loeb Classical Library, 1916. Vol. 1.

Evers, Alf. *Kingston: The City on the Hudson.* Woodstock, NY: Overlook Press, 2005.

Faig, Kenneth W., Jr. *Lovecraftian Voyages.* New York: Hippocampus, 2017.

Faulkner, William. *Absalom, Absalom!* New York: Modern Library, 1951.

Fischer, David Hackett. *Paul Revere's Ride.* New York: Oxford University Press, 1994.

France, Anatole. "The Procurator of Judaea" and "Crainquebille." In *Bedside Book of Famous French Stories,* ed. Belle Becker and Robert N. Linscott. New York: Random House, 1945.

Freud, Sigmund. *The Interpretation of Dreams.* Tr. and ed. James Strachey. New York: Avon Books, 1965.

Goethe, Johann Wolfgang von. *Werke.* Vol. 1. Ed. Erich Trunz. Hamburg: Christian Wegner, 1948.

Graves, Robert. *The Greek Myths.* Baltimore: Penguin, 1955. 2 vols.

Haeckel, Ernst. *The Riddle of the Universe at the Close of the Nineteenth Century.* Tr. Joseph McCabe. New York: Harper & Brothers, 1900.

Hale, Edward Everett. *The Man without a Country.* Boston: Little, Brown, 1915.

Hardy, Thomas. *The Dynasts.* New York: Macmillan, 1965.

Hegel, G. W. F. *Phaenomenologie des Geistes.* Ed. Gerhard Goehler. Frankfurt am Main: Ullstein, 1973.

Hesiod. *Theogonia Opera et Dies Scutum.* Ed. Friedrich, Solmsen, R. Merkelbach, and M. L. West. Oxford: Oxford University Press, 1970.

Hill, Geoffrey. *Broken Hierarchies: Poems 1952-2012.* Ed. Kenneth Haynes. Oxford: Oxford University Press, 2013.

Hillman, James. *The Myth of Analysis: Three Essays in Archetypal Psychology.* New York: Harper Perennial, 1992.

Horace. *Opera.* Ed. Edward C. Wickham and H. W. Garrod. Oxford: Clarendon Press, 1901.

Irving, Washington. *Selected Writings of Washington Irving.* Ed. Saxe Commins. New York: Modern Library, 1945.

Joshi, S. T. *I Am Providence: The Life and Times of H. P. Lovecraft.* New York: Hippocampus Press, 2010. 2 vols.

———. *A Subtler Magick: The Writings and Philosophy of H. P. Lovecraft.* San Bernardino, CA: Borgo Press, 1996.

———, ed. *H. P. Lovecraft: Four Decades of Criticism.* Athens: Ohio University Press, 1980.

———, ed. "Introduction and Notes." In H. P. Lovecraft, *The Call of Cthulhu and Other Weird Stories.* New York: Penguin, 1999.

Joyce, James. *Finnegans Wake.* New York: Viking, 1960.

———. *A Portrait of the Artist as a Young Man.* Ed. Seamus Deane. New York: Penguin Books. 2003.

———. *Ulysses.* Ed. Walter Gabler. New York: Random House, 1986.

Keats, John. *The Poems*. Ed. Jack Stillinger, Cambridge, MA: Harvard University Press, 1978.

———. *The Letters: 1814-1825*. Ed. Hyder E. Rollins. Cambridge, MA: Harvard University Press, 1958. 2 vols.

Kipling, Rudyard. *Kim*. New York: Dell, 1959.

———. "The Phantom 'Rickshaw." In *The Best Short Stories of Rudyard Kipling*. Garden City, NY: Hanover House, 1961.

———. *Rudyard Kipling's Verse: Inclusive Edition, 1885-1918*. Garden City, NY: Doubleday, Page, 1921.

Kleist, Heinrich von. *Penthesilea*. In *Werke*. 2nd Band. Ed. Heinrich Kurz. Leipzig: Verlag des Bibliographischen Instituts, n.d. 2 vols.

Lagerlöf, Selma. *The Saga of Gösta Berling*. Tr. Paul Norlen. Introduction by George C. Schoolfield. New York: Penguin, 2009.

Laxdaela Saga. In *Islendinga Sögur*. Ed. Guđni Jonsson. Reykavik: State Hrappseyjprent, 1946.

Leiber, Fritz. *The Big Time*. New York: Ace, 1961.

———. *Changewar*. New York: Ace, 1963.

———. "A Literary Copernicus." In Joshi, *Four Decades* 50-62.

———. *The Sinful Ones*. New York: Pocket Books, 1980.

———. *The Wanderer*. New York: Tor, 1964.

Leopardi, Giacomo. *Canti*. Ed. Franco Brioschi. Milano: Biblioteca Universale Rizzoli, 1983.

Lévy, Maurice. *Lovecraft: A Study in the Fantastic*. Tr. S. T. Joshi. Detroit: Wayne State University Press, 1988.

Lewis, Sinclair. *Babbitt*. New York: Harcourt, Brace & World, 1922.

———. *Main Street*. New York: Harcourt, Brace & World, 1920.

Liddell, Henry George, and Robert Scott, ed. *A Greek-English Lexicon Abridged*. Oxford: Oxford University Press, 1891.

Longfellow, Henry Wadsworth. *The Complete Poetical Works*. Boston: Houghton Mifflin, 1902.

"Loom." In *The Compact Edition of the Oxford English Dictionary.* Oxford: Clarendon Press, 1971.

Lopez, Barry. *Arctic Dreams: Imagination and Desire in a Northern Landscape.* New York: Charles Scribner's Sons, 1986.

Lovecraft, H. P. *The Ancient Track: Complete Poetical Works.* Ed. S. T. Joshi. 2nd ed. New York: Hippocampus Press, 2013.

———. *Collected Essays.* Ed. S. T. Joshi. New York: Hippocampus Press, 2004–06. 5 vols.

———. *Collected Fiction: A Variorum Edition.* Ed. S. T. Joshi. New York: Hippocampus Press, 2015–17. 4 vols.

———. *Letters to Alfred Galpin.* Ed. S. T. Joshi and David E. Schultz. New York: Hippocampus Press, 2003.

———. *Letters to F. Lee Baldwin, Duane W. Rimel, and Nils Frome.* Ed. David E. Schultz and S. T. Joshi. New York: Hippocampus Press, 2016.

———. *Letters to Family and Family Friends.* Ed. S. T. Joshi and David E. Schultz. New York: Hippocampus Press, 2020.

———. *Letters to J. Vernon Shea, Carl F. Strauch, and Lee McBride White.* Ed. S. T. Joshi and David E. Schultz. New York: Hippocampus Press, 2016.

———. *Letters to Maurice W. Moe and Others.* Ed. David E. Schultz and S. T. Joshi. New York: Hippocampus Press, 2018.

———. *Letters to Rheinhart Kleiner and Others.* Ed. S. T. Joshi and David E. Schultz. New York: Hippocampus Press, 2020.

———. *Letters to Robert Bloch and Others.* Ed. David E. Schultz and S. T. Joshi. New York: Hippocampus Press, 2015.

———. *Letters to Elizabeth Toldridge and Anne Tillery Renshaw.* Ed. David E. Schultz and S. T. Joshi. New York: Hippocampus Press, 2014.

———. *Selected Letters.* Ed. August Derleth, Donald Wandrei, and James Turner. Sauk City, WI: Arkham House, 1965-76. 5 vols.

———. *The Spirit of Revision: Lovecraft's Letters to Zealia Brown Reed Bishop.* Ed. Sean Branney and Andrew Leman. Glendale, CA: The H. P. Lovecraft Historical Society, 2015.

"Luis Muñoz Rivera." Web. Accessed 29 September 2010.

McAleer, Neil. *Arthur C. Clarke: The Authorized Biography.* Chicago: Contemporary Books, 1992.

MacDiarmid, Hugh. *A Drunk Man Looks at the Thistle.* Ed. John C. Weston. Amherst: University of Massachusetts Press, 1971.

MacDonald, George. *Lilith.* Grand Rapids, MI: William B. Eerdmans, 1981.

Mann, Thomas. *Buddenbrooks: Verfall einer Familie.* Berlin: G. B. Fischer, 1960.

———. "Mario und der Zauberer." In *Die Erzählungen.* Frankfurt am Main: S. Fischer, 1966.

March, Harold. *Romain Rolland.* New York: Twayne, 1971.

Marsden, George M. *The Soul of the American University: From Protestant Establishment to Establishment Nonbelief.* New York: Oxford University Press, 1994.

Matthews, Gareth B. "Si Fallor, Sum." In R. A. Markus, ed. *Augustine: A Collection of Critical Essays.* Garden City, NY: Doubleday/Anchor Books, 1972. 151-67.

Milton, John. *Complete Poems and Major Prose.* Ed. Merrit Y. Hughes. New York: Odyssey Press, 1957.

"Mirage." In *Encyclopaedia Britannica.* 9th ed. 1875-98.

"Morris-Dance." In *Encyclopaedia Britannica.* 9th ed. 1875-98.

"Mummers." In *Encycopaedia Britannica.* 9th ed. 1875-98.

"MUNOZ—Name Meaning & Origin." Web. Accessed 20 November 2010.

Murphy, Patricia O'Reilly. *Kingston.* Charleston, SC: "Postcard History Series," Arcadia, 2013.

Needham, Joseph, and Arthur L. Peck. "Molly Dancing in East Anglia." *Journal of English Folk Dance and Song Society* 1, No. 2 (December 1933): 79-85.

Neumann, Erich. *The Great Mother: An Analysis of the Archetype.* Tr. Ralph Manheim. Princeton, NJ: Princeton University Press, 1972.

The New Cassell's German Dictionary. Ed. Harold T. Betteredge. New York: Funk & Wagnalls, 1958.

Newman, John Henry. *The Idea of a University.* Garden City, NY: Image Books, 1959.

Njáls Saga. Ed. Magnús Finnbogason. Reykjavík: Menningarsjóðs ok Þjóðvinafélagsins, 1944.

O'Neill, Eugene. *Long Day's Journey into Night.* New Haven: Yale University Press, 1962.

———. *The Plays.* New York: Random House, 1955. 3 vols.

———. *Mourning Becomes Elektra.* In *Nine Plays.* New York: Modern Library, 1932.

Opfell, Olga S. *The Lady Laureates: Women Who Have Won the Nobel Prize.* Metuchen, NJ: Scarecrow Press, 1978.

Österling, Anders. "The Literary Prize." In H. Schück et al. *Nobel: The Man and His Prizes.* Stockholm: Sohlmann, 1950.

Paul, Simpson-Housley. *Antarctica: Exploration, Perception, and Metaphor.* London: Routledge, 1992,

Pindar. *Carmina cum Fragmintis.* Ed. Bruno Snell. 3rd ed. Leizig: Teubner, 1959.

Pirandello, Luigi. *Sei personaggi in cerca d'autore; Enrico IV.* Milan: Arnoldo Mondadori, 1970.

Pliny the Younger. *Epistulae*. Ed. R. A. B. Mynors. Oxford: Oxford University Press, 1963.

Pokorny, Julius. *Indogermanisches Etymologisches Wörterbuch*. Bern: Francke, 1948–59. 2 vols.

Pope, Alexander. *The Dunciad in Four Books*. Ed. Valerie Rumbold. Edinburgh: Pearson, 2009.

Pynchon, Thomas. "Entrope." In *Slow Learner*. New York: Bantam, 1984.

The Real Mother Goose. Chicago: Rand McNally, 1916.

Rickman, Gregg. *To the High Castle: Philip K. Dick—A Life 1928–1962*. Long Beach, CA: Fragments West/The Valentine Press, 1989.

Ridley, Hugh. *Thomas Mann: Buddenbrooks*. (Landmarks of World Literature.) Cambridge: Cambridge University Press, 1987.

Rolland, Romain. *Jean-Christoph*. Paris: Albin Michel, 1966.

Rollins, Hyder Edward, ed. *The Keats Circle: Letters and Papers*. 2nd ed. Cambridge, MA: Harvard Unversity Press, 1969. 2 vols.

Rudolph, Frederick. *The American College and University: A History*. New York: Alfred A. Knopf, 1962.

Schultz, David E., and S. T. Joshi, ed. *An Epicure in the Terrible: A Centennial Anthology of Essays in Honor of H. P. Lovecraft*. 2nd ed. New York: Hippocampus Press, 2011.

Scott, Robert F. *The Voyage of the 'Discovery.'* 1905. New York: Greenwood Press, 1962. 2 vols.

Scott, Sir Walter. *Marmion*. In *Complete Poetical Works*. Ed. Horace E. Scudder. Boston: Houghton Mifflin, 1900.

Shackleton, Ernest. *South: The Endurance Expedition*. 1919. New York: New American Library, 1999.

Shakespeare, William. *The Norton Shakespeare*. Ed. Stephen Greenblatt. New York: W. W. Norton, 1997.

Shaw, George Bernard. *Back to Methuselah: A Metabiological Pentateuch.* London: Constable, 1931.

———. *Man and Superman.* Baltimore: Penguin, 1952.

Shelley, Percy Bysshe. *Poetical Works.* Ed. Thomas Hutchison. London: Oxford University Press, 1923.

Simpson-Housley, Paul. *Antarctica: Exploration, Perception, and Metaphor.* London: Routledge, 1992.

Smith, William. *Chambers/Murray Latin-English Dictionary.* Ed. John Lockwood. Edinburgh: Chambers; London: John Murray, 1976.

Smyrnaeus, Quintus. *The Fall of Troy.* Tr. Arthur S. Way. Cambridge, MA: Harvard University Press/Loeb Classical Library, 1913.

Sohlmann, Ragnar, and Henrik Schück. *Nobel, Dynamite and Peace.* Tr. Brian and Beatrix Lunn. New York: Cosmopolitan Book Corp., 1929.

Spinoza, Benedict de. *Die Ethik.* Tr. Jakob Stern. Ed. Bernhard Lakebrink. Stuttgart: Reclam, 1977.

Stesichorus. In *Lyra Graeca.* Ed. J. M. Edmonds. 2nd ed. London: William Heinemann/Loeb Classical Library, 1921.

Sutin, Lawrence. *Divine Invasions: A Life of Philip K. Dick.* New York: Citadel Press, 1991.

Tagore, Rabindranath. *Gitanjali.* New York: Macmillan, 1952.

Tennyson, Alfred, Lord. *The Poetic and Dramatic Works.* Boston: Houghton Mifflin, 1927.

"Transvaal." In *Encyclopaedia Britannica.* 11th ed. 1911. 27.186-210.

Triber, Jayne E. *A True Republican: The Life of Paul Revere.* Amherst: University of Massachusetts Press, 1998.

Ullman, James Ramsey, *High Conquest: The Story of Mountaineering.* London: Travel Book Club, 1943.

Undset, Sigrid. *Kristin Lavransdatter.* Tr. Charles Archer. New York: Alfred A. Knopf, 1942.

Verne, Jules. *Les Aventures du capitaine Hatteras.* Paris: Livre de Poche, 1966.

Virgil (P. Vergilius Maro). *Opera.* Ed. Frederick Arthur Hirtzel. Oxford: Oxford University Press, 1900.

Wagner, Richard. *Gesammelte Schriften.* Ed. Julius Kapp. Leipzig: Hesse & Becker, 1914. 14 vols.

Waugh, Robert H. "The Lament of the Midwives: Arthur C. Clarke and the Tradition." *Extrapolation* 31, No. 1 (Spring 1990): 40–47.

———. "Landscapes, Selves, and Others in Lovecraft." In Schultz and Joshi 230–55.

———. *The Monster in the Mirror: Looking for H. P. Lovecraft.* New York: Hippocampus Press, 2006, rpt. 2021.

———. *A Monster of Voices: Speaking for H. P. Lovecraft.* New York: Hippocampus Press, 2011, rpt. 2021.

Washington, Margaret. *Sojourner Truth's America.* Urbana: University of Illinois Press, 2009.

Webster's New Collegiate Dictionary. Springfield, MA: Merriam, 1960.

Widmer, Edward L. *Brown: The History of an Idea.* New York: Thames & Hudson, 2015.

Yeats, W. B. *The Poems.* Ed. Richard J. Finneran. New York: Macmillan, 1983.

Index

"A se stesso" (Leopardi) 214
Aeneid (Virgil) 24-25, 217
Aeschylus 133-34, 135, 179
Alhazred, Abdul 207
"Alle Fonti del Clitumno" (Carducci) 157
American Heritage Dictionary 127, 128
"Among School Children" (Yeats) 166
Amundsen, Roald 64, 66, 67
"Anna Livia Plurabelle" (Joyce) 164, 171, 208
Aquinas, Thomas 76, 210
Ars Poetica (Horace) 132
At the Mountains of Madness 15, 32, 33, 34-36, 37, 59-60, 61, 67-74, 93, 138, 140, 141
Augustine, St. 92, 210, 211
Aventures du capitaine Hatteras, Les (Verne) 64

Babbitt (Lewis) 164, 175-76
Back to Methuselah (Shaw) 168, 171
Baring-Gould, William S. 101
Barrack-Room Ballads (Kipling) 158
Baudelaire, Charles 155, 184, 185, 186-87, 214-15, 218, 219
Baum, L. Frank 34
"Bazaar of the Bizarre, The" (Leiber) 151
Beethoven, Ludwig van 163
Bergson, Henri 169, 170-71
Bible 27-28, 74, 85, 115, 138, 150, 189, 204
Big Time, The (Leiber) 145-46, 152
Bishop, Zealia 30
Blavatsky, Helena P. 168
Boer War 101-2
Book of the Dead 29
Boston, MA 15-22, 74
Brown University 8, 75-76, 78-81, 82, 85-86, 92

Browning, Robert 21-22
Buddenbrooks (Mann) 173, 174
Burr, Aaron 47-48
Burroughs, Edgar Rice 34
Byrd, Richard E. 66-67

"Call of Cthulhu, The" 43, 53, 79, 80, 85-86, 92, 113, 142, 145, 149-50
Callaghan, Gavin 95, 97, 102
Cambridge, MA 15, 74
Campbell, John W. 74
Camus, Albert 172
Cannon, Peter 41, 121
Carducci, Giosué 157-58, 180
Carlyle, Thomas 160
Carroll, James 54
Case of Charles Dexter Ward, The 42, 57-59, 91, 130, 147, 196
Catullus (C. Valerius Catullus) 108, 109, 157
Chaucer, Geoffrey 54
"Celephaïs" 194-95, 199-200
Childhood's End (Clarke) 141, 142, 143
Christianity 53-54
City and the Stars, The (Clarke) 141
Clarke, Arthur C. 140-43, 147, 150-51
"Colour out of Space, The" 53-57, 84-85, 86, 89, 91, 142, 143, 147
Complete Poems (Hill) 180
"Cool Air" 8, 113-39
Creative Evolution (Bergson) 170-71
"Crime of the Century, The" 100
Crying of Lot 49, The (Pynchon) 125
Crypt of Cthulhu 41

"Dagon" 141
Dance of the Machines, The (O'Brien) 147
Dante Alighieri 103, 128

Darwin, Charles 168-69, 171
Dee, John 87-88
"Diary of Alonzo Typer, The" (Lovecraft-Lumley) 45
Dick, Philip K. 140, 147-50, 152-53
Disney, Walt 113
Divine Invasion, The (Dick) 147, 152
Doktor Faustus (Mann) 174
Doyle, Sir Arthur Conan 95-110
Drayton, Michael 167
Dream-Quest of Unknown Kadath, The 8, 17, 71, 73, 161, 183-210
"Dreams in the Witch House, The" 89-91, 122-23, 125, 127, 129, 135, 136, 148
Dreiser, Theodore 175
Drunk Man Looks at the Thistle, A (MacDiarmid) 179, 180
Dunsany, Lord 161, 166, 184, 193
"Dunwich Horror, The" 86-88, 122, 123, 124, 126, 127, 135, 136

"Earthlight" (Clarke) 143
"Easter, 1916" (Yeats) 166
Eckhardt, Jason C. 7, 61, 199
Eclogues (Virgil) 157
Eliot, T. S. 81
Emperor Jones, The (O'Neill) 188
Encyclopaedia Britannica 75
Endymion (Keats) 211, 212
"Entropy" (Pynchon) 114, 124-27
Etymological Dictionary of Latin 128
Euripides 158, 183

Fall of Hyperion, The (Keats) 217-18
Faust (Goethe) 183
Finnegans Wake (Joyce) 163, 206-8, 209
"Five Orange Pips, The" (Doyle) 102
France, Anatole 165
Frankenstein (Shelley) 156
French Revolution, The (Carlyle) 160
Freud, Sigmund 177, 186, 207

"Gaudeamus" 76
George III (King of England) 42
Georgics (Virgil) 217
Gérard de Nerval 83
"Ginestra, La" (Leopardi) 213-14, 217
Gitanjali (Tagore) 161

"Gladius Dei" (Mann) 174
Goethe, Johann Wolfgang von 27, 134, 137, 183
"Gouffre, Le" (Baudelaire) 214-15
Greene, Sonia H. 168
Gulliver's Travels (Swift) 148

Haeckel, Ernst 83, 168
Haggard, H. Rider 208
Hale, Edward Everett 48
Hamilton, Alexander 47-48
Harvard University 82, 87, 88
"Haunter of the Dark, The" 153
Heaney, Seamus 180
Helen (Euripides) 183
Henry IV (Pirandello) 176, 177
"Herbert West—Reanimator" 83-84
Hesiod 132
Hill, Geoffrey 180
Hillman, James 216
Horace (Q. Horatius Flaccus) 132, 133, 135, 157, 158
"Horror at Red Hook, The" 115-16
"Hound, The" 34, 83, 95, 113
Hound of the Baskervilles, The (Doyle) 95-110
"How They Brought the Good News from Ghent to Aix" (Browning) 21-22
Howard, Robert E. 23
Hurley, N.Y. 43-44, 46, 47
Hyperion (Keats) 33, 212, 217

Iceman Cometh, The (O'Neill) 178
Idea of a University, The (Newman) 75, 77-78
"Idle Days on the Yann" (Dunsany) 193
"In the Walls of Eryx" (Lovecraft-Sterling) 140
Indiana University 82
Inferno (Dante) 103
"Irrémédiable, L'" (Baudelaire) 186-87
Irving, Washington 45

James I (King of England) 98
Jean-Christophe (Rolland) 162
Johnson, Samuel 73, 191
Joshi, S. T. 25, 41, 168

Joyce, James 136, 163-64, 166, 180, 206-8
Jungle Books (Kipling) 159

Keats, John 32-33, 184, 187, 211-13, 216-19
Kim (Kipling) 159
King Lear (Shakespeare) 191
Kingston, N.Y. 41-46
Kipling, Rudyard 158-60
Kirk, George 115
Kleist, Heinrich von 26-27
Kristin Lavransdatter (Undset) 172-73

Ladd Observatory (Brown University) 81
"Lady Wentworth" (Longfellow) 16
Lagerlöf, Selma 155, 160-61, 172
Lamia (Keats) 212, 213
Leiber, Fritz 140, 144-47, 151-52
Leopardi, Giacomo 157, 184, 213-14, 217, 219
Lévy, Maurice 130
Lewis, Sinclair 163, 175-76
Lexicon Pentaglotton 79
Lilith (MacDonald) 115, 122, 123
"Literary Copernicus, A" (Leiber) 144
"Locksley Hall" (Tennyson) 33
Long Day's Journey into Night, A (O'Neill) 178, 179
Longfellow, Henry Wadsworth 15, 16, 17, 18, 20-22
Lovecraft Studies 41
"Lycidas" (Milton) 119

Maass, Joachim 27
Macbeth (Shakespeare) 54
MacDiarmid, Hugh 179-80
MacDonald, George 114-15, 122, 123, 129-30, 133
MacLeish, Archibald 81
Magna Mater 107-10
Main Street (Lewis) 163, 164, 175
Man in the High Castle, The (Dick) 152-53
"Man of Stone, The" (Lovecraft-Heald) 45
Mann, Thomas 155, 173-74
"Mario und der Zauberer" (Mann) 174
Martian Time-Slip (Dick) 148

Mather, Cotton 17, 55
"Meeting with Medusa, A" (Clarke) 143
Memnon 25-26, 27, 31
Milton, John 55, 119, 134
"Minnaloushe" (Yeats) 166
Miskatonic University 75, 78, 80, 82-83, 87-88, 89, 91-92
Mistral, Frédéric 157
Modest Proposal, A (Swift) 197
Morris-dance 131-32
"Mound, The" (Lovecraft-Bishop) 27, 30-34
Mourning Becomes Electra (O'Neill) 178-79
"Music of Erich Zann, The" 121, 125, 126, 129, 135, 136

"Nameless City, The" 23, 25, 28-29, 31, 32, 34, 37, 38, 148
Necronomicon (Alhazred) 25, 79, 80, 142, 207
Neumann, Erich 107-8, 110
New Dunciad, The (Pope) 97
New Paltz, N.Y. 41, 43-44, 45, 46
Newman, John Henry 75, 77-78, 89
Nietzsche, Friedrich 24
Nobel, Alfred 156

O'Brien, Edward J. 147
"Ode on a Grecian Urn" (Keats) 184, 212
Odi Barbare (Carducci) 157, 180
Odyssey (Homer) 164
"On First Looking into Chapman's Homer" (Keats) 32-33
O'Neill, Eugene 178-79, 188
"Outsider, The" 25, 48, 81

Paradise Lost (Milton) 55, 122
Parsifal (Wagner) 110, 128-29
Pascal, Blaise 215
"Paul Revere's Ride" (Longfellow) 16, 55
Petrarch (Francesco Petrarca) 178
"Phanrom 'Rickshaw, The" (Kipling) 159
"Pickman's Model" 15-17, 20, 22, 55-56, 73
"Picture in the House, The" 20, 120, 121, 125, 126, 129, 135, 136
Pindar 132

Pirandello, Luigi 176-78
Plato 120-21
Poe, Edgar Allan 86, 218
Political Economy (Wayland) 79
Pope, Alexander 97
Princess and the Goblin, The (MacDonald) 114-15
"Procurator of Judaea, The" (France) 165
"Prometheus" (Goethe) 134
Prometheus Bound (Aeschylus) 133-34, 179
Prometheus Unbound (Shelley) 156
Proust, Marcel 163
Prudhomme, Sully 155, 156
Purgatorio (Dante) 128
Pynchon, Thomas 114, 124-25

"Rats in the Walls, The" 56, 95-110, 130, 150
Rendezvous with Rama (Clarke) 143
Republic (Plato) 120
"Retreat from Earth" (Clarke) 141
"Rêve Parisien" (Baudelaire) 185
Revere, Paul 15, 16, 17-18, 20
Reynolds, John Hamilton 212
Right You Are (if you think you are) (Pirandello) 176
Rime of the Ancient Mariner, The (Coleridge) 18-19
"Rip Van Winkle" (Irving) 45-46
Roerich, Nicholas 63-64, 68-69
Rolland, Romain 155, 162-63

Saga of Gösta Berling, The (Lagerlöf) 160
Saint Joan (Shaw) 168
Scott, Robert 62-63, 66, 67
"Sept Vieillards, Les" (Baudelaire) 215
Shackleton, Ernest 64-66, 67
"Shadow out of Time, The" 34, 37-39, 92-93, 140, 141
"Shadow over Innsmouth, The" 60, 141, 142
Shakespeare, William 54
Shaw, George Bernard 168-69, 171
She (Haggard) 208
Shelley, Percy Bysshe 156
"Shunned House, The" 45
Sinful Ones, The (Leiber) 147
Six Characters in Search of an Author (Pirandello) 175

Smyrnaeus, Quintus 26
Somerset (ship) 18, 19
Spinoza, Benedict de 163
Stesichorus 183, 184, 201
Strindberg, August 169, 178
Swift, Jonathan 148, 169
Synge, J. M. 167

Tagore, Rabindranath 161-62
Tales from the White Hart (Clarke) 147
Tales of a Wayside Inn (Longfellow) 16
"Thing on the Doorstep, The" 92, 120
Tennyson, Alfred, Lord 33a
Three Stigmata of Palmer Eldritch, The (Dick) 152, 153
"Tod in Venedig, Der" (Mann) 174
Transmigration of Timothy Archer, The (Dick) 152
Truth, Sojourner 48-49

Ulysses (Joyce) 164, 206, 208
Undset, Sigrid 155, 172-73

Vanderlyn, John 47
Verne, Jules 64
Virgil (P. Vergilius Maro) 24, 26, 27, 157, 217
Voyage of the 'Discovery,' The (Scott) 62-63

Wagner, Richard 110, 128-29, 163
"Wall of Darkness, The" (Clarke) 142-43
Wanderer, The (Leiber) 144-45, 151-52
Waste Land, The (Eliot) 205
Wayland, Francis 79-80, 92
Webster's Dictionary 53, 73, 91
Wells, H. G. 30
"Whisperer in Darkness, The" 88-89
"Who Goes There?" (Campbell) 74
Williams, Roger 45, 78
Wilson, Edward 63, 64
Woodhouse, Richard 211

Yeats, W. B. 162, 166-68, 180

Zauberberg, Der (Mann) 173, 174
Zola, Émile 172

www.ingramcontent.com/pod-product-compliance
Lightning Source LLC
Chambersburg PA
CBHW051047160426

43193CB00010B/1091